"This is a unique example of a masterful combination of legal and political science scholarship on a topic seldom researched in such a comprehensive way. Pablo Castillo constructs a compelling case for interdisciplinary research on courts."

Carlos Closa, European University Institute, Italy

"This book offers a unique analysis of the role played by national Supreme and Constitutional Courts in the process of ratification of European Union treaties. By combining traditional research and empirical data, a deep knowledge of the legal processes and political science's instruments, this book manages to deliver an excellent piece of scholarship based on sound research and rigorous methodology."

Giuseppe Martinico, European University Institute, Italy

EU Treaties and the Judicial Politics of National Courts

Cases such as the Maastricht ruling by the German Federal Constitutional Court or the *Crotty* decision by the Irish Supreme Court have gone down in the history of European integration as outstanding examples of intervention by judicial actors in important political processes. In this book, Dr. Castillo Ortiz conducts for the first time a comprehensive analysis of all such rulings by national higher courts on European Union treaties issued during their processes of ratification.

Using an interdisciplinary law and politics approach and a sophisticated methodological strategy, the book describes the political dynamics underlying some of the most relevant judicial episodes in the process of European integration during the last decades: litigation strategies by Europhile and Euro-sceptic actors, relations between the judiciary and the other branches of government, and clashes of power between national courts and the European Court of Justice. By offering empirical evidence and by relying on scientific rigour, the book seeks to provide both experts and the general public with an accessible account of one of the most salient but least studied aspects of current European law and politics.

Pablo José Castillo Ortiz is Lecturer in Law at The University of Sheffield, UK.

Law, Courts and Politics
Edited by Robert M. Howard
Georgia State University

In *Democracy in America*, Alexis de Tocqueville famously noted that 'scarcely any political question arises in the United States that is not resolved, sooner or later, into a judicial question'. The importance of courts in settling political questions in areas ranging from health care to immigration shows the continuing astuteness of de Tocqueville's observation. To understand how courts resolve these important questions, empirical analyses of law, courts and judges, and the politics and policy influence of law and courts have never been more salient or more essential.

Law, Courts and Politics was developed to analyze these critically important questions. This series presents empirically driven manuscripts in the broad field of judicial politics and public law by scholars in law and social science. It uses the most up-to-date scholarship and seeks an audience of students, academics, upper division undergraduate and graduate courses in law, political science and sociology, as well as anyone interested in learning more about law, courts and politics.

1. **The Dual System of Privacy Rights in the United States**
   Mary McThomas

2. **Making Law and Courts Research Relevant**
   Brandon L. Bartels and Chris W. Bonneau

3. **The Europeanization of Judicial Review**
   Nicola Corkin

4. **The New Myth of the Court**
   The Media, the Court, and the Misrepresentation
   Rorie Spill Solberg and Eric N. Waltenburg

5. **EU Treaties and the Judicial Politics of National Courts**
   A Law and Politics Approach
   Pablo José Castillo Ortiz

EU Treaties and the Judicial Politics of National Courts

A Law and Politics Approach

Pablo José Castillo Ortiz

Routledge
Taylor & Francis Group
NEW YORK AND LONDON

First published 2016
by Routledge
711 Third Avenue, New York, NY 10017, USA

and by Routledge
2 Park Square, Milton Park, Abingdon, Oxfordshire OX14 4RN

First issued in paperback 2017

Routledge is an imprint of the Taylor & Francis Group, an informa business

Library of Congress Cataloging-in-Publication Data
Castillo Ortiz, Pablo José, author.
EU treaties and the judicial politics of national courts : a law and politics approach / Pablo José Castillo Ortiz.
pages cm. — (Law, courts and politics ; 5)
Includes bibliographical references and index.
1. Treaty-making power—European Union countries. 2. European Union countries—Foreign relations—Treaties. 3. European Union. 4. Treaties—Political aspects. 5. Treaties—Ratification. 6. Courts—European Union countries. 7. Judicial process—European Union countries. 8. Judicial independence—European Union countries. I. Title. II. Title: European Union treaties and the judicial politics of national courts.
KJE5106.C37 2016
341.242'24—dc23
2015008576

ISBN 13: 978-1-138-06674-8 (pbk)

ISBN 13: 978-1-138-88558-5 (hbk)

Typeset in Sabon
by Apex CoVantage, LLC

A mi familia

Contents

List of Figures viii
List of Tables ix
Acknowledgements x

1 National Higher Courts and Processes of Ratification of European Union Treaties 1

2 Constructing a Model of Judicial Behavior: Theoretical Framework 20

3 EU Primary Law Before the Guardians of the Constitution: Courts' Decisions on the Merits 48

4 *Kompetenz-Kompetenz*—The Doctrine of the Last Say: The Interpretative Decisions of Courts 66

5 The Legal Dimension: Assessing Judicial Behaviour from the Viewpoint of Legal Rules 98

6 The Political Dimension: A Pro-ratification Context 126

7 The Judicial Dimension: Institutional Design and Decisional Dynamics 158

8 Judicial Behaviour as a Result of Complex Causation: A QCA Approach to the Juridical Dynamics of Treaty Ratification 187

9 Conclusions and Some Final Reflections 205

10 Methodological Appendix 215

Index 227

Figures

2.1 Solving the problem of coordination between NHCs regarding the reception of the *Kompetenz-Kompetenz* doctrine 30
2.2 Increase in coordination costs 39
3.1 Judicial decisions on the merits by treaty 59
3.2 Judicial decisions on the merits by courts 61

Tables

1.1 Rulings on European Union treaties issued during their processes of ratification 8
4.1 Courts' statements of *Kompetenz-Kompetenz* 71
4.2 Evolution of statements of *Kompetenz-Kompetenz* 78
4.3 Topics addressed by the courts in their rulings 87
5.1 European clauses by case and correlations with judicial decisions 110
6.1 Judicialization of the processes of treaty ratification 127
6.2 Status and stance of the claimants 129
6.3 Claimants and their stances by decisions on the merits 131
6.4 Claimants and their stances by statement of *Kompetenz-Kompetenz* 133
6.5 Procedures of constitutional amendment and alternative procedures for ratification 137
6.6 Positions towards the treaties in the lower chamber and threshold for amendment 139
6.7 Positions of citizens regarding the treaties/the EU 142
6.8 Consequences of declarations of unconstitutionality and decisions on the merits 149
7.1 Institutional design and degree of independence 160
7.2 Correlations between judicial independence and courts' decisions 163
8.1 Intermediate solution for the presence of '*Kompetenz-Kompetenz*' 190
8.2 Intermediate solution for the absence of '*Kompetenz-Kompetenz*' 193
8.3 Intermediate solution for declarations of unconstitutionality 196
8.4 Intermediate solution for declarations of constitutionality 199
9.1 The four 'types' of rulings 208
A.1 Truth table for presence of '*Kompetenz-Kompetenz*' 222
A.2 Truth table for absence of '*Kompetenz-Kompetenz*' 223
A.3 Truth table for '*declaration of unconstitutionality*' 224
A.4 Truth table for '*declarations of constitutionality*' 224
A.5 QCA data matrix 225

Acknowledgements

This book is the result of a PhD dissertation entitled 'The Judicial Politics of National Courts in the Processes of Ratification of European Union Treaties', which was defended at the *Universidad Autónoma de Madrid* in 2014. My first acknowledgement is for my PhD supervisor, Professor Carlos Closa. Professor Closa trained me in the virtues of academic rigour and supported me in the difficult moments. With his help I have discovered what it means to do real research and how to enjoy it. I also would like to thank the Spanish *Consejo Superior de Investigaciones Científicas* (CSIC) which supported my PhD thesis through its JAE program. Since the start of the economic crisis in Europe and Spain, this institution has suffered serious financial cutbacks. I think that this is the perfect occasion to insist that investing in the training of new researchers is essential for the progress of any country and that investment in research is especially necessary in societies in need of economic and social development.

In addition to CSIC, this book was written in a number of institutions: the *Universidad Autónoma de Madrid*, the *Universitat Pompeu Fabra*, the *Centre d'études Européennes* of Sciences-Po, the *Euskal Herriko Unibertsitatea*, the *Université Catholique de Louvain* and the University of Sheffield. Among those who helped me by reading and commenting on earlier versions of this manuscript, I want emphasize the essential help of Irene Martin, Renaud Dehousse, Joxerramon Bengoetxea, Javier Arregui, Benoit Rihoux, Victor Ferreres Comella, Arthur Dyevre, Giuseppe Martinico, Ignacio Molina, Federico Crehuet, Daniel García, Daniela Vintila, Juan Antonio Mayoral, Iván Medina, Aleksandra Maastch, Cecilia Güemes, Patricio Galella and so many other friends and colleagues who supported me during the writing process.

Finally, the most deserved acknowledgment is for my family: *sin vuestro amor y vuestro apoyo una aventura como esta nunca habría sido posible.*

Sheffield
14 January 2015
Pablo José Castillo Ortiz

1 National Higher Courts and Processes of Ratification of European Union Treaties

Introduction

National higher courts with powers of constitutional review – hereinafter NHCs – have played a protagonist role in the political integration of the European continent. A couple of significant examples are sufficient to illustrate this. In 1987, at the request of Mr. Raymond Crotty, the Irish Supreme Court issued a ruling on the constitutionality of the ratification of the Single European Act. After the court declared the treaty unconstitutional, the Irish Constitution had to be amended in referendum in order to complete ratification. From that moment, every ratification of a major European Union (EU) treaty was deemed to require previous constitutional amendment in the country. The *Crotty* ruling was thus responsible for a number of referendums in Ireland whose ultimate goal was the ratification of EU treaties. Furthermore, some of these referendums failed for treaties such as Nice or Lisbon, giving rise to often criticized, complex political manoeuvres intended at circumventing the negative vote. In the long run, the decision of the Irish Supreme Court had political consequences of a continental dimension.

The second example took place just a few years later, this time in Germany. After accepting the complaint filed by Manfred Bruner against the Maastricht Treaty, the German Federal Constitutional Court issued a ruling that made European history. Although the court declared the treaty to be constitutional, it challenged the European Court of Justice. Karlsruhe presented itself as the ultimate guardian of the rights of German citizens against EU law and stated it would watch that the EU would not exercise its competencies *ultra vires*. Two of the core principles of EU law, primacy and direct effect, had been put into question.

Rulings on EU treaties during their processes of ratification are thus critical events. They show how NHCs behave under strong political pressures and how they articulate their relations with other judicial and political actors. These episodes allow the exploration of dynamics of conflict and cooperation in which law and politics merge. This book is intended to provide the first comprehensive, in-depth review and analysis of all such cases, combining a number of research efforts in the field.

Towards a Better Understanding of Judicial Behaviour in Processes of Ratification of EU Treaties

The pair of examples that have just been mentioned show the relevance of national courts' rulings on EU treaties. Precisely because of this salience, it is striking that not much attention has historically been devoted to such rulings in law and politics literature. In general, in political science studies until the seventies, courts were often excluded from the agendas of European integration researchers, and when they paid attention to these actors, they mainly focused on the Court of Justice of the European Union (Dehousse, 2000:16). In its original narrative, neofunctionalism focused on the interaction between the political development of European integration and the needs created by this integration (Haas, 1958, 1964; see also Schmitter, 2005; Rosamond, 2005). The neofunctionalist narrative is widely known: The integration in certain sectors of the European economy created incentives for further integration in other sectors. The growth in the number of transactions among member states created a need for supranational institutions, to which wide regulatory powers had to be bestowed, and which deepened the process (see *inter alia* Haas, 1958, 1964). In this narrative, judiciaries – especially national judiciaries – were mainly absent. After the classic writings of this school of thought, however, a number of authors (Stein, 1981; Weiler, 1981; Mancini, 1989) began to pay attention to the role of the European Court of Justice in the process of integration. Probably that is why, when Haas' neofunctionalist school was renewed by a body of literature led by Alec Stone Sweet (2000, 2004, 2010; with Brunell, 1998), the Court of Justice of the European Union and its role in furthering the integration became core elements of the analysis. However, on the one hand, these later writings focused on the Court of Luxembourg and its relation with national lower courts, with NHCs being less explored. And, on the other hand, such literature has generally referred to the everyday functioning of EU politics and not to the more concrete processes of treaty ratification.

Intergovernmentalism paid more attention to processes of treaty ratification (Moravsik, 1995, 1998; Moravsik and Nikolaides, 1999). Unlike neofunctionalism, intergovernmentalism defends that it is the states – in particular national governments – who are the key actors when trying to understand the political evolution of the EU (Moravsik, 1995). Although intergovernmentalism paid attention to processes of treaty ratification, conceiving periods of transformation of the EU as moments of convergence in national preferences, in this case, the emphasis was put especially on 'political' actors in the narrowest meaning of the word: in governments, negotiations, etc., with the role of NHCs being unexplored. As Stone Sweet and Brunnel (1998) suggested on a footnote of the end of their piece: 'Intergovernmentalist approaches to European integration are all but irrelevant to the concerns of this article ["The European Court and the national courts"], not least because they ignore the role of national judges and litigants'. The only offspring of this school of thought – if this can be so considered – which has paid attention to judicial actors has been Garret's (1992, 1995) 'structural modified realism', which has focused mainly on the European Court, but has neglected its agency to a large extent, as this theory conceives the decisions of the court as the result of the preferences of European states.

Despite this, the role of NHCs in processes of ratification of EU treaties is, for a number of reasons, a theoretically relevant phenomenon. The participation of NHCs in processes of treaty ratification involves interaction in the judicial arena between a number of convergent, juxtaposed or divergent interests: those of actors supporting ratification, those of actors opposing it or those of the very courts. For that reason, the decisions made in these rulings, far from being mere legal constructions, will be the expression of the dense political context in which they are framed. In studying national courts' rulings on EU treaties, this book is therefore one on judicial decision making in a clearly defined political frame: processes of ratification. In general, researches like this one have tried to answer general questions about judicial behaviour:

> [W]hy does a judge vote for one litigant instead of the other in a particular case? Does the judge base his or her decision on the legal principles governing the dispute, or is he or she affected by ideological, policy, or strategic considerations?
>
> (Weiden, 2010:335)

In the case of this research, however, judicial behaviour is greatly conditioned by the scenario in which it takes place and by the object of judicial review. The episodes that will be analyzed raise concrete problems and research questions regarding the context in which judicial behaviour operates. This book addresses in particular two important theoretical puzzles, which relate to the two most important decisions that courts made in these rulings: decisions on the merits and decisions of *Kompetenz-Kompetenz*. These two different research questions relate to two different branches of literature in judicial politics. Whereas the first question poses a problem of 'inter-branch interaction' – how courts interact with other branches of government – the second one poses a problem of 'intra-branch interaction' – how courts interact with each other (Friedman, 2005).

Intra-Branch Interaction: Kompetenz-Kompetenz *Decisions*

The role of NHCs in processes of ratification of EU treaties is salient, first, because the ratification of a new EU treaty may provide for new rules about how EU law and internal law will interact in the future. These new rules might implicitly set a certain role for NHCs under the new legal frame, even if only because they do not modify the preexisting status quo. Their participation in processes of treaty ratification gives national courts the possibility to have their say regarding their new position in the context of European legal integration. And NHCs have often used that possibility for their voice to be heard (see *inter alia* MacCormick, 1995; Claes, 2006; Kruma, 2010).

The first research question refers thus to how national courts have interpreted their own relation with EU law and with the Court of Justice. From the beginning of the process of integration, the Court of Justice has created with its praetorian case law the principles of primacy and direct effect of EU law (see Weiler, 1999). According to these principles, EU secondary law must take precedence over national law in cases of conflict between them. In addition, the interpretation of rules of EU law and their validity would correspond exclusively with that of the Court of Justice. Strictly following these principles was considered by the European Court as a guarantee for the functioning of the common market (Komarek, 2005) and as the very foundations of European law (Maduro, 2003:13–14). However, in their rulings on EU treaties, some national courts have challenged this interpretation, creating the doctrine of their own *Kompetenz-Kompetenz*: their capacity to make an exception to the application of secondary law in cases of conflict with core constitutional provisions (v. *inter alia* MacCormick, 1995; Weiler, 1995; Kiiver, 2010). In so doing, national courts have challenged the doctrine of the Court of Justice of the EU and the status quo of European legal integration. The question that arises therefore is: Which circumstances allowed national courts to challenge the doctrine and the power of the European Court of Justice by citing the Kompetenz-Kompetenz doctrine?

Statements of *Kompetenz-Kompetenz* have been studied by law scholars in many works (*inter alia* Everling, 1994; Weiler, 1995; Přibáň, 2009; Kruma, 2009). However, the only attempt to study such statements in a systematic and causal way has been the work recently published by Dyevre (2013). Using econometric models, the author has analyzed the variation in national courts' approaches to the issue of their own *Kompetenz-Kompetenz*. This book, however, only partially overlaps with his approach, as I have opted for a different methodology, a different theoretical framework, different explanatory variables and a different unit of analysis: Whereas Dyevre uses courts as units of analysis, this book uses statements of *Kompetenz-Kompetenz* in individual rulings. This has some consequences. On the one hand, this research does not exhaust the issue of *Kompetenz-Kompetenz*, but just makes a contribution to the more general debate, as a number of such doctrinal statements have been made in rulings which fall outside the object of research. My research strategy, however, has also some positive aspects. On the one hand, a large number of context-related variables are automatically controlled for, as such context is homogeneous for all the cases covered by the book. On the other hand, this implies that the study is carried out at a micro level – concrete rulings – instead of a meso–macro level – courts in general. This allowed me to analyze in more detail each ruling and to describe the micro politics of judicial decisional activity: I could analyze variables whose importance can only be understood by reviewing individual cases, variables which would otherwise go unnoticed, hidden in the greater generalization of analyses carried out at the level of courts.

Inter-Branch Interaction: Decisions on the Merits

The second research question refers to courts' decisions on the merits. Following Closa (2013a), the role of national courts in processes of EU treaties ratification can be understood in the light of Putnam's (1988) 'two-level game' theory. According to this theory, agreements in processes of ratification must be reached at two levels: the negotiation (level I) and the ratification (level II), so that an agreement cannot be modified at the ratification level without reopening the level of negotiation. This situation confers to NHCs great power in the ratification of treaties so that they can enjoy a de facto veto power (Closa and Castillo, 2012). Given that each ratification of an EU treaty requires the unanimous consent of all member states, and given that the giving of state consent is regulated by the internal legal systems of each member state (Maduro, 2003), the participation of NHCs may affect such giving of consent, making it easier, more complicated or even blocking it. Thus, the courts' role is relevant both for supporters and opponents of the ratification of the treaty. In his recent piece, Closa (2013a) studied the impact of Putnam's theory on the work of other authors, who in some cases have analyzed even processes of ratification of EU treaties (König and Hug, 2000; König and Slapin, 2004). But the object of study of this book presents a special feature in which it diverges from other applications of Putnam's theory. The participation of NHCs in processes of treaty ratification normally takes place once negotiation has already concluded and the content of the treaty has already been agreed to. For that reason, political actors have just two options to avoid what Lida (1993) called 'involuntary defection': They can either anticipate the reactions of NHCs before the text of the treaty is agreed to – and thus make the text of the treaty compatible with the expected preferences of courts – or they can try to constrain and control the reactions of NHCs to prevent them from vetoing the treaty once it has already been agreed to.

Processes of treaty ratification require agreement by all member states (Closa, 2013a), so the failure of ratification in one single state can become a setback of a continental-wide dimension (De Witte, 2004). In this sense, two types of results of the process of constitutional review are innocuous – declarations of constitutionality and rejections of the petitions on formal grounds – as these give green light to the process of ratification (Closa and Castillo, 2012). In fact, these types of outcomes are the most expected ones because, according to some studies on judicial behaviour, judicial actors do not usually challenge majority policy preferences (Dahl, 1957: 265; Keck, 2007: 513). Consequently, declarations of unconstitutionality can be expected to be avoided because they make the route of ratification more complex and can call into question the success of the entire process (Closa and Castillo, 2012; Closa, 2013b). However, the paradox is that decisions of this type are relatively frequent. The second research question is, therefore: *Which combinations of circumstances explain courts' decisions on the merits?*

NHCs' decisions on the merits have gone, until recently, essentially unnoticed. It is true, though, that such decisions have been analyzed by law scholars in some doctrinal pieces (*inter alia*, Herdegen, 1994; Luchaire, 2004; Chaltiel, 2009; Briza, 2009; Grimm, 2009); however, these types of works have been characterized by the analysis of a single ruling or a small group of rulings, which were approached from a purely doctrinal perspective. Very recently, however, in a few studies in political science (Closa and Castillo, 2012; Closa, 2013a, 2013b; Castillo, 2013) we have begun to approach the topic. This book complements such research in a number of ways. First, using the larger length of this book, a more detailed analysis of the cases will be carried out. Second, the impact of explanatory variables will be reassessed and new explanatory variables will be proposed. Third, instead of focusing only on declarations of unconstitutionality, I will also analyze declarations of constitutionality, which in the view of this book were caused by different and asymmetric explanatory paths. And fourth, a different methodology – qualitative comparative analysis (QCA) – will be used, which will allow us to understand judicial behaviour from different epistemological assumptions, this book being one of the first applications of QCA to judicial politics.

Judicial Decisions on EU Treaties: The Object of Study of This Book

As already suggested, this book studies *judicial decisions made by higher national courts with powers of constitutional review on EU treaties issued during their processes of ratification.* As this definition of the object of study is essential to understanding the rest of this volume, a number of preliminary clarifications are necessary.

First, by national higher courts with powers of constitutional review – 'NHCs' – I mean judicial-type organs with the last word regarding constitutional review in their countries. Thus, the analysis includes centralized constitutional courts like the German Federal Constitutional Court or even the *sui generis* French Constitutional Council, but also institutions like the Irish Supreme Court. It does not include, however, political organs such as constitutional committees in national parliaments or councils of state whose decisions are not binding. British courts are excluded because of a specificity of the legal system in this country: the supremacy of the Parliament, which is not subject to the decisions of organs with constitutional review powers (see Ferreres, 2004: 462). In addition, when referring to 'decisions of judicial-type organs', I also mean that the focus of the book is on courts' decisions and not decisions of individual magistrates. Two reasons justify this. First, not all NHCs' dissenting opinions are allowed, so in many cases it was not possible to obtain information about the decisions of individual justices (see Redher, 2007: 18). Second, the decisions of courts as collegiate organs are the ones with real political implications, as was noted by Volcansek (2001: 348–49): 'Individual judges vote, as do individual legislators or cabinet ministers, but the policy that governs is the one that achieves the winning majority'.

In addition, the focus is on processes of treaty ratification, as the aim of this book is to make a contribution to both the study of such processes and to the study of judicial behaviour in the context of high political pressures. A number of important rulings on EU treaties issued outside these processes[1] do not belong to the object of study in a strict sense, but given their obvious importance, they will often be commented on in this book.

Finally, it is important to note that, according to the definition of the object of study, this book does not study rulings in general, but concrete decisions contained in those rulings. The focus is on rulings in which courts entered into the merits of the case instead of rejecting the petition on formal grounds. In these rulings, in particular, the aim is to understand courts' decisions on the merits (declarations of constitutionality/unconstitutionality) and some courts' interpretative decisions (declarations of *Kompetenz-Kompetenz*). The goal is to provide for an innovative understanding of judicial behaviour, which is understood as a set of interrelated decisions contained in the ruling.

This book does not simply study judicial decisions contained in *some* rulings on EU treaties issued during their processes of ratification, but decisions included in *all* such rulings, which have all been systematically registered and analyzed. In this regard, this research has an important feature with deep methodological implications: it reviews the entire population of cases included in its object of study and not just a sample of them. In total, NHCs intervened in processes of treaty ratification on twenty-four occasions, and in seventeen of these occasions, a decision on the merits of the cases was issued (see Table 1.1). The importance of these rulings

Table 1.1 Rulings on European Union treaties issued during their processes of ratification

Period of accession	*Court*	*EDC Treaty*	*SEA*	*Maastr. Treaty*	*Amst. Treaty*	*Const. Treaty*	*Lisbon Treaty*	*Total cases*	*Share of claims rejected on formal grounds*	*Share of countries in which a claim was presented, by wave of enlargement*
Founding Member States	French C.C.	*	0	2 (+*1*)	1	1	1	5(+*1*)	17%	50%
	German F.C.C.	(+*1*)	0	1	0	0	1	2 (+*1*)	33%	
	Belgian C.C.	*	0	0	0	0	2 (+*1*)	2 (+*1*)	33%	
1973 enlargement	Irish S.C.	*	1	0	0	0	0	1	0%	33%
1986 enlargement	Spanish C.C.	*	*	1	0	1	0	2	0%	50%
1995 enlargement	Austrian C.C.	*	*	*	0	(+*1*)	(+2)	(+3)	100%	33%
2004 enlargement	Czech C.C.	*	*	*	*	0	2	2	0%	50%
	Slovak C.C.	*	*	*	*	1	0	1	0%	
	Slovenian C.C.	*	*	*	*	0	(+*1*)	(+*1*)	100%	
	Polish C.C.	*	*	*	*	0	1	1	0%	
	Latvian C.C.	*	*	*	*	0	1	1	0%	
Total		(+*1*)	1	4 (+*1*)	1	3 (+*1*)	8 (+4)	17 (+7)	29%	
Share claims rejected on formal grounds		100%	0%	20%	0%	25%	33 %	29%		

*Not an EU member state or court did not exist in that period
(+) Cases rejected on formal grounds

Sources: Primary sources, Closa and Castillo (2012), Closa (2013b). Author's elaboration.

is not limited to the most famous cases, such as those of the German Federal Constitutional Court, which had an enormous impact on legal literature (inter alia, Everling, 1994; Herdegen, 1994; MacCormick, 1995; Baquero, 2008; Lock, 2009), but also reaches other, less commented on episodes, such as the claims against the Lisbon Treaty in Latvia or Poland.

Table 1.1 shows the participation of NHCs in the processes of ratification of EU treaties, indicating for each institution and treaty the number of rulings with a decision on the merits and, in parentheses, the number of additional cases that were rejected on formal grounds. The series started in the fifties with the failed European Defense Community (EDC) Treaty, for which one complaint was presented and rejected on formal grounds[2] (Loewestein, 1955; Kommers, 1976; Closa, 2013b). Next, during the process of ratification of the Single European Act, the Irish Supreme Court issued the first ruling with a decision on the merits: the famous *Crotty* ruling.[3] In the process of ratification of the Maastricht Treaty, the number of rulings with a decision on the merits increases to four[4], plus one complaint rejected on formal grounds.[5] For the Amsterdam Treaty there was one more ruling in France.[6] Although the Nice Treaty was not judicialized, during the process of ratification of the Constitutional Treaty there were three rulings entering the merits of the case,[7] including the Slovak case, in which the claim was filed during the process of ratification but the court did not issue a ruling until 2008, when the ratification of the treaty had already been discarded (Bartovik, 2010: 53). In addition, for this treaty one complaint was rejected on formal grounds in Austria[8] and one complaint was presented in Germany for which the court never made a decision, after the treaty failed in the French and Dutch referendums (Wendel, 2011: 108). Finally, for the Lisbon Treaty the number of petitions dramatically increased. Eight rulings with a substantive decision on the merits were issued,[9] including one ruling in Poland pronounced when the treaty had already been ratified, but whose proceedings had started during the process of ratification.[10] In addition, four more claims were presented but rejected on formal grounds: two before the Austrian Constitutional Court,[11] one before the Belgian Constitutional Court[12] and one more before the Slovenian Constitutional Court.[13] It is worth noting that the share of rejection of petitions for the Lisbon Treaty is the highest one since the EDC Treaty: 33 per cent. In addition, at least two more rulings were issued regarding the treaty, but they were initiated when such treaty had already entered into force: one by the Hungarian Constitutional Court, and a third ruling before the Austrian Constitutional Court,[14] after a claim presented by thirty-seven members of the Freedom Party (FPÖ). As shown in the table, 29 per cent of the petitions were rejected on formal grounds, but in the majority of cases (71 per cent), the complaints gave rise to a judicial proceeding in which the constitutionality of the treaty was assessed. However, if the ECD Treaty is excluded, a clear trend of an increase of the share of petitions rejected on formal grounds can be observed.

Table 1.1 also shows the share of countries in which a claim was presented by waves of accession to the EU. For the founding member states, as well as for the member states of the 1986 and 2004 enlargements, the share of countries in which a claim was presented is notably high: 50 per cent. For the countries of the 1973 and 1995 enlargements, the share is 33 per cent, although this count excludes the United Kingdom (see earlier in this section). It is worth noting that only a few enlargements are not represented in the table: those taking place in 1981 (Greece), 2007 (Romania and Bulgaria) and 2013 (Croatia).

In total, seventeen rulings deciding on the merits of the cases could be observed, distributed among nine countries, over various decades of European integration. This distribution will allow us to study the functioning of NHCs in a high number of EU member states. Western and Eastern European countries are included in this book, as well as Northern and Southern European ones. The research also includes countries that joined the EU in different waves and epochs and thus have different historical backgrounds. The variation reaches even the types of state, including parliamentary monarchies (Spain and Belgium), semi-presidential republics (France) and parliamentary republics. Even more importantly, variation also exists with regard to the type of court studied; centralized constitutional courts in line with the Kelsenian tradition will be studied, but also supreme courts, such as the Irish one, or *sui generis* institutions such as the French Constitutional Council. Finally, France and Germany can be found among the countries with the highest number of cases: these countries have frequently been called the 'engine' of integration for historic, socioeconomic and political reasons.

Approaches to the Study of European Judicial Integration

The field of study of European judicial integration is defined by the multiplicity of approaches and interwoven theories. As Chalmers and Chaves (2012: 25) have suggested, '[M]ost recent accounts accept that no single narrative fully explains European Union judicial politics'. In this context, it is difficult to speak about dominant and omni-comprehensive approaches: a great variety of theories and approaches, contrasting or complementary, legal and political, coexist without each of them necessarily having the aspiration to offer a complete, self-sufficient explanation of all aspects of the behaviour of each of the different judicial actors in Europe. With this said, from an analytical perspective, it can be argued that there have been three main explanatory patterns in the field of studies about judicial behaviour in the European integration process: the political–contextual, the institutional self-empowering and the legalist:

- Political–contextual. This first explanatory pattern deals with the relationships between courts and political actors, as well as with the political context in which the courts behave. Whether because magistrates are selected by political actors, because courts have an interest in the stability of the broader political framework where they act or simply because the magistrates sympathize with certain actors or political ideas, the preferences of political actors and the political context of courts are considered here as an explanatory factor of judicial behaviour. Different approaches have embraced this political–contextual pattern as an explanation of judicial behaviour: for example, the 'modified structural realism' by Garret (1992), the liberal approach of Slaughter and Mattli (1997) or the approaches based on the political cost and the 'implementation costs' of which this work is a culmination (Closa and Castillo, 2012; Closa, 2013b). Although deeply divergent in other respects, all these studies converge in pointing to and using this link among preferences of political actors and judicatures as an explanation of judicial behaviour.

- Institutional self-empowering. Clearly, a great part of the research in this field has accepted the idea that courts seek the reinforcement of their own institutional power as a premise to understand their behaviour. Usually rooted in neoinstitutionalism, the main idea in this heterogeneous group of studies is that courts have an interest in self-empowerment and they do so by using their main working tool: their rulings. This pattern of behaviour has been adduced in reference to national lower courts (Stone Sweet, 2004), to high national courts (Baquero, 2008; Weiler, 1999) or to the Court of Justice of the European Union. This idea, in my opinion, is also the main explanatory pattern underlying the theory of 'inter-court competition' of Karen Alter (1997).
- Legalist. According to this approach, judicial decisions are fundamentally the result of the application of what is provided by the legal system (Garoupa and Grembi, 2012). Said in other terms, courts simply apply the law, and therefore the law explains judicial behaviour. This approach can fundamentally be found in the more orthodox legal–doctrinal studies, but also – combined with socio-political explanations – in some scientific–social and political studies, which accept, to some extent, 'role-oriented' behaviour in the courts. An example of a sophisticated use of explanations based on legal factors in combination with political variables can be found, for instance, in the liberal approach of Slaughter and Mattli (1997). Law-related explanations of judicial behaviour can also be found in some parts of the *sui generis* work of Weiler (1999).

One way or another, explicitly or implicitly, almost all explanations about this subject use one or more of these patterns that cross-cut the field. For example, it is evident that doctrinal works, given their concrete theoretical assumptions, privileged the legalist interpretative pattern. The leap to 'law in context' approaches – not to mention socio–political ones – allowed for the reception of other types of interpretative patterns.

Connoisseurs in the field will concede that, even if only because of the broadness of the terms used to formulate them, these three interpretative patterns, combined in different ways, constitute the raw staple material of the majority of the theories of European judicial integration.

In general, the analyses of NHCs' decisions on EU treaties in the framework of their ratification processes have had a legal–doctrinal bias, as well as a descriptive rather than explanatory intention. Political or hybrid approaches of an explanatory character have opted for the Court of Justice of the European Union as a preferential object of study. For this reason, this research finds itself compelled to build its own theoretical framework. However, the theoretical framework I will construct uses the three explanatory patterns described earlier as a basis to build a theory. In the case of this book, these three patterns serve as reference points and will structure the theoretical framework and the general hypotheses of the research. This will be seen in detail in the next chapter.

A Few Words on Methodology

Courts have been the realm of legal scholars only for a long time. This means that the tools for their research have been those of the doctrinal analysis: the assessment of the rulings, including the analysis of their compatibility with the constitutional or legal systems; their relation with other rulings of the same or different courts and so on. For a long time the methodology in the analysis of courts has remained unaltered. Maybe that is why in 1959, more than half a century ago, French lawyer and sociologist Jean Carbonnier (2001[1949]: 415) tried to imagine how a shift in the study of 'legal things' could be: he suggested that one day law schools would substitute the doctrinal analysis of the codes and of the rulings with laboratory instruments and experiments.

Maybe Carbonnier went too far in pretending that the logic of 'hard sciences' could be used to understand the dynamics of the juridical field. But his view is not that far from what works in judicial politics are doing nowadays: trying to understand judicial behaviour from a scientific–positivist perspective, looking for causal relations in the observation of the phenomena. For this reason, a book focusing on courts, as this is, has to devote some words to methodological questions. Tools for understanding courts and rulings are no longer only doctrinal reflections, but standardized, protocolized and replicable analyses whose technique requires an explanation.

This research comprises both theoretical and empirical considerations about the role of NHCs in the processes of ratification of EU treaties. It contains doctrinal analyses that follow the basic rules of legal research. However, the book also emphasizes trying to understand and to describe empirical causal relations, following the Cartesian principle of conducting reviews so general that nothing is omitted (Descartes. 2008[1637]). In doing so, the methods of empirical social sciences research are respected and followed, so that they are one of the main pillars structuring the whole book. This includes the formulation of hypotheses and the creation and operationalization of 'variables' or 'explanatory conditions'. Given the nature of the research, a 'medium-N' research in which the object of study was composed of only seventeen cases, the strategy followed was the combination of qualitative, quantitative and QCA analysis.

First, qualitative research was used in order to construct and test the variables. The central chapters of this book – Chapters 3 to 7 – are devoted to the qualitative analysis of the cases. In small-N and medium-N research, precision in the utilization of data is particularly important, since deviations in small details may lead to biased results, which, in larger-N research, may be counterbalanced by the very size of the datasets. In this sense, discussing the variables individually, offering qualitative information on each of them, constitutes a guarantee of rigour. This is particularly important, given that the data matrix in which subsequent quantitative and QCA analyses are based was, to a large extent, original: most of its content has been developed and used for the first time in this research. The qualitative analysis of the cases allowed me to show and justify the information regarding each of the variables for each of the cases in the data matrix. That information was gathered from a variety of sources: from doctrinal to social sciences academic writings, from legal provisions to the websites of the actors. The source of information is quoted in each case. This qualitative information was the basis of some modest quantitative analyses in the form of bivariate correlations, as well as of the QCA analyses.

QCA was used in order to assess the interaction of the explanatory conditions in producing courts' decisions. Note that in QCA there are no 'independent and dependent variables', but 'conditions and outcomes'; however, given that this research uses not only QCA but also other techniques, both pairs of concepts will be used in different parts of the book to refer to the phenomena explored. Given that QCA is particularly well suited for small- and medium-N studies, this tool was useful in dealing with the cases: QCA is a powerful methodology when trying to overcome the 'many variables, few cases' impasse (Delreux and Hesters, 2010: 3). In addition, QCA helped to approach the interplay between the explanatory conditions in a configurational way and furnished the research with a richer and more complex view and helped to 'go back to the cases' (see, e.g., Rihoux and Lobe, 2009) at a later stage in the research. Given its core role in the rest of the book, a few clarifications on QCA are necessary. QCA aims at discovering necessary and/or sufficient conditions for an outcome to occur. In a QCA solution, conditions might be present – in this book, represented with the name of the condition in uppercase – or absent – represented with the name in lowercase. This has a translation in set theory: the presence of a condition means inclusion of a case in the set of cases in which the condition is present, and absence of a condition means exclusion from that set. Since this book uses also 'fuzzy sets', inclusion or exclusion of cases from the sets may sometimes be a question of degree. In the solutions, it is usually the combination of conditions that leads to the outcome. The combination being represented by the symbol '*' that leads to the outcome. Sometimes, different combinations of conditions – represented by the symbol '+'– may alternatively drive to the outcome. The consistency of the solution indicates the share of cases included in it that had the outcome of interest. The coverage of the solution indicates the share of cases with the outcome of interest that is explained by that solution.

For the sake of clarity, during the rest of this book I will avoid methodological specifications as much as possible. To ensure rigour, however, I have included a methodological appendix at the end of this book, which includes raw data, operationalization decisions, truth tables and so on. Readers interested in a deeper understanding of configurational analysis beyond the essential indications made in this section and in the appendix will find it useful to check some of the basic works on QCA techniques (*inter alia* Ragin, 2008; Rihoux and Ragin, 2009).

Approach and Structure of This Book

As has been already mentioned, this book takes an interdisciplinary law and politics approach in which doctrinal analysis is combined with the discovery of causal relations from a social sciences perspective. After this introduction, Chapter 2 sets out the theoretical framework of the book and presents some preliminary hypotheses. Chapters 3 and 4 analyze, respectively, the two 'dependent variables' – or, in QCA jargon, 'outcomes' – of the research: decisions on the merits and statements of *Kompetenz-Kompetenz*. Chapters 4 to 7 make a qualitative analysis of the causal impact of explanatory conditions of legal, political and institutional types, and Chapter 8 presents the QCA analyses where the interactions between these explanatory conditions are made explicit. Chapter 9 presents some final conclusions. At the end of the book, readers will find a methodological appendix in which operationalization decisions and databases used are displayed and commented on.

Notes

1 *Inter alia* Danish Supreme Court, case UfR 1998, 800 Maastricht, decision of 6 April 1998.
2 German Federal Constitutional Court, case 1 BvG 396, *Treaty of the European Defense Community*, decision of 30 July 1952. A number of other complaints were presented, but for different reasons the court never made a decision on them.
3 Irish Supreme Court, case *Crotty v. An Taoiseach* [1987] IESC 4; [1987 IR 713], decision of 9 April 1987.

4 French Constitutional Council, cases 92–308 DC *Maastricht I*, decision of 9 April 1992 and 92–312 DC *Maastricht II* decision of 2 September 1992. Spanish Constitutional Court, Declaration 001/1992 on the *Treaty of Maastricht*, decision of 1 July 1992. German Federal Constitutional Court, case 2 BvR 2134 et al. *Treaty of Maastricht*, decision of 12 October 1993.
5 French Constitutional Council, case 92–313 DC *Maastricht III*, decision of 23 September 1992.
6 French Constitutional Council, case 97–394 DC *Amsterdam*, decision of 31 December 1997.
7 French Constitutional Council, case 2004–505 DC *Constitutional Treaty*, decision of 19 November 2004. Spanish Constitutional Court, declaration 1/2004 on the *Treaty Establishing a Constitution for Europe*, decision of 13 December 2004. Slovak Constitutional Court, case II.U.S. 171/05–175 *Constitutional Treaty*, decision of 27 February 2008.
8 Austrian Constitutional Court, case G 62/05 *Constitutional Treaty*, decision of 18 June 2005
9 French Constitutional Council, case 2007–560 DC *Treaty of Lisbon*, decision of 20 December 2007. Czech Constitutional Court, cases PL US 19/08 *Treaty of Lisbon I*, decision of 30 September 2008; and PL US 29/09 *Treaty of Lisbon II*, decision of 3 November of 2009. Latvian Constitutional Court, case 2008–35–01 *Treaty of Lisbon*, decision of 7 April 2009. German Federal Constitutional Court, case 2 be 2/08 et al. *Treaty of Lisbon*, decision of 30 June 2009. Belgian Constitutional Court, case 58/2009 *Treaty of Lisbon I*, decision of 19 March 2009; and case 125/2009 *Treaty of Lisbon II*, decision of 16 July 2009.
10 Polish Constitutional Court, case K32/09 *Treaty of Lisbon*, decision of 23 November 2010.
11 Austrian Constitutional Court, cases SV 2/08–3, 80/08–3 G SV 3/08–6, G 81/08–6 SV 3/08–6, 81/08–6 G, decision on 30 September 2008; and case G 149–152/08–5, decision of 11 March 2009.
12 Belgian Constitutional Court, case 156/2009 *Treaty of Lisbon III*, decision of 17 October 2008.
13 Slovenian Constitutional Court, case Ul-49/08 *Treaty of Lisbon*, decision of 17 October 2008.
14 Austrian Constitutional Court, case SV 1/10–9, decision of 12 June 2010.

References

Alter, K. (1997) 'Explaining National Courts Acceptance of European Court Jurisprudence: A Critical Evaluation of Theories of Legal Integration', in Slaughter, A-M, Stone Sweet, A., and Weiler, J. H. H., *The European Court and National Courts – Doctrine and Jurisprudence. Legal Change in Its Social Context*, Oxford: Hart, pp. 227–52.

Baquero, J. (2008) 'The legacy of the Maastricht-Urteil and the pluralist movement', *European Law Journal* 14(4): 389–422.

Bartovic, V. (2010) 'National Council of the Slovak Republic in the EU Agenda: Giant in Theory, Dwarf in Practice', in Král, D. and Bartovic, V., *The Czech and the Slovak Parliaments After the Lisbon Treaty*, European Institute for European Policy, at www.europeum.org/doc/publications/Narodni_parlamenty_ENG_Web.pdf (02.03.2011).

Bříza, P. (2009) 'The Czech Republic. The constitutional court on the Lisbon Treaty. Decision of 26 November 2008', *European Constitutional Law Review* 5(1): 143–64.

Carbonnier, J. (2001 [1949]) *Flexible Droit. Pour une sociologie du droit sans rigueur*, Paris: L.G.D.J.
Castillo, P. (2013) 'La Política Judicial del Tribunal Constitucional en los procesos de ratificación de tratados de la Unión Europea: aproximación desde un nuevo realismo jurídico', *Revista de Estudios Políticos* 159: 107–38.
Chalmers, D. and Chaves, M. (2012) 'The reference points of EU judicial politics', *Journal of European Public Policy* 19(1): 25–42.
Chaltiel, F. (2009), 'Droit constitutionnel européen', *Revue Française de Droit Constitutionnel* 82: 367–75.
Claes, M. (2006) *The National Courts Mandate in the European Constitution*, Oxford: Oxford University Press.
Closa, C. (2013a) *The Politics of Ratification of European Union Treaties*, London: Routledge.
Closa, C. (2013b) 'National Higher Courts and the Ratification of European Union Treaties', *West European Politics* 36(1): 97–121.
Closa, C. and Castillo, P. (2012), 'National Courts and Ratification of European Union treaties', in Evas, T., Lord, C., and Liebert, U. *Multilayered Representation in the European Union. Parliaments, Courts and the Public Sphere*, Berlin: Nomos, pp.129–57.
Dahl, R. (1957) 'Decision-Making in a Democracy: The Supreme Court as a National Policy-Maker', *Journal of Public Law* 6: 279–95.
De Witte, B. (2004) 'The process of ratification of the Constitutional Treaty and the crisis options: A legal perspective', *EUI Working Paper LAW No. 2004/16*, at http://cadmus.eui.eu/bitstream/handle/1814/2831/law04–16.pdf;jsessionid=05EE3A663DA3DCCBDF286C9341335439?sequence=1 (23.04.2012).
Dehousse, R. (2000) 'Integration Through Law Revisited: Some Thoughts on the Juridification of the European Political Process', in Snyder, F. (ed.) *The Europeanisation of Law. The Legal Effects of European Integration*, Oxford: Hart, pp. 15–29.
Delreux T. and Hesters D. (2010) 'Solving contradictory simplifying assumptions in QCA: Presentation of a new best practice', *Compass Working Paper*, at www.compasss.org/files/WPfiles/Delreux2010.pdf (11.01.2011).
Descartes, R. (2008[1637]) *Discourse on the Method of Rightly Conducting the Reason and Seeking the Truth in the Sciences*, at www.gutenberg.org/files/59/59-h/59-h.htm (11.04.2012).
Dyevre, A. (2013) 'European integration and national courts: Defending sovereignty under institutional constraints?', *European Constitutional Law Review* 9(1):139–68.
Everling, U. (1994) 'The Maastricht judgement of the German Federal Constitutional Court and its significance for the development of the European Union', *Yearbook of European Law* 14(1): 1–19.
Ferreres, V. (2004) 'The European model of constitutional review of legislation: Toward decentralization?', *International Journal of Constitutional Law* 2(3): 461–91.
Friedman, B. (2005) 'The politics of judicial review', *Texas Law Review* 84(2): 287–337.
Garoupa, N. and Grembi, V. (2012) 'Judicial Review and Political Bias: Moving from Consensual to Majoritarian Democracy?', at SSRN http://papers.ssrn.com/sol3/papers.cfm?abstract_id=2097259 (26.09.2012).

Garret, G. (1992) 'International cooperation and institutional choice: The European community's internal market', *International Organization* 46(2): 533–60.

Garret, G. (1995) 'The politics of legal integration in the European Union', *International Organization* 49(1): 171–81.

Grimm, D. (2009) 'Defending sovereign statehood against transforming the European Union. Comments on the German Constitutional Court's decision on the Lisbon Treaty', *European Constitutional Law Review* 5(3): 353–73.

Haas, E. B. (1958) *The Uniting of Europe: Political, Social and Economic Forces, 1950–1957*, Stanford: Stanford University Press.

Haas, E. B. (1964) *Beyond the Nation State: Functionalism and International Organization*, Stanford: Stanford University Press.

Herdegen, M. (1994) 'Maastricht and the German Constitutional Court: Constitutional restraints for an ever closer union', *Common Market Law Review* 31(2): 235.

Keck, T. (2007) 'Party politics or judicial independence? The regime politics literature hits the law schools', *Law & Social Inquiry* 32(2): 511–44.

Kiiver, P. (2010) 'The Lisbon judgment of the German Constitutional Court: A court-ordered strengthening of the national legislature in the EU', *European Law Journal* 16(5): 578–88.

Komarek, J. (2005) 'Federal elements in the community judicial system: Building coherency in the community legal order', at http://mosquito-net.eu/documents/Komarek_Federal_Elements-CMLRev-final.pdf (21.04.2012).

Kommers, D. P. (1976), *Judicial Politics in West Germany. A Study of the Federal Constitutional Court*, Los Angeles: Sage.

König, T. and Simon H. (2000), 'Ratifying Maastricht: Parliamentary votes on international treaties and theoretical solution concepts', *European Union Politics* 1(1): 93–124.

König, T. and Slapin J. (2004), 'Bringing parliaments back in the sources of power in the European treaty negotiation', *Journal of Theoretical Politics* 16(3): 357–94.

Kruma, K. (2009) 'Constitutional Courts in the Europeanisation of National Constitutions', in Closa, Carlos (ed.) *The Lisbon Treaty and National Constitutions. Europeanisation and Democratic Implications*, at www.astrid-online.it/Riforma-de/Studi-e-ri/Archivio-25/ARENA-Report-3_2009.pdf#page=145 (12.06.2012).

Kruma, K. (2010) 'Constitutional courts and the Lisbon Treaty. The future based on mutual trust', Centre for European Policy Studies, at www.isn.ethz.ch/isn/Digital-Library/Publications/Detail/?ots591=0c54e3b3–1e9c-be1e-2c24-a6a8c7060233&lng=en&id=117517 (12.06.2012).

Lida, K. (1993) 'When and how do domestic constraints matter? Two-level games with uncertainty', *Journal of Conflict Resolution* 37(3): 403–26.

Lock, T. (2009) Why the European Union is not a state. Some critical remarks. Comments on the German Constitutional Court's decision on the Lisbon Treaty, *European Constitutional Law Review* 5(3): 407–20.

Loewestein, K. (1955) 'The Bonn Constitution and the European community treaties. A study on judicial frustration', *The Yale Law Journal* 64: 805–39.

Luchaire, F. (2004) 'Le conseil constitutionnel devant la constitution pour l'Europe', *Revue Française de Droit Constitutionnel* 59: 465–71.

MacCormick, N. (1995) 'The Maastricht-Urteil: Sovereignty now', *European Law Journal* 1(3): 259–66.

Maduro, M. (2003) 'Las formas del poder constitucional de la Unión Europea', *Revista de Estudios Políticos* 119: 11–55.
Mancini, F. (1989) 'The making of a constitution for Europe', *Common Market Law Review* 26(4): 595–614.
Moravsik, A. (1995) 'Liberal intergovernmentalism and integration: A rejoinder', *Journal of Common Market Studies* 33(4): 611–28.
Moravsik, A. (1998), *The Choice for Europe: Social Purpose and State Power from Messina to Maastricht*, London: UCL Press.
Moravsik, A. and Nikolaides K. (1999) 'Explaining the treaty of Amsterdam: Interests, influence, institutions', *Journal of Common Market Studies*, 37(1): 57–85.
Přibáň, J. (2009), 'From "which rule of law?" to "the rule of which law"? Post-communist experiences of European legal integration', *The Hague Journal on the Rule of Law* 1(2): 337–58.
Putnam, R. D. (1988) 'Diplomacy and domestic politics: The logic of a two-level game', *International Organization* 42(3): 427–60.
Ragin, C. (2008) *Redesigning Social Inquiry: Fuzzy Sets and Beyond*, Chicago: University of Chicago Press
Redher, B. (2007) 'What is political about jurisprudence? Courts, politics, and political science in Europe and the United States', MPIfG Discussion Paper, Max Planck Institute for the Study of Society, Cologne (Germany).
Rihoux, B. and Lobe, B. (2009) 'The case for qualitative comparative analysis (QCA): Adding leverage for thick cross-case comparison', in Byrne, D. and Ragin, C. (eds.) *The Sage Handbook of Case-Based Methods*, Los Angeles: Sage, pp. 222–42.
Rihoux, B. and Ragin C. (2009) *Configurational Comparative Methods*, Los Angeles: Sage.
Rosamond, B. (2005) 'The uniting of Europe and the foundation of EU studies: Revisiting the neofunctionalism of Ernst B. Haas', *Journal of European Public Policy* 12(2): 237–54.
Schmitter, P. (2005) 'Ernst B. Haas and the legacy of neofunctionalism', *Journal of European Public Policy* 12(2): 255–72.
Slaughter, A.-M. and Mattli, W. (1997) 'The Role of National Courts in the Process of European Integration: Accounting for Judicial Preferences and Constraints', in Slaughter, A.-M., Stone Sweet, A. and Weiler, J. H. H., *The European Court and National Courts: Doctrine and Jurisprudence. Legal Change in Its Social Context*, Oxford: Hart Publishing, pp. 253–77.
Stein, E. (1981) 'Lawyers, judges, and the making of a transnational constitution', *American Journal of International Law* 75(1):1–27.
Stone Sweet, A. (2000) *Governing with Judges. Constitutional Politics in Europe*, Oxford: Oxford University Press.
Stone Sweet, A. (2004) *The Judicial Construction of Europe*, Oxford: Oxford University Press.
Stone Sweet, A. (2010) 'The European Court of justice and the judicialization of EU governance', *Living Reviews in European Governance* 5(2): 1–50.
Stone Sweet, A. and Brunell, T. (1998) 'Constructing a supranational constitution: Dispute resolution and governance in the European community', *American Political Science Review* 92(1): 63–81.

Volcansek, M., (2001) 'Constitutional courts as veto players: Decrees and divorce in Italy', *European Journal of Political Research* 39(3): 347–72.

Weiden, D. (2010) 'Judicial politicization, ideology, and activism at the high courts of the United States, Canada, and Australia', *Political Research Quarterly* 64(2): 335–47.

Weiler, J. H. H. (1981) 'The community system: The dual character of supranationalism', *Yearbook of European Law* 1(1): 268–306.

Weiler, J. H. H. (1995) *Europa, fin de siglo*, Madrid: Centro de Estudios Constitutionales.

Weiler, J. H. H. (1999) *The Constitution of Europe. "Do the New Clothes Have an Emperor?" and Other Essays on European Integration*, Cambridge: Cambridge University Press.

Wendel, M. (2011) 'Lisbon before the courts: Comparative perspectives', *European Constitutional Law Review* 7(1): 96–137.

2 Constructing a Model of Judicial Behaviour

Theoretical Framework

The Theoretical Approach: Some General Ideas

In their work on European legal integration, Slaughter and Mattli (1997: 257) decided to 'move away from contending paradigms such as realism and neo-functionalism and toward the development of mid-range hypotheses that are both theoretically sophisticated and empirically informed'. In my view, that strategy is particularly advisable in the case of this book. Given the object of study, the great narratives of European integration, or even of European legal integration, do not provide already-made theories and hypotheses with which to answer the research questions, even if this study has gathered their abundant contributions. And this is so for two reasons:

- First, as I suggested previously, the greatest part of literature on EU law and politics (among the exceptions, see Closa and Castillo, 2012; Closa, 2013) has focused its attention on the Court of Justice of the European Union, and not on the national higher courts (NHCs), when explaining judicial behaviour. Even more so, the majority of studies that have addressed the behaviour of NHCs – see especially Slaughter, Stone Sweet and Weiler (1997) – have not done it on the concrete processes of ratification of treaties. I think that the singularity of the actors (NHCs with powers of constitutional review) and context (ratification processes) researched require a *sui generis* explanation that allows a grasp of such specificity.
- Second, the dominant methodological approaches in the field are either qualitative or quantitative. In general, there is always an interaction between the methodology employed and the type and nature of theories and hypotheses that are possible to falsify using said methodology. The main methodology I will use in this research – configurational analysis with qualitative comparative analysis (QCA) – is determinist and conjunctural, and focuses on the interaction between explanatory conditions. This creates the need for an

enunciation of theories and phrasing of hypotheses coherent with the configurational nature of the methodology chosen.

Ultimately, the theoretical framework of this book is novel to a great extent, even if it takes inspiration from some of the most relevant literature in the field. Such theoretical approach is the result of an iterative process of dialogue between theory and qualitative analysis of the cases that has allowed for the formulation of hypotheses of medium range which are adapted to the uniqueness of the object of study.

At the same time, the theoretical framework of this research is built around three fundamental pillars. First, this research analyzes judicial behaviour as a complex phenomenon, as a set of decisions that are expressed in the ruling and that are not limited to the decision on the merits. Second, this research combines the three patterns of judicial behaviour identified in the first chapter of this book: political-contextual, self-empowering and legalistic. Therefore, it can be considered an instance of what the law theorist Brian Tamanaha (1997) described as 'integrative approaches', in which legal variables are integrated in empirical social sciences research. Third, and related to the foregoing, this research combines explanatory variables of diverse types – political/contextual, institutional and legal – so that, instead of privileging a certain approach over the others, it tries to scrutinize how explanatory conditions of different natures are combined and interact in order to cause certain results.

The structure of this chapter takes into account the three aforementioned characteristics of this research. After this brief introduction, I will present the two types of 'judicial decisions' covered by the book: 'interpretative decisions' and 'decisions on the merits'. In the third section I refer to three institutional objectives that, in my view, courts seek when issuing their rulings, and which constitute the most general explanation for their behaviour. Once I have done this, I go into detail about the explanatory conditions and configurational hypotheses regarding the 'dependent variables' of the research: decisions of *Kompetenz-Kompetenz* and decisions on the merits.

Judicial Behaviour Studied in Its Complexity: Interpretative Decisions and Decisions on the Merits

One of the original aspects of the approach of this book is that it aims to offer a comprehensive analysis of judicial behaviour, and to do so it analyzes not only courts' decisions on the merits – as the major part of literature on judicial politics does – but also some interpretative decisions adopted in the legal reasoning of the rulings. Judicial behaviour is thus studied in this book at a high level of complexity, by understanding it as a set of decisions expressed in different parts of the ruling.

General literature on judicial politics usually focuses on courts' decisions on the merits (*inter alia* Herron and Randazzo, 2003; Carruba et al, 2008; Hönnige, 2009). Decisions on the merits are, in general, the most relevant part of the outcome of a judicial proceeding. In its decision on the merits, the court decides the case at stake. For instance, in the cases analyzed by this book, courts declare the constitutionality or unconstitutionality of a treaty, which is obviously a question of enormous political salience. The analysis of judicial behaviour focusing only on decisions on the merits is, however, insufficient. Although a number of studies have tried to pay attention to the legal argumentation and doctrine of courts from a scientific–social perspective (see *inter alia* Clark and Lauderdale, 2012), this aspect of judicial behaviour is still under-analyzed. This is, however, surprising, given the importance of judicial argumentation and interpretation of law. As Edouard Lambert warned almost one century ago, the ability to declare the unconstitutionality of certain rules is a judge's most powerful tool, but alongside it judges have a second tool available to them: their 'more simple and less noisy' interpretation of the text (Lambert, 2010 [1921]: 145 et seq.). Through such interpretation, courts can make decisions with important political implications which are sometimes binding on other actors. This research considers that such interpretative decisions must also be analyzed in order to complete a comprehensive exploration of judicial behaviour.

Of course, not all interpretative decisions of the courts have the same salience. However, there is a type of interpretative decision that can be found in many of the cases analyzed by this book: the *Kompetenz-Kompetenz* statements of NHCs. Although the *Kompetenz-Kompetenz* doctrine will be explained in depth later on – Chapter 4 is devoted in its entirety to it – it is worth noting that such a doctrine is a construction according to which NHCs claim to have the last word about the constitutionality of European Union law. In their rulings, some NHCs have claimed the authority to declare EU secondary law non-applicable in certain cases, thus potentially breaching the principles of primacy and direct effect of EU law, as well as the interpretative authority of the Court of Justice of the European Union (see MacCornick, 1995). If there is a type of interpretative decision that is politically relevant, this is it.

This work rests upon this dialectic between decisions on the merits and interpretative decisions of *Kompetenz-Kompetenz*. From the perspective of this book, judicial behaviour has a complex expression through both of them, so both will be studied in detail. I will suggest that when it comes to reaching their legal and political objectives – which will be presented in the following section – courts can use decisions of one type or the other, or combinations of them both.

A Complex Motivational Background: Institutional Objectives of the Courts

The most recent literature on judicial politics has overcome purely psycho-sociological explanations of judicial decision making. It now focuses on strategic accounts about the rational behaviour of courts when trying to pursue certain institutional objectives. According to Epstein and Knight (2000: 625), within this approach (1) actors act in order to achieve certain objectives; (2) such actors act strategically in the sense that their decisions depend on their expectation of other actors' behaviour and (3) these decisions are structured by the institutional framework within which they act (see also Elster, 1986). It is thus necessary to define which were those institutional objectives in cases on EU treaties, taking into account that magistrates pursue as a general rule not one but a multiplicity of simultaneous objectives that are potentially relevant to explain their behaviour (Baum, 1994: 760).

In the previous chapter I suggested that there are three different explanatory patterns that cross-cut the literature on judicial behaviour in the field of European integration studies: political–contextual, self-empowering and legalist. Now, I aim at highlighting how each of those three explanatory patterns puts forward the existence of an institutional objective of the courts. Although in the field of European judicial politics the aforesaid patterns have been used more often – although not uniquely – to explain the behaviour of the European Court of Justice (ECJ), I believe that they are in general also applicable to the NHCs. In fact, I think these three patterns can be considered, not mutually incompatible, but complementary, as each of them points at goals that all courts are usually interested in pursuing. As I said, each of these patterns of behaviour reveals the existence of one institutional goal: first, a contextual objective referring to the stability of the broader political context in which their activity is developed; second, an objective of institutional self-empowerment relating to the maximization of the authority of the court; and third, a legal-type objective, rooted in the ordinary functions of courts in their facet [or dimension, or aspect] of legal actors, which refers to the application of law.

(1) *Stability of the political framework*. The first objective has a political character and points at a relation between judicial behaviour and the general context in which the court operates. The general literature on political science suggests that when pursuing their own objectives, courts must take into consideration the interests and preferences of other actors (*inter alia* Lindquist and Solberg, 2007; Clark, 2009). Accordingly, the enormous importance that NHCs acquire in the context of the processes of ratification of European Union treaties must be noted. Judicial institutions are sometimes characterized by the literature on judicial politics as actors holding veto power (Brouard, 2009; Kaiser, 1998; Tsebelis, 2002;

Volcansek, 2000). That is often the case in processes of ratifying EU treaties, in which an unfavourable decision by a court can imply in some cases the failure of the whole ratification process at the EU level (Closa and Castillo, 2012; Closa, 2013). A scenario of this type could become enormously costly in political terms, as it could challenge the preferences of other actors, imposing on the courts a burden difficult to assume by a judicial actor.

From this perspective, it can be argued that NHCs want to avoid creating problems for the broader institutional framework that legitimates their very existence and action. Courts will therefore behave with a 'responsible' behaviour regarding such institutional framework (see Closa, 2013). In general, then, it is predictable that courts incorporate the preferences of the generality of the political actors as one of their own institutional objectives. As will be showed in the empirical part of this book, such preferences point directly to the correct and easy ratification of the treaties, an objective on which there was a notable consensus among the national political elites in almost all the cases.

(2) *Empowerment of the court.* The second institutional objective of the courts refers to their interest in strengthening their authority and power. This can be understood as a form of 'empowerment' as Stone Sweet (2004: 20) described it, in which 'given the opportunity, judges will work to enhance their own authority and legal control and, therefore, policy outcomes, and to reduce the control of other institutional actors, such as national executives, parliament, and other judges'.

Prior to the beginning of the process of European integration, NHCs were at the peak of their respective judicial systems, and they were therefore the most powerful actors in relation to what Bourdieu (2001:169) defined as the most important characteristic of the juridical field: the power to '*dire le droit*'[1] ('to say the law'). The emergence of the European integration process, however, changed this situation radically. Together with the internal legal systems governed by the national constitutions, another overlapping legal system – the European one – was born. The EU legal system claimed to have an independent source of legitimacy based on European Union treaties through which member states had agreed to the transfer of sovereign competences. The Court of Justice of the European Union was created as a legal guarantor of said treaties, and in this way it defied the previous interpretative monopoly by NHCs over the entire legal system. It was for that reason that they perceived the ECJ as a threat (Slaughter and Mattli, 1997). As Konrad Hesse (Voßkuhle, 2010: 176) – ex-magistrate in Karlsruhe – acknowledged, the growing importance of the European Court meant 'a change of the Federal Constitutional Court's tasks, its position and its possibilities of action'.

For many years, NHCs seemed to slowly adapt to the new situation. At a certain point, though, this trend started to change. In its *Maastricht-Urteil* decision, the German Federal Constitutional Court threatened to declare EU secondary law contrary to the constitution, in a movement that was seen as a challenge to the ECJ, its interpretative authority and the principles slowly established by its case law (Weiler, 1999; Baquero, 2008). The decision of the German Federal Constitutional Court was self-empowering and enlarged its sphere of power, and its doctrine would soon spread across other European courts. Ultimately, what is underlying this is a fight for the power to provide an ultimate interpretation of what is law in each case (‘*dire le droit*’). That is, there is a fight of power between the ECJ and the NHCs, which crystallized in their competing doctrinal views about the relation between European and constitutional laws. This conflict shows that institutional self-empowerment is also one of the objectives guiding the behaviour of national courts, even if not the only one.

(3) *Appropriate application of law to case*. The third institutional objective is of the legal type, and it is connected with what Merton (1949) would have called the ‘manifest’ function of the institution: the application of the legal system to the concrete case; what Baum (1994: 751) has denominated as the objective of making ‘good law’, that is, the precise application of legal rules. Even if courts seek other more political goals, they do not ignore their function of applying the law to the cases. What happens is simply that those other institutional objectives and a ‘good’ application of the legal system to the case are not mutually incompatible. The ‘open texture of law’ (Hart, 1997 [1961]) has a lot to do with this.

It can be expected, especially from those courts with powers of constitutional review, that they will try to guarantee the supremacy of the constitution when assessing EU treaties. This is, after all, the main function entrusted to them. In his controversy with Carl Schmitt, Hans Kelsen (2009 [1931]) stated that the defense of the constitution had to be trusted to an independent court. Kelsen’s view was that this would help to maintain the coherence and the hierarchical structure of the legal system around a positive constitution. A legalist vision would suggest that courts are then limited to fulfil the legal function that was entrusted to them. This slightly ‘legalist’ vision is, however, compatible with a socio-political approach to judicial behaviour. From the perspective of the historical–sociological neo-institutionalism, it can be stated that certain values and principles related to the neutral application of law to the cases belong to courts as institutions, and therefore guide judicial behaviour (see Whittington, 2000: 623 et seq.). Magistrates have been socialized in law faculties (Baum, 1994: 756) and probably believe in the construction of the legal system and in the functions of constitutional review entrusted to the courts, more or less in the manner in which Kelsenian positivism does. This is what Dyèvre (2008) called the ‘formal-positivist’ model of thinking about the law. Magistrates share a particular legalist ethos or, as Shapiro (2002) acknowledged, belong to the *epistemic* community of law. A central legal value, such as making ‘correct’ rulings from a legal perspective, especially relevant when the aim is to integrate two overlapping legal systems, very likely is taken into account by the magistrates.

At the same time, legal norms can have different degrees of definiteness. In many cases, law, and specifically constitutional law, is relatively indeterminate. This indefiniteness facilitates the existence of different interpretations of the 'right' solution to the case, all of them equally defensible in legal terms. This allows courts to satisfy their two first institutional objectives without neglecting their obligations as guardians of the constitution: the chosen interpretation in these cases is simply as 'legal' as any other alternative one. On the other hand, however, it is indeed possible to find concrete norms that are precise and determinate enough as to notably reduce the margin of interpretation of the court and to impose, or at least induce, a concrete solution. Some of these norms, such as those contained in European clauses, are because of their transversality – they can be found in a great number of constitutions and cases – susceptible to offer cross-case explanations and causal patterns.

In this book, these three institutional goals are considered to be the general motivational frame of courts when adopting decisions. They are the broad explanation for why certain variables have an impact on judicial behaviour. The first institutional objective, referring to the stability and congruence with the broader political context in which the courts operate, would explain the eventual importance of variables such as the preferences of the other political actors or the calculation by courts of the political cost of their decisions. The second institutional objective, the maximization of their institutional power, would clarify why some courts pronounce decisions of *Kompetenz-Kompetenz*, and it also would help to explain the impact on the cases of certain explanatory variables such as cross-fertilization or courts' powers of review. Lastly, the third institutional objective, the correct application of law and the maximization of coherence between the two overlapping legal systems, would explain why courts integrate into their decision making certain legal norms, such as European clauses.

Nevertheless, these institutional objectives only act as a general framework of judicial behaviour. In order to understand the specific judicial decisions, such behaviour must be analyzed using what configurational language calls 'explanatory conditions'. These conditions are related to said institutional objectives and interact with one another, creating causal paths.

The Decisions of *Kompetenz-Kompetenz*: Explanatory Conditions and Configurational Hypotheses

Kompetenz-Kompetenz statements are a challenge to the Court of Justice. It could be said that these decisions are mainly motivated by what was defined as the second institutional objective of the courts: the will for self-empowerment. However, an explanation based solely on this element is insufficient: although all NHCs should have a priori an equal tendency to try to empower themselves, not all of them have adopted *Kompetenz-Kompetenz* decisions, so there must be more factors in play. This forces this book to take into consideration other elements, from explanatory conditions of legal character to others of an institutional type, that allow the research to complete the general picture and to understand the variations between rulings regarding this issue.

The European Clauses

As said earlier, law in general is undetermined and allows for different interpretations, but some concrete rules can be definite enough as to condition judicial behaviour, and, therefore, it is worth scrutinizing them. When taking legal and judicial variables into consideration, this research moves towards the area of 'integrative approaches' (Tamanaha, 1997), which include legal-type variables in social sciences analyzes of judicial behaviour. Unlike most research in judicial politics, which rely almost exclusively on socio-political variables – as Martin Shapiro (2002: 37) acknowledged – this book uses sociological neoinstitutionalism (see Hall and Taylor, 1996) to emphasize the role of courts as applicators of law to the cases, in line with Whittington (2000).

In this book it is suggested that a type of legal norm is especially relevant when assessing the constitutionality of EU treaties: the 'European' or 'integration' clauses in national constitutions. European clauses in national constitutions offer a great variation regarding their content (Claes, 2005, 2007). In many cases, they are limited to a concise acknowledgment of the membership of the country to the European Union. In other cases, detailed descriptions of the connections between the political bodies of the country and the European Union legal system are made. Although in certain cases national constitutions have an integration clause from the very moment of the accession of the country to the European Union, in other cases, the incorporation of said clause was made some time later through constitutional reform (Claes, 2005, 2007). Following Claes (2007), four issues were analyzed in European clauses: explicit mention of the EU, specific regulation of the process of ratification for EU treaties, conditioning of membership to the respect by the EU for certain political principles and declaration of primacy of EU law. As Whittington (2000: 620) acknowledges, if law matters in judicial behaviour, 'it must have been because it was explicit, specific, determinate and coercive'. Each of the four issues analyzed in European clauses shares these characters, except perhaps the one referring to coercion. Throughout an iterative process of dialogue between the theory and the cases, these four issues were analyzed – see in particular Chapter 5 – and preliminary evidence was found that two of them could have an impact on judicial behaviour:

- *Substantive principles in European clauses.* As Claes (2007) shows, some constitutions introduce within their integration clauses the express provision that the European Union will respect certain principles or substantive conditions when exercising the transferred powers. Thus, constitutions could demand respect for fundamental rights or the democratic principle, as it happens in Article 23 of the German constitution, perhaps the clearest example of this kind of clause. These material or substantive limits, then, would act as a criterion for the assessment of the constitutionality of the treaty. This type of substantive condition can also have some impact on the *Kompetenz-Kompetenz* decisions, to the extent in which they would become a constitutional grounding for such doctrine. Empirical evidence shows that, in many cases, declarations of *Kompetenz-Kompetenz* are inserted into the argumentations of the courts in the framework of a discourse in which the idea of 'substantive conditions' plays a core role. Such clauses could thus offer NHCs a constitutional basis for their challenge to the Court of Justice.
- *Acknowledgement of primacy in European clauses.* Claes (2007) also shows that some national constitutions include a clause acknowledging the primacy of the law of the European Union over internal law – with or without specifying whether this primacy also applies to the national constitution. The most noted example is that of Article 29.4 of the constitution of Ireland. Obviously, a clause of this type has implications for the question of courts' declarations of *Kompetenz-Kompetenz.* Constitutional clauses stating the primacy of European law can favour a behaviour of self-restraint by NHCs: once the national constitution establishes the primacy of European law, the national court will find it more difficult to argue that it reserves for itself the right to a 'last word' precisely to protect said constitution.

Previous Declarations of Kompetenz-Kompetenz *by Other Courts: 'Cross-Fertilization'*

Recently, a growing body of literature (Lax and Rader, 2010; Richards and Kritzer, 2002; Richards, Smith and Kritzer, 2006) has analyzed the role of preceding rulings in subsequent judicial decisions, both horizontally – on later jurisprudence of the same court – and vertically – on the jurisprudence of other lower/inferior courts. In the case of this research, the value of previous rulings is taken into account in an oblique direction: I will analyze how the decisions of *Kompetenz-Kompetenz* of some courts influence later *Kompetenz-Kompetenz* decisions of other courts. In line with Gelter and Siems (2012), crossed citations between NHCs will be studied. After all, the capacity of the previous case-law to legitimate new decisions (Whittington, 2000: 620) can also act at an inter-judicial level, so that the decisions of some national courts are legitimated by similar previous case law of significant courts of other countries.

The full meaning of this theory can be observed in a long-term scenario. National courts, through their *Kompetenz-Kompetenz* declarations, have tried to reinforce their power at the expense of the Court of Justice. The interaction between national courts and the ECJ, for which metaphors such as 'judicial dialogue' (Stone Sweet, 2010) have been used, has in reality much to do with a judicial arm wrestling and is characterized by asymmetry: whereas on one side of the 'dialogue' a sole institution can be found, the Court of Justice, on the other side there are a myriad of national higher courts. These share the same interest – the maintenance of their power to '*dire le droit*', which can only be reached through coordination.

Figure 2.1 illustrates the coordination problem between NHCs. Its remote precedent is Weiler's (1999) writings about the relation between NHCs. A unique challenge to the Court of Justice in the form of a declaration of *Kompetenz-Kompetenz* by an isolated national court would be risky and probably of little success. It would be perceived, very probably, as little more than a legal heterodoxy, with little relevance in a general context of national courts that accept the doctrine of the Luxembourg Court. Such a single and isolated challenge would probably be reverted in the medium term. The higher the number of NHCs joining the challenge against the interpretative authority of the Court of Justice and the status quo, the more serious such a challenge would appear to be, and therefore the higher the probabilities of success and the lower the costs of losing the bet – that could at least be shared among the courts. This means that the first court issuing a challenging ruling would have the highest risks: if the rest of the courts do not follow its doctrine, it would have to bear the cost of a defeat alone. At a certain point after it has been repeated by many NHCs, the *Kompetenz-Kompetenz* doctrine is sufficiently settled on the outlook of European legal integration so as to ensure the probability of success exceeds the risks, and as a consequence, the incentives to join the doctrinal challenge increase (see point 'i' in the figure).

The coordination problem begins to disappear, then, when a court has taken the risk of declaring the first challenge against the Court of Justice, and point 'i' is probably reached in the moment in which a couple of relatively important courts have repeated such a challenge. At this point, the doctrine should have already been accepted as a matter of fact by the rest of the judicial actors, and maybe by European law scholars. Once this happens, the uncertainty regarding the costs of the challenge is lower for the rest of the NHCs, which still have an incentive to join

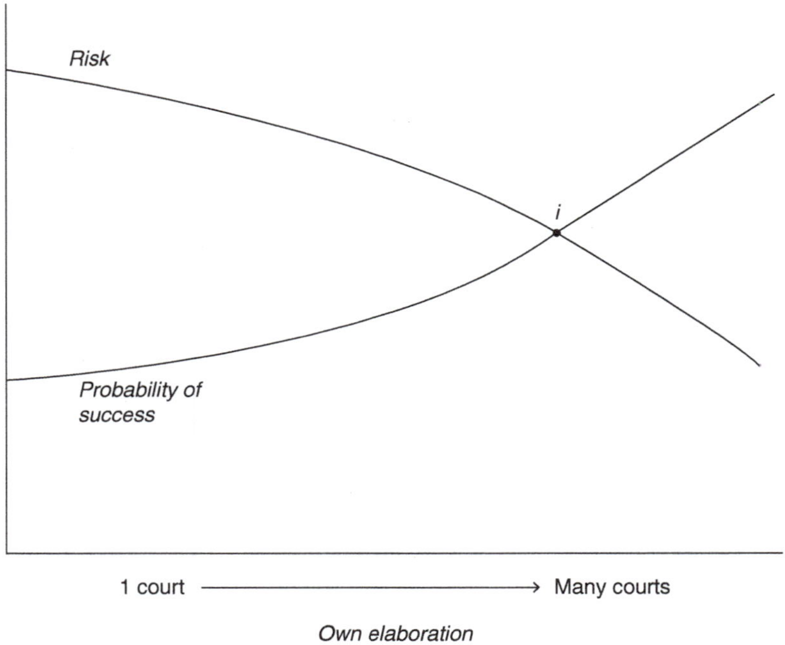

Figure 2.1 Solving the problem of coordination between NHCs regarding the reception of the *Kompetenz-Kompetenz* doctrine

this doctrine: their own empowerment. This theory has, in fact, a close precedent: in his review of the history of the relationships among NHCs and the ECJ, Davies (2012: 425) remembered how the German political elites were afraid of an imitation effect on other courts after the *Solange* decision.

Judicial Independence

Neoinstitutionalism suggests that the design of an institution modulates the behaviour of the actors when pursuing their institutional goals (see Hall and Taylor, 1996). In judicial politics literature, neoinstitutionalism has evolved into the dominant theoretical trend (Redher, 2007). At the same time, the evaluation of the independence of the courts has been the prevailing subject in a large part of the studies in the field (Herron and Randazzo, 2003; Larkins, 1996; Melone, 1997; Vanberg, 2000). Part of the literature has maintained that the institutional design of the courts modulates the way in which political actors can exert pressure upon them, through mechanisms such as the magistrates' re-election procedures, the threat of removal from office or the threat of the suspension of the whole court (Epstein et al, 2001b).

If statements of *Kompetenz-Kompetenz* are a challenge to the Court of Justice, it can be expected that institutionally stronger courts will be more prone to make such a challenge. Although institutional strength is hard to measure, institutional guarantees of independence might be a good proxy for it. First, more independent courts have a higher capacity to pursue their own agenda. As Herron and Randazzo (2003: 425) put it, '[C]ourts with greater guarantees of independence should be freer to exercise their own will and consequently should have more opportunities to engage in judicial review'. Second, judicial independence is a necessary and core element of the wider concept of judicial strength. Third, empirical evidence (see Chapter 7) suggests that courts which are usually considered to be the most powerful in the continent are also those with higher guarantees of independence, as showed by the example of the German Federal Constitutional Court. And fourth, judicial independence can be in itself, regardless of other elements of institutional strength, an important explanatory factor for decisions of *Kompetenz-Kompetenz*: only independent courts can resist pressures by other actors that would prefer to avoid judicial clashes in the EU.

Powers of Review

The institutional design of the court, however, can affect the occurrence of statements of *Kompetenz-Kompetenz* in a more direct way. The *Kompetenz-Kompetenz* doctrine implicitly assumes a certain institutional design of the courts, one that allows them to perform a concrete and *ex post* constitutional review of EU legislation. For the court to actually exercise *Kompetenz-Kompetenz* powers, it would have to declare European Union secondary legislation unconstitutional once it has already come into force. For courts whose powers of review are limited in this regard – for instance, to *ex ante* review of legislation – the declaration of *Kompetenz-Kompetenz* would make little sense: the court would assume all the costs and risks of challenging the Court of Justice without being able to expect real benefits in the form of empowerment in exchange. Dyevre (2013) already anticipated a hypothesis in this direction, comparing the French Constitutional Council and the German Federal Constitutional Court. The powers of review of the French Constitutional Council were limited until a recent reform, as they were restricted to constitutional review *in abstracto* and a priori, so a law could not be declared unconstitutional once it had been promulgated: 'as regards to EU law, this meant that the Council could not rule on directives and norms based on the EC Treaty' (Dyevre, 2013: 158). Contrary to the French Council, the German Federal Constitutional Court did not suffer all these restrictions, which would contribute to explaining its doctrinal position.

What has been said regarding the French Constitutional Council is also valid for any court whose constitutional design limits its capacity to assess the constitutionality of European Union secondary legislation. Furthermore, it is not only the formal institutional design of the court that matters, but also the framework of conventions that de facto regulates – either by doctrinal interpretation or by legal custom – which are the court's powers of review: in the case of some countries, the dominant doctrinal approaches exclude European Union secondary law from the scope of review of the courts, thus reducing the incentives for the statement of the *Kompetenz-Kompetenz* doctrine. On the other hand, other NHCs whose powers of review are interpreted by the dominant doctrinal approaches as including European Union secondary law will still have higher incentives to state their *Kompetenz-Kompetenz*.

Sequences of Cases Before the Same Court About the Same Treaty

A last explanatory condition would suggest that when a court has to assess the same treaty on successive occasions, its pronouncements will vary: once its own *Kompetenz-Kompetenz* is declared in a first ruling on a treaty, it is expected that it will not declare it again in subsequent rulings on the same treaty. Said in these terms, the idea seems to be counterintuitive and even contrary to the widespread theories of path dependency, but as I expect to show, it is not. In general, theories of path dependency point to actors tending to persevere in their decisions in time, so that once a decision is adopted, repeating it is less costly (Levi, 1997; see also Stone Sweet, 2004). One application of this theory has to do with the role of the precedent in judicial decisions, which has been theorized, for instance, at the level of analysis of individual magistrates: 'It is fairly costless for a dissenting justice to continue to dissent; it is a rather more significant step for a justice to cast a decisive vote that abandons an existing precedent' (Whittington, 2000: 608). The theory in this subsection does not contradict this; nevertheless, the precedent of one or two cases is, in reality, too small to speak about the existence of a fixed pattern of behaviour. On the other hand, the phenomenon to which this research refers – sequences of rulings by the same court on exactly the same treaty – occurs only rarely and requires a more specific theorization. In this research, such theorization is created inductively after the observation of the Czech case, which stated the doctrine in its first Lisbon case and softened the approach in the second one. The explanation for this could refer, again, to the costs of such a doctrine. *Kompetenz-Kompetenz* declarations are an open challenge to the Court of Justice, so once its own *Kompetenz-Kompetenz* has been stated in a wave of ratification, the court can save repeating a movement that is relatively costly. By establishing the *Kompetenz-Kompetenz* doctrine in a ruling, it is possible that the court decides on subsequent rulings about the same treaty to soften its attitude. Courts can in these subsequent rulings emphasize their cooperative relationships with the

Court of Justice or underline the existing alternatives to the exercise of its *Kompetenz-Kompetenz*, as the 'red line' has been already marked in a previous decision, thus appearing as a collaborative actor without giving up its quest for self-empowerment.

Configurational Hypotheses About Kompetenz-Kompetenz *Decisions*

Kompetenz-Kompetenz declarations must be read especially in light of two of the institutional objectives of courts: the strengthening or 'empowerment' of the institution, and the application of the law. On one hand, *Kompetenz-Kompetenz* declarations mean for the courts an increase of their capacity to, as Bourdieu (2001) put it, '*dire le droit*'; that is, an increase of their capacity to make binding interpretations of the legal rules, which, according to the *Kompetenz-Kompetenz* doctrine, would also include the assessment of constitutionality of EU secondary legislation. In this sense, as MacCormick (1999: 9) acknowledged in explicit reference to the dialogue between NHCs and Court of Justice, the underlying theme is a matter of power, a political question:

> Whoever can make a judgement prevail in the last resort, in the sense of its being carried out through by main force if necessary, and can reliably and predictable enforce such judgements in the general run, has political power.

On the other hand, the declarations of *Kompetenz-Kompetenz* play an important role in the judicial function of constructing a coherent relation between the legal systems. Through this doctrine, the relationship between the law of the European Union and the national law is interpreted in a particular way. Specifically, the issue of how to proceed in case of conflict between these two orders is solved: it gives NHCs the capacity to solve such conflict in favour of the internal constitutional rules.

Kompetenz-Kompetenz declarations, then, have a complex causation. Two factors appear as quasi-necessary conditions. First, a condition is linked to the more purely legal dimension of the judicial action: the non-existence of a constitutional clause acknowledging the primacy of the European Union law. The *Kompetenz-Kompetenz* doctrine, with its special way of approaching the articulation between European Union and internal law, no longer makes sense if the national constitution already foresees how a possible conflict with EU law must be solved, and particularly if it does so by acknowledging the primacy of European law. Second, a condition linked to the incentives of the court to declare its own *Kompetenz-Kompetenz* could also be relevant: the presence of sufficient powers of constitutional review so that the court is able to assess European Union secondary legislation. It is useless for a court to declare its own *Kompetenz-Kompetenz* if it actually has no capacity to review the cases in which a conflict between internal law and the EU secondary law needs to be settled.

Therefore, these two conditions – the lack of constitutional acknowledgement of the primacy of EU law and the presence of broad powers of constitutional review – need to interact in order to allow courts to declare their own *Kompetenz-Kompetenz.* But alone they are insufficient to produce such a result, since they do not provide incentives for NHCs to challenge the Court of Justice. For a national court to dare formulate such a challenge, a triggering factor must also exist. According to the theory defended in this book, this factor could consist in being a powerful institution which can reasonably go ahead with the challenge against the ECJ and which could resist pressures by other actors that would prefer to avoid such a clash. Judicial independence allows the court to form its own agenda and pursue its own goals. For that reason, the first configurational hypothesis would be that *the lack of a constitutional clause that acknowledges the primacy of European Union law, combined with sufficient power of review of the court and with high independence, would lead to the declaration of Kompetenz-Kompetenz.*

There does exist, however, an alternative way through which NHCs could declare their own *Kompetenz-Kompetenz.* For this second path to lead to the previously mentioned result, the two first conditions should be kept unaltered: the lack of a declaration of primacy of EU law in the national constitution and the presence of enough powers of review. However, there is an alternative to the third condition, that is to say, a different incentive. A *Kompetenz-Kompetenz* declaration would be risky for the first court stating it, as the scenario would still be one of unconditional acceptance by all other NHCs of the doctrines of the ECJ. Such a court should be a highly independent and powerful institution. However, for courts that simply follow and repeat the *Kompetenz-Kompetenz* doctrine, once established in previous rulings by other courts, the existence of a precedent by a more powerful institution would be enough to reduce the costs associated with the statement of such a doctrine. Because of that, a second hypothesis would postulate that *the lack of constitutional clause acknowledging the primacy of European Union law, combined with sufficient powers of review by the court, and with the existence of – at least – a prior declaration of* Kompetenz-Kompetenz *by some other institution, would lead to the declaration of Kompetenz-Kompetenz by a new institution.*

Decisions on the Merits: Explanatory Conditions and Configurational Hypotheses

If, regarding the decisions of *Kompetenz-Kompetenz*, the main explanatory key is the institutional goal of judicial empowerment, in regard to decisions on the merits, that role is performed by the institutional goal of conservation of stability of the institutional framework of the court. However, again, if that goal was enough to explain judicial behaviour, all courts would have always avoided risky declarations of unconstitutionality, which is not the case. A more subtle analysis of certain explanatory conditions is thus necessary in order to provide a sophisticated account of judicial behaviour.

Type of Claimant: Executives

A part of the literature in judicial politics, or even critical legal studies, has referred to certain characteristics of the actors that participate in the judicial proceedings as one of the explanatory variables of judicial behaviour (Raymond, 2010). The literature in the field has tried to find evidence regarding whether factors such as the race (Kleck, 1981; Hagan, 1974; Peterson and Hagan, 1984; Spohn, Gruhl and Wech 1981) or gender (Myers, 1988; Kritzer and Uhlman, 1977) of the parties to the proceedings are relevant when explaining the judicial decisions. These studies, however, usually focused on criminal cases. More directly related to this research, in their work, Herron and Randazzo (2003: 431) have tried to figure out whether the status of the claimant – executives, citizens, legislatives and parliamentarian minorities – could have an impact on the decisions of constitutional courts in post-socialist European countries. Finally, in their studies, Galanter (1974) and Handler (1978) have shown variations in the results of the judicial proceedings as a result of the resources and the experience in litigation of the parties.

This study, then, had to take into consideration the status of the complainants. But it has done so in light of certain empirical preliminary evidence, through an 'inductive' process of selection of explanatory conditions, which is usual in QCA studies (Yamasaki and Rihoux, 2009:125). In the exploration of the cases and in former studies (Closa and Castillo, 2012; Closa, 2013) a relatively striking phenomenon was noticed: many of the declarations of unconstitutionality were issued in cases initiated by executives who had taken part in the process of elaboration of the treaty and were, therefore, a priori committed to its ratification. A first hypothesis regarding this observed pattern could point to a challenging attitude by the courts. Once the proceedings were initiated by heads of state or government, courts took the chance to declare the unconstitutionality of the treaty against the interests of those heads of state. But this theorization, however, does not seem to be solid. First, it does not explain why courts did not do the same in the case of claims presented by other actors, such as citizens, for which the declarations of unconstitutionality were an exception rather than the rule. And second, this hypothesis presumes that executives behave in an irrational manner: Heads of state and government would deliberately activate a judicial proceeding whose result would go against their interests. In order to avoid such a paradox, the role of the heads of state and government must be understood from another perspective and, overall, in light of its configurational combination with other explanatory conditions such as the political cost of the case (Closa and Castillo, 2012; Closa, 2013). Although it is paradoxical, by raising a question to the court about the constitutionality of the treaty, executives are sending a signal to the court that in this case – and only in this case – it is possible to declare the unconstitutionality of the treaty, provided that the court acts prudently in its declaration, thereby avoiding political costs (Closa and Castillo, 2012; Closa, 2013).

Avoiding Political Costs: The Consequences of Decisions

As it was said, the previous explanatory condition must be understood in its interaction with the consequences of the decisions of the courts (Closa and Castillo, 2012; Closa, 2013).

As the institutionalist-externalist model (Dyèvre, 2010: 304) suggests, courts take into consideration the preferences of other actors. In particular, some studies have analyzed the explanatory power of the preferences of actors in the legislative and the executive branches (Eskridge, 1991; Volcansek, 2001) or the support of the citizens (Lijphart, 1999; Volcansek, 2000; Vanberg, 2001, 2005) when explaining judicial behaviour (see Dyevre, 2010). In general, the relevance of the preferences of the political actors finds resonance in a great part of the literature on judicial politics, according to which 'judicial decisions are almost fully determined by the agendas of partisan elites' (Keck, 2007: 513). The idea can be found in judicial politics researches about the U.S. Supreme Court; thus, in his noted study, Dahl stated that 'the policy views dominant on the court are never out of line for long with the policy views dominant among the law-making majorities of the United States' (Dahl, 1957: 265). The approach taken by Robert McCloskey was similar to that taken by Dahl, and that according to Keck (2007) McCloskey said that 'the Supreme Court has seldom, if ever, flatly and for very long resisted a really unmistakable wave of public sentiment' (McCloskey, 1960: 23). It must be taken into account, as the literature in the field shows, that political actors have a direct influence on the courts when choosing their magistrates, reverting their decisions or expanding or reducing the extension of their jurisdiction. Research grouped under the category of Regime Politics Approach suggests that 'governing regimes or partisan coalitions, ensure that the Court promotes their interests by appointing like-minded justices who vote based on their policy preferences' (Hall, 2012: 878). In the case of this research, political actors' preferences focused on the ratification of the treaties. If, according to the literature of the Regime Politics Approach, 'the values of the justices mirror and certainly lie within the range of those values currently or recently receiving official representation in other branches of government' (Peretti, 1999: 5), it is expected that the consequences of the courts' decisions do not go against the interests of political elites, especially when there is a broad consensus among these, as is the case of the ratifications of treaties of the European Union.

In this regard, one of the core premises of the literature in the field is the understanding of courts as 'strategic' actors (Epstein and Knight, 2000: 625). As Chalmers and Chaves (2012: 27) have stated, in the field of European judicial politics 'actors must factor into their decision-making a calculus of legal risk which anticipates responses to their decisions'. Many studies have empirically documented a pattern in judicial behaviour, according to which courts try to avoid decisions that could later be overturned by political actors (Ferejohn et al, 2004: 181) through mechanisms such as parliamentarian revision of the ruling (Epstein et al, 2001a; Ferejohn and Wiengast, 1992; Hausegger and Baum, 1999; Whittington, 2006) or the veto to its implementation (Vanberg, 2001, 2005). This research (following Closa and Castillo, 2012) inverts this general theory: courts will declare treaties unconstitutional precisely when such a decision can be overturned, or at least circumvented, by political actors. In this sense, the range of consequences of a declaration of unconstitutionality is relatively broad. In previous studies (Closa and Castillo, 2012; Closa, 2013), it was considered that once the unconstitutionality of the treaty was declared, to proceed to its ratification, it was necessary to reform the national constitution. In such studies, however, a second possibility was not considered: the possibility that the claim questions the ratification procedure and not the substantive content of the treaty, so that in cases of declaration of unconstitutionality, not constitutional amendment, but an alternative ratification – usually in referendum – follows. In both cases, the route of the ratification is altered, imposing new requirements (Closa and Castillo, 2012; Closa, 2013): reform of the constitution in the parliamentary arena or in a referendum, new elections necessary to reform the constitution or even the possibility of constitutional deadlock in the case of constitutional provisions protected by an 'eternity clause'. Among these possibilities, the least costly is the first one because only in this case is control over the process given back to the political elites (Closa and Castillo, 2012; Closa, 2013).

A Holistic Approach to the Ruling: The Interaction Between Kompetenz-Kompetenz *Declarations and Decisions on the Merits*

A peculiarity of this study is that one of the 'outcomes' analyzed, the declaration of *Kompetenz-Kompetenz*, acts simultaneously as an explanatory condition for the other 'outcome', the declaration of unconstitutionality. More than as an argumentative 'strategy' of courts (Closa,

2013), the presence or absence of the *Kompetenz-Kompetenz* doctrine could act as an explanation for decisions on the merits. This theoretical expectation shows the link between the two dimensions of the judicial behaviour analyzed in this research – decisions on the merits and interpretative decisions – which, far from being parallel and disconnected phenomena, interact among themselves and allow judicial behaviour to be expressed in a complex manner. Although Closa (2013: 97) theorized that 'This [decisions on the merits] happens regardless of the substantive contents of the arguments given [by courts]', it is defended here that the legal reasoning does matter when explaining decisions on the merits. In a somehow counterintuitive way, the presence of *Kompetenz-Kompetenz* declarations is deemed to favour declarations of constitutionality of the treaty. There are a number of reasons supporting such expectation.

First, if the court declares its own *Kompetenz-Kompetenz*, this can ultimately serve to mitigate the risk of friction between the constitution and the treaty once the latter has come into force. The possible inconsistences between European and national law deriving from the treaty would not have to be pointed at in a preventive manner through a declaration of unconstitutionality of the treaty. Instead, they could be settled afterwards, even after the treaty enters into force, through an eventual corrective action of the court in the exercise of its *Kompetenz-Kompetenz* (see Closa, 2013: 112). In a certain sense, the *Kompetenz-Kompetenz* declaration could be understood as a lighter substitute for the more costly unconstitutionality declaration.

Second, if national courts want to satisfy their objective of self-empowerment through *Kompetenz-Kompetenz* declarations, they can make the declaration of constitutionality, which other actors need, conditional to the respect of the courts' right to have a last say regarding EU law. Paradoxically, the declaration of constitutionality reinforces the statement of *Kompetenz-Kompetenz*. This theory finds support in the usual phrasing of this type of ruling. NHCs such as the German Federal Constitutional Court seem to have implicitly suggested that treaties are declared constitutional *to the extent* to which they are interpreted as admitting and respecting the *Kompetenz-Kompetenz* of the court, and precisely because of that.

Third, as Figure 2.2 shows, if after a *Kompetenz-Kompetenz* declaration the court declares the unconstitutionality of the treaty, the ruling as a whole will take on an excessively challenging look. That will increase the coordination costs described previously: the *Kompetenz-Kompetenz* doctrine will be seen as an excessively costly heterodoxy as it goes together with the declaration of unconstitutionality in the ruling, and therefore the incentives for other courts to later reproduce this doctrine will be reduced. It must be recalled that this doctrinal reception in other countries is indispensable for the legitimation *a posteriori* of the first *Kompetenz-Kompetenz* declarations. As Figure 2.2 shows, the risks

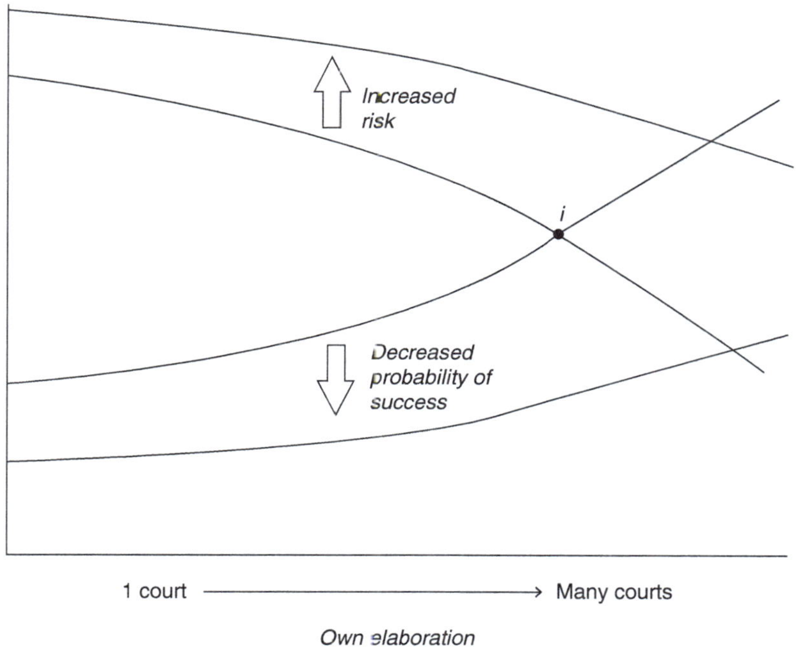

Figure 2.2 Increase in coordination costs

would increase and the probabilities of success would diminish, thus reducing the incentives for other NHCs to join the challenge – so point 'i' might not be reached.

Finally, in an extreme case, if the court declares the treaty to be unconstitutional with the argument that it does not respect its own *Kompetenz-Kompetenz*, only two options exist. The first one is reforming the treaty to acknowledge the NHC's 'last say', which does not seem to be a realistic option, since that would require the creation of a new consensus among all member states. The second is reforming the national constitution to curtail the NHC's jurisdiction, excluding EU law from it, so that the constitution and treaty can become compatible. But this option, of course, is detrimental to the interests of NHCs, so they have an incentive to avoid this combination.

Type of Court

The diverse institutional designs and the different idiosyncrasies associated with the distinct types of NHCs can also be relevant in explaining the behaviour of these actors and their decisions on the merits, as Closa (2013) suggested. The most classic taxonomy (see Cappelletti, 1970) classifies NHCs in centralized constitutional courts of the Kelsenian-style, including in this category the *sui generis* French Constitutional Council, and decentralized systems of constitutional review.

The centralized model is the most widespread among the courts studied in this book. In this model, the power of constitutional review is concentrated in a unique body that is left out of the structure of the judicial branch (see Garlicki, 2007: 44); in the model of centralized constitutional review, only the constitutional court has the capacity to make an assessment of the constitutionality of a statute, so that in cases of doubt, lower courts must refer the question to the constitutional court. On the contrary, in the decentralized model of constitutional review, 'any judge of any court, in any case, at any time, at the best of any litigating party, has the power to declare a law unconstitutional' (Stone Sweet, 2000). In the model of decentralized review, the superior body of the court system – usually a supreme court – only has the last word on constitutional matters, so that courts of lower hierarchical range can also assess the constitutionality of rules, even if their decisions are appealable. But together with this fundamental difference, the centralized and decentralized models usually also differ in an important number of other details (Favoreu, 1990; Navia and Ríos-Figueroa, 2005): professional judges, in the case of decentralized models, against jurists of reputable competence, in the case of the centralized ones; lifelong mandates against limited mandates; etc.

All systems analyzed in this research follow the centralized model with the exception of one, the Irish Supreme Court. However, Ireland does not strictly follow a model of decentralized review, but it constitutes an intermediate model (see Ferreres, 2004: 462). In this country, only the Supreme Court and the High Court have the capacity to assess the constitutionality of rules. Nevertheless, the Irish Supreme Court shares other characteristics with the decentralized model, such as being part of the ordinary jurisdiction, even if it is at the top of the court system. It also follows the peculiar design which consists of professional judges having lifelong mandate. This set of institutional differences converges to create a different institutional ethos that goes beyond the simple addition of guarantees of judicial independence and that can, in its interaction with other explanatory conditions, contribute to the production of different outcomes of judicial behaviour, in particular of challenging declarations of unconstitutionality.

Judicial Independence

Judicial independence can also play a role with regard to the decisions on the merits. As said before, the institutional design of a court modulates the way in which political actors can exert pressure on it (Epstein et al, 2001b). Thus, protective designs which maximize the independence of the court can facilitate the making of decisions which defy the preferences of political actors. After all, as the literature suggests, an independent court should be able to freely adopt decisions without having to worry about their effects in connection to other political actors (Ferejohn, Rosenbluth and Shipan, 2004: 3).

In this research, a high level of judicial independence could act as an explanatory condition of unconstitutionality declarations. More independent courts could be less likely to try to please political actors with decisions on the merits that satisfy their preferences – which, as will be seen, pointed at costless ratification of the treaty. In short, judicial independence plays a role in the pursuit of the first institutional objective of the court: a court which is barely independent would avoid declarations of unconstitutionality that could put the ratification of the treaty in danger, whilst a more independent court would have more incentives to do so.

Configurational Hypothesis for Decisions on the Merits

Courts' decisions on the merits must be seen overall in light of the first of the courts' institutional goals: maintaining the stability of the framework in which judicial activity is based. According to this, courts take into consideration the preferences of the rest of the political actors in their activity (see *inter alia* Eskridge, 1991; Volcansek, 2001). The relevance of this institutional objective for the decisions on the merits is explained by the impact that such decisions can have in the process of ratification of the treaty (Closa and Castillo, 2012; Closa, 2013). However, NHCs can simultaneously seek their other institutional goals. The second institutional objective, the empowerment of the court, is satisfied to the extent to which the rulings, together with decisions on the merits and interacting with them, also incorporate in some cases decisions of *Kompetenz-Kompetenz*. The tertiary objective, the building of legal coherence, is also satisfied to the extent to which the open texture of law provides the court with a margin of manoeuvre broad enough as to be able to adopt decisions compatible with the rest of the objectives.

For declarations of unconstitutionality, in principle, it could be considered that the lack of declarations of *Kompetenz-Kompetenz* acts as a quasi-necessary condition. As the combination of *Kompetenz-Kompetenz* declarations and unconstitutionality declarations is highly challenging and costly (see earlier), only in the absence of the first one will there appear for the courts the possibility of adopting the second. But the absence of *Kompetenz-Kompetenz* declarations just offers the possibility, not the incentive, to declare the treaty unconstitutional. The incentive is created with the combination of that condition and other ones. In principle, unconstitutionality declarations could be a challenge to the political elites that have negotiated the treaty. However, this approach to declarations of unconstitutionality is based on a vision of the relation between courts and political actors featured by conflict. However, in this research, and in line with the literature on the Regime Politics Approach (Gillmam and Clayton, 1999; Clayton, 2002), the relation between these two types of actors can also be sometimes be considered a cooperative one. This translates into unconstitutionality declarations being issued when their consequences are meant to be innocuous; that is, when the ratification of the treaty can still be carried out after a simple reform of the constitution in the parliamentary arena (Closa and Castillo, 2012; Closa, 2013). For these cases, the process as a whole would not escape the control of the political pro-European elites. And in addition, a process of ratification fully protective of the internal constitutional system would be staged, with certain solemnity, in front of the civil society, endorsed by the intervention of the constitutional court and the subsequent constitutional reform. The first configurational hypothesis for this outcome thus links two explanatory conditions: the lack of declarations of *Kompetenz-Kompetenz* and the consequences of the decision on the merits: *the absence of a declaration of* Kompetenz-Kompetenz *combined with a low political cost of a declaration of unconstitutionality would lead to such outcome.*

As already mentioned, the previous configurational hypothesis is framed in the general assumption of cooperative relations between political actors and constitutional courts. However, an intervening element can modify this relationship: judicial independence (see Larkins, 1996; Vanberg, 2000). As an alternative to the previous hypothesis, then, the cause of the declaration of unconstitutionality can be the high independence of the court (see Herron and Randazzo, 2003: 425). In this case, the 'inter-branch interactions' (Friedman, 2005) would go from being based on cooperation to being based on conflict, and courts could declare the unconstitutionality of the treaty, regardless of the preferences of the political elites. These more independent courts could, in fact, privilege the tertiary objective of 'making good law' and declare the unconstitutionality of the treaty if they are honestly convinced that they must do so. This hypothesis would thus suggest that *the absence of a declaration of* Kompetenz-Kompetenz *combined with a high judicial independence would lead to declarations of unconstitutionality.*

Note

1 'The legal field is where a concurrence for the monopoly of law of the "rule on legal matters" happens, that is, the good distribution (*nomos*) or the good order in which agents vested with an inseparably social and technical competence are confronted, which consists essentially in the socially acknowledged capacity of interpreting (in a way more or less free or authorised) a corpus of texts that establish the legitimate, sound vision, of the social world.'

References

Baquero, J. (2008) 'The legacy of the Maastricht-Urteil and the pluralist movement', *European Law Journal* 14(4): 389–422.

Baum, L. (1994) 'What judges want: Judges' goals and judicial behavior', *Political Research Quarterly* 47(3):749–68.

Bourdieu, P. (2001) *Poder, derecho y clases sociales*, Bilbao: Desclee.

Brouard, S. (2009), 'The politics of constitutional veto in France: Constitutional council, legislative majority and electoral competition', *West European Politics* 32(2): 384–403.

Cappelletti, M. (1970) 'Judicial review in comparative perspective', *California Law Review* 58(5): 1017–53.

Carruba, C., Gabel M. and Hamkla C. (2008) 'Judicial behavior under political constraints: Evidence from the European Court of Justice', *The American Political Science Review* 102(4): 435–52.

Chalmers, D. and Chaves, M. (2012) 'The reference points of EU judicial politics', *Journal of European Public Policy* 19(1): 25–42.

Claes, M. (2005) 'Constitutionalizing Europe at its source: The "European" clauses in the national constitutions: Evolution and typology', *Yearbook of European Law* 24(1): 81–125.

Claes, M. (2007) 'The Europeanisation of national constitutions in the constitutionalisation of Europe: Some observations against the background of the constitutional experience of the EU-15', *Croatian Yearbook of European Law and Policy* 3: 1–38.

Clark, T. (2009) 'The separation of powers, court curbing, and judicial legitimacy', *American Journal of Political Science* 53(4): 971–89.

Clark, T. and Lauderdale, B. (2012) 'The genealogy of law' *Political Analysis* 20(3): 329–50.

Clayton, C. (2002) 'The supply and demand sides of judicial policy-making', *Law and Contemporary Problems* 65(3): 69–85.

Closa, C. (2013) 'National higher courts and the ratification of European Union treaties', *West European Politics* 36(1): 97–121.

Closa, C. and Castillo, P. (2012), 'National Courts and Ratification of European Union Treaties', in Evas, T., Lord, C., and Liebert, U. *Multilayered Representation in the European Union. Parliaments, Courts and the Public Sphere*, Berlin: Nomos, pp. 129–57.

Dahl, R. (1957) 'Decision-making in a democracy: The supreme court as a national policy-maker', *Journal of Public Law* 6: 279–95.

Davies, B. (2012) 'Pushing back: What happens when member states resist the European Court of Justice? A multi-modal approach to the history of European law', *Contemporary European History* 21(3): 417–35.

Dyevre, A. (2008) 'Making sense of judicial lawmaking: A theory of theories of adjudication', *EUI Working Papers 2008/9* at http://cadmus.eui.eu/bitstream/handle/1814/8510/MWP_2008_09.pdf?sequence=1 (03.06.2010).

Dyevre, A. (2010) 'Unifying the field of comparative judicial politics: Towards a general theory of judicial behaviour', *European Political Science Review* 2(2): 297–327.

Dyevre, A. (2013) 'European integration and national courts: Defending sovereignty under institutional constraints?', *European Constitutional Law Review* 9(1): 139–68.

Elster, J. (1986) *Rational Choice*, New York: University Press.

Epstein, L. and Knight, J. (2000) 'Toward a strategic revolution in judicial politics: A look back, a look ahead', *Political Research Quarterly* 53(3): 625–61.

Epstein, L., Knight, J. and Martin, A. D. (2001a) 'The supreme court as a strategic national policymaker', *Emory Law Journal* 50: 583–611.

Epstein, L., Knight, J. and Shvetsova, O. (2001b) 'The role of constitutional courts in the establishment and maintenance of democratic systems of government', *Law & Society Review* 35(1): 117–63.

Eskridge, W. (1991) 'Reneging on history? Playing the court/congress/president civil rights game', *California Law Review* 79(3): 613–74.

Favoreu, L. (1990) 'American and European models of constitutional justice', in Clark, D. S. (ed.) *Comparative and Private International Law: Essays in Honor of John Merryman*, Germany: Humboldt, pp. 105–20.

Ferejohn, J. A., and Weingast, B. R. (1992) 'A positive theory of statutory interpretation', *International Review of Law and Economics* 12(2): 263–79.

Ferejohn, J., Rosenbluth, F., and Shipan, C. (2004) 'Comparative judicial politics', at www.yale.edu/polisci/rosenbluth/Papers/comparative%20judicial%20politics.pdf (16.10.2011).

Ferreres, V. (2004) 'The European model of constitutional review of legislation: Toward decentralization?', *International Journal of Constitutional Law* 2(3): 461–91.

Friedman, B. (2005) 'The politics of judicial review', *Texas Law Review* 84(2): 287–337.

Galanter, M. (1974) 'Why the "haves" come out ahead: Speculations on the limits of legal change', *Law & Society Review* 9(1): 95–160.

Garlicki, L. (2007) 'Constitutional courts versus supreme courts', *International Journal of Constitutional Law* 5(1): 44–68.

Gelter, M. and Siems, M. (2012), 'Networks, dialogue or one-way traffic? An empirical analysis of cross-citations between ten of Europe's highest courts', *Utrecht Law Review* 8(2): 88–99.

Gillman, H., and Clayton, C. (1999) 'Beyond judicial attitudes: Institutional approaches to Supreme Court decision-making', in Clayton, C. and Gillman, H. (eds.) *Supreme Court Decision-Making: New Institutionalist Approaches*, Chicago: Chicago University Press, pp. 1–15.

Hagan, J. (1974) 'Extra-legal attributes and criminal sentencing: An assessment of a sociological viewpoint', *Law & Society Review* 8(3): 357–83.

Hall, M. (2012), 'Rethinking regime politics', *Law & Social Inquiry* 37(4): 878–907.

Hall, P. and Taylor, R. C. R., (1996), 'Political science and the three new institutionalisms', *MPIfG Discussion Paper 99/6* Cologne: Max Planck Institute for the Study of Societies.

Handler, J. (1978) *Social Movements and the Legal System: A Theory of Law Reform and Social Change*, Waltham: Academic Press.

Hart, H. L. A. (1997 [1961]) *The Concept of Law*, New York: Oxford University Press.

Hausegger, L., and Baum, L. (1999) 'Inviting congressional action: A study of supreme court motivations in statutory interpretation', *American Journal of Political Science* 43(1): 162–15

Herron, E. S. and Randazzo, K. A. (2003) 'The relationship between independence and judicial review in post-communist courts', *Journal of Politics* 65(2): 422–38.

Hönnige, C. (2009) 'The electoral connection: How the pivotal judge affects oppositional success at European constitutional courts', *West European Politics* 32(5): 963–48.

Kaiser, A. (1998) 'Institutional Regimes' in Deth, J. W. V. (ed.) *Comparative Politics. The Problem of Equivalence*, London: Routledge, pp. 205–21.

Keck, T. (2007) 'Party politics or judicial independence? The regime politics literature hits the law schools', *Law & Social Inquiry* 32(2): 511–44.

Kelsen, H., (2009[1931]), '¿Quién debe ser el defensor de la Constitución?' in Lombardi, G., (ed.), *La polémica Schmitt-Kelsen sobre justicia constitucional*, Tecnos: Madrid.

Kleck, G. (1981) 'Racial discrimination in criminal sentencing: A critical evaluation of the evidence with additional evidence in death penalty', *American Sociological Review* 46(6): 783–805.

Kritzer, Herber M., and Uhlman, T. M. (1977) 'Sisterhood in the courtroom: Sex of judge and defendant in criminal cases disposition', *Social Science Journal* 14(2): 77–88.

Lambert, E. (2010 [1921]) *El gobierno de los jueces*, Madrid: Tecnos.

Larkins, C. M. (1996) 'judicial independence and democratization: A theoretical and conceptual analysis', *The American Journal of Comparative Law* 44(4): 605–26.

Lax, J., and Rader, K.T. (2010) 'Legal constraints in Supreme Court decision making: Do jurisprudencial regimes exist?', *The Journal of Politics* 72(2): 273–84.

Levi, M. (1997) 'A Model, a Method, and a Map: Rational Choice in Comparative and Historical Analysis', in Lichbach M. and Zuckerman, A., *Comparative Politics: Rationality, Culture and Structure*, Cambridge: Cambridge University Press, pp. 19–41.

Lijphart, A. (1999) *Patterns of Democracy – Government Forms and Performance in Thirty-Six Countries*, New Haven: Yale University Press.

Lindquist S. and Solberg R. (2007) 'Judicial review by the Burger and Rehnquist courts: Explaining justices' responses to constitutional challenges', *Political Research Quarterly* 60(1): 71–90.

MacCormick, N. (1995) 'The Maastricht-Urteil: Sovereignty now', *European Law Journal* 1(3): 259–66.

MacCormick, N. (1999) *Questioning Sovereignty*, Oxford: Oxford University Press.

McCloskey, R. (1960) *The American Supreme Court*, Chicago: University of Chicago Press.

Melone, A. P. (1997) 'Judicial independence and constitutional politics in Bulgaria' *Judicature* 80(6): 280–85.

Merton, R. (1949) *Social Theory and Social Structure*, New York: Free Press.

Myers, M. A. (1988) 'Social background and the sentencing behaviour of judges', *Criminology* 26(4): 649–75.

Navia, P. and Rios-Figueroa, R. (2005) 'The constitutional adjudication mosaic of Latin America', *Comparative Political Studies* 38(2): 189–217.

Peretti, T. (1999) *In Defense of a Political Court*, Princeton: Princeton University Press.

Peterson, R. D. and Hagan, J. (1984) 'Changing conceptions of race: Towards an account of anomalous findings of sentencing research', *American Sociological Review* 49(1): 56–70.

Raymond, S. (2010) 'Judicial politics and medical device preemption after Riegel', *New York University Journal of Law & Liberty* 5: 745–85.

Redher, B. (2007) 'What is political about jurisprudence? Courts, politics, and political science in Europe and the United States', MPIfG Discussion Paper, Max Planck Institute for the Study of Society, Cologne (Germany).

Richards, M.J. and Kritzer, H.M. (2002) 'Jurisprudencial regimes in the Supreme Court decision making', *American Political Science Review* 96(2): 305–20.

Richards, M.J., Smith, J.L. and Kritzer, H.M. (2006) 'Does Chevon matter?', *Law and Policy* 28(4): 444–69.

Shapiro, M. (2002) 'The success of judicial review and democracy' in Shapiro, M. and Stone Sweet, A. *On Law Politics and Judicialization*, Oxford: Oxford University Press, pp. 149–208.

Slaughter, A.-M. and Mattli, W. (1997) 'The role of national courts in the process of European integration: Accounting for judicial preferences and constraints', in Slaughter, A.-M., Stone Sweet, A. and Weiler, J. H. H., *The European Court and National Courts: Doctrine and Jurisprudence. Legal Change in Its Social Context*, Oxford: Hart Publishing, pp. 253–77.

Slaughter A.-M., Stone Sweet A. and Weiler, J. H. H. (1997) *The European Court and National Courts: Doctrine and Jurisprudence. Legal Change in Its Social Context*, Oxford: Hart Publishing.

Spohn, C., Gruhl, J., and Welch, S. (1981) 'The effect of race on sentencing: A re-examination of an unsettled question', *Law & Society Review* 16(1): 71–88.

Stone Sweet, A. (2000) *Governing with Judges. Constitutional Politics in Europe*, Oxford: Oxford University Press.

Stone Sweet, A. (2004) *The Judicial Construction of Europe*, Oxford: Oxford University Press.

Stone Sweet, A. (2010) 'The European Court of Justice and the judicialization of EU governance', *Living Reviews in European Governance* 5(2): 1–50.

Tamanaha, B. (1997) *Realistic Socio-Legal Theory*, New York: Oxford University Press.

Tsebelis, G. (2002) *Veto Players: How Political Institutions Work*, Los Angeles: Sage.

Vanberg, G., (2000) 'Establishing judicial independence in West Germany – The impact of opinion leadership and the separation of powers', *Comparative Politics* 32(3): 333–56.

Vanberg, G., (2001) 'Legislative-judicial relations: A game theoretic approach to constitutional review', *American Journal of Political Science* 45(2): 346–61.

Vanberg, G., (2005) *Constitutional Politics in Germany*, Oxford: Oxford University Press.

Voßkuhle, A. (2010) 'Multilevel cooperation of the European constitutional courts, Der Europäische Vergassungsgerichtsverbund', *European Constitutional Law Review* 6(2): 175–98.

Volcansek, M., (2000) *Constitutional Politics in Italy. The Constitutional Court*, Houndmills: Macmillan Press.

Volcansek, M., (2001) 'Constitutional courts as veto players: Decrees and divorce in Italy', *European Journal of Political Research* 39(3): 347–72.

Weiler, J. H. H. (1999) *The Constitution of Europe. 'Do the New Clothes Have an Emperor?' and Other Essays on European Integration*, Cambridge: Cambridge University Press.

Whittington, K. (2000) 'Once more unto the breach: Postbehavioralist approaches to judicial politics', *Law & Social Inquiry* 25(2): 601–34.
Whittington, K. (2006) 'Legislative sanctions and the strategic environment of judicial review', *International Journal of Constitutional Law* 1(3): 446–74.
Yamasaki, S. and Rihoux, B. (2009) 'A commented review of applications', in Rihoux, B. and Ragin, C., *Configurational Comparative Methods*, Los Angeles: Sage, pp. 123–46.

3 EU Primary Law Before the Guardians of the Constitution

Courts' Decisions on the Merits

Introduction: Exploring Courts' Decisions on the Constitutionality of European Union Treaties

Constitutional review is a common feature in modern democracies (Cole, 1959: 956; Lijphart, 1999), and is particularly widespread across European countries (Ferreres, 2004). In contemporary versions of constitutionalism, the safeguard of the national constitution – the foundational element of the polity – is usually entrusted to an independent court, be it part of the judicial branch or an autonomous constitutional court. In many occasions, pieces of legislation are assessed by such organs, which may declare them contrary to the constitution. Even if their nature differs from that of internal statutes, international treaties – including European Union treaties – can also be the object of constitutional review. Indeed, during the processes of ratification of European Union treaties, this has happened in a number of occasions.

As has already been explained, judicial behaviour is presented in this book as a complex set of decisions on the merits and interpretative decisions. Decisions on the merits, however, have clearer and more immediate political implications: when deciding on the constitutionality of treaties of the European Union, courts participate in a political process, such as the process of ratification of the treaty (Closa and Castillo, 2012). Thus, review of European treaties, far from being a cold, legalistic operation, is also a political activity. Judicialization – a phenomenon increasingly studied in the literature (Vallinder, 1994; Blichner and Molander, 2005) – becomes an important dimension of the political process of renewal of the European institutions. Once processes of ratification have been judicialized, political actors frame and interpret judicial decisions according to their preferences, whatsoever these decisions may be. Precisely because of this, it is obvious that trying to understand judicial behaviour in the processes of ratification of European Union treaties means, to a large extent, knowing which were courts' decisions on the merits of the treaties and understanding the factors underlying the variation in such judicial decisions (Closa and Castillo, 2012; Closa, 2013a).

In this chapter I introduce the topic of constitutional review of European Union treaties and explain and discuss judicial decisions on the merits, the first of the dependent variables of this research. After this introduction, the nature of constitutional review and its salience to modern democratic systems will be briefly explained, showing that the implementation of constitutional review in general has been the result of slow processes in which normative and empirical resistances have been overcome. Subsequently, the specific nature of treaties of the European Union and the implications of constitutional review will be assessed. In the fourth section, the possible outcomes of constitutional review of European Union treaties will be analyzed, and the political reactions that may follow after each of them will be described. In a fifth section, empirical information regarding the evolution of courts' decisions on the merits over the history of European Union integration will be provided for the rulings issued within the processes of ratification of the treaties. The chapter will end with some final conclusions.

The Birth of Constitutional Review

Although constitutional review is probably one of the newest features of democratic systems, it has already become one of their core elements (Habermas, 2001; Stone Sweet, 2002). In Europe, after World War II, constitutional review – particularly of a Kelsenian type – spread throughout the continent (Stone, 1990; Ferreres, 2004: 461). Where they exist, constitutional courts have the capacity and the duty to review pieces of legislation in order to guarantee that they respect constitutional mandates. In addition, they carry out other important functions, such as the defense of the constitutional rights of citizens or the mediation as referees in problems regarding the distribution of powers between different organs and levels of government (see Shapiro, 2002; Stone Sweet, 2002). Indeed, where constitutional courts do not exist, these functions are usually carried out by the organs of the judicial branch, especially by supreme courts; this phenomenon even pre-exists in some cases the creation of the first Kelsenian courts (see Shapiro, 2002). Constitutional review is thus today one of the central aspects of constitutional architecture in contemporary societies (see Ackerman, 1997; Lijphart, 1999; Whittington, 2002). But in order to achieve its current role as guarantor of the constitutional text in democratic systems, the very idea of constitutional review has had to overcome two different but interrelated obstacles, the first of a theoretical nature and the second of practical one.

First, constitutional review has had to overcome difficulties of a normative and theoretical nature; namely, constitutional review implies that in a democratic system, a non-democratically elected organ has the capacity to review and eventually overturn pieces of legislation passed by a democratically elected assembly (Kyritsis, 2012), what has been called the 'countermajoritarian difficulty' (Stone, 2008; Friedman, 1998). Democratic systems are based *grosso modo* on the idea that elected representatives of the people have the legitimacy to make decisions on public policies, which crystallize in pieces of legislation. The link between representatives and their constituencies is renewed in universal elections taking place regularly, which thus are a source of political legitimacy. Courts, conversely, are not legitimized by ballot; courts and justices obtain legitimacy precisely in the absence – and due to the absence – of a direct political link with the citizens by asserting that they are committed to the neutral, non-partisan and independent enforcement of the law (Kyritsis, 2012). For that reason, the legitimacy of courts to intervene in political processes remained contested for a long time. As said by Zurn (2002: 468) following Bickel (1986),

> Since representative forms of democracy must involve the legislative enactment and executive enforcement of the will of the people, and since the will of the people is expressed in the majoritarian decisions of their elected representatives, any governmental agency that overrules the outcomes of legislative practices appears not only undemocratic, but fundamentally anti-democratic.

Curiously enough, it has been precisely the needs of the democratic systems that gave courts and constitutional review of legislation a growing role in political processes. At some point, certain judicial type-organs became a 'negative legislator', as Kelsen put it (Stone Sweet, 2002: 81). To a large extent, the clash between totalitarian and democratic systems in the twentieth century showed the need for constitutional review. It gave rise to a change of mentality after which the problems associated with the 'countermajoritarian difficulty' were overcome. In Europe, one of the most representative episodes of this change of mentality is the discussion between Hans Kelsen, the father of modern constitutionalism, and Carl Schmitt, who was for a long time one of the main theorists of the national–socialist legal system (Zarka, 2008). In their debate, they argued about who should be the 'guardian of the constitution'. Schmitt supported a model in which a charismatic leader – the 'President of the Reich' – was in charge of interpreting and enforcing the legal system (Schmitt, 2009 [1931]: 239 ff.). Against this option Hans Kelsen defended the idea of entrusting this role to a constitutional court, so that the function of the defense of the constitution could be transferred to an independent judicial organ (Kelsen, 2009 [1931]: 302). After the horrors of World War II, the Kelsenian model became dominant. This probably marked the transition towards the so-called model of 'neoconstitutionalism' (Weiler, 1996; Stone Sweet, 2007), in which the countermajoritarian nature of the constitutional review of legislation, far from being a weakness, is considered one of the main strengths of courts' action and one of their sources of legitimacy (see Ferrajoli, 2010).

The understanding of democratic systems under the assumptions of neoconstitutionalism is slightly more complex than under those of the traditional model. According to Stone Sweet (2007: 74–75), neoconstitutionalism could be defined by five main features: the authority of state organs derives from a constitution; the constitution attributes the power to the people through regular elections; the exercise of public power is legitimate only to the extent that it is adapted to what is established by the constitution; the constitution foresees a catalogue of rights and a judicial system to defend them; constitutional courts have the power and the duty to enforce this system of justice. In neoconstitutionalism, therefore, beyond the periods of ordinary politics in which general elections legitimate political action, 'constitutional moments' (on this concept, see Ackerman, 1989) acquire prominence. Constitutions, usually the result of a deeper democratic process of constitution making, are deemed to be the very foundations and source of legitimacy of the entire legal and political systems, as well as the general framework within which the periods of ordinary politics can be democratically organized (see *inter alia* Porras, 1981). In this context, constitutions become not only a superior rule in legal terms – as theorized by Kelsen – but also the core element of political life in political terms, whose mandates need to be respected and enforced. Here is where constitutional review finds its legitimacy: courts, theoretically independent from partisan politics, have precisely for that reason the capacity to enforce the constitutional text (see Kyritsis, 2012).

But together with these theoretical and normative obstacles, constitutional review of legislation had to overcome obstacles of a practical nature. In this regard, two different paths seem to have led to constitutional review of legislation. In some legal systems, constitutional review was established after a slow process of reform and empowerment of pre-existing judicial-type organs, whereas in other systems, it was the result of a dramatic transformation of the entire political edifice of the state (see Shapiro, 2002). In the former, constitutional review of legislation was the result of the pressure put by existing judicial institutions in order to gain powers vis-à-vis other branches of government. In such cases, powers of constitutional review of legislation were achieved after political struggles carried out by courts by means of path-breaking jurisprudential developments. The United States is probably the best-known example. In this country, the Supreme Court gained powers of constitutional review after its *Marbury v. Madison* decision of 1803[1] (Schwartz, 1999:145). The background to this decision relates to the struggle of power between the federalists, who had lost the majority in the legislature and the presidency of the government, and Jefferson's new republican majority, which was in power. Before leaving office, the outgoing federalist cabinet made a number of moves in order to keep control of the judiciary. President Adams nominated John Marshall, his secretary of state, as chief justice and passed the Judiciary Act of 1801. According to the act, the next vacancy in the Supreme Court would not be covered so the number of justices would be reduced and the new president's first nominations would be postponed. In addition, he created sixteen new circuit courts for which only federalists judges were nominated – the 'midnight appointments' (Rose, 2003). William Marbury was one of them. Although Marbury and the rest of judges had been nominated by President John Adams and confirmed by the Senate, the secretary of state had not delivered all their commissions, and Jefferson's new government gave the order to not do so. Marbury brought the case before the Supreme Court, asking it to issue a writ to the government so that his commission could be delivered (Rose, 2003). In so doing, he put a dilemma before the court: had the court found that Marbury's commission had to be delivered, Madison, as the new secretary of state, could still ignore the writ, leaving the court with no means to enforce its decision. The other option was to make a pronouncement against Marbury's petition, but in this case, the judicial power would have been surrendered to the control of the republicans. To overcome the impasse, the Supreme Court declared that Section 13 of the Judiciary Act of 1789, which gave the court powers to writ the requested mandamus, was unconstitutional and null and void (see Lijphart, 1999; Rose, 2003). Judicial review of legislation had been established.

In Europe, the process was far more dramatic. Contrary to what happened in the United States, where constitutional review of legislation was the result of a development of judicial politics, in Europe, it was the result of developments of constitutional politics (see Shapiro, 2002). In historical terms, the Austrian Constitutional Court, in whose creation the jurist Hans Kelsen had a prominent role, is deemed to be the first modern centralized court for the review of legislation (Schwartz, 1999; Kommers, 1975) and the model for subsequent constitutional courts across Europe (Garlicki, 2007). But constitutional courts did not spread across the continent until the end of World War II; as was suggested earlier, it is against the background of the totalitarian period how a consensus is reached around the need to complement the democratic systems with a new organ for the enforcement of the constitution (Cole, 1959). The failure of the Weimar Constitution revealed that the former organization of democratic systems allowed for democracies to be subverted from inside. In addition, the massive violations of human rights of the Nazi period put at the forefront of the agenda the need for an organ to safeguard the fundamental rights of citizens in any situation and even against the action of the public authorities. After the war, the new German and Italian constitutions included the creation of Kelsenian-type constitutional courts. The trend continued with the subsequent waves of democratization. In the seventies and early eighties Portugal and Spain created constitutional courts based on the German model. After the fall of the Iron Curtain, almost every Central and Eastern European country included in its constitution the creation of a new constitutional court or, at least, renewed and democratized existing ones (see Closa, 2013a:101).

At the moment, the problems of the theoretical and practical nature of constitutional review can be said to be overcome. As said before, in the era of neoconstitutionalism, constitutional review of legislation is widely accepted as a fundamental part of the democratic system of government. And in practical terms, at least in Europe, the historical background has facilitated the creation of political edifices which, in the majority of cases, include a system of constitutional review.

Constitutional Review in the Processes of Ratification of European Union Treaties

In order to understand the participation of national higher courts (NHCs) in the processes of ratification of European Union treaties, it is adequate to begin by analyzing the relation between the internal and European legal systems. The paradox is that the understanding of this relation is different when assessed from the viewpoint of internal law than when assessed from the viewpoint of European law (see MacCormick, 1999). As recently said by Martinico (2013: 135), '[B]oth the Constitutional Courts and the ECJ [European Court of Justice] perceive their own reference documents (. . .) as the supreme law and claim ultimate authority for them'. From the perspective of national legal systems, (a) the national constitution plays a crucial role, since it is the basis for any transfer of powers to the European Union (Posch, 2008); from the perspective of European law (b) however, the founding treaties and the stability of the European Union are the starting point of the analysis (see Claes, 2007).

(a) The viewpoint of national constitutionalism emphasizes the importance of the consent given by the member states of the European Union to the founding treaties. This consent has permitted the transfer of powers to the European Union and the creation of the European institutions (de Búrca, 1996: 350). Although it has been suggested that the European Union points towards the superseding of the Westphalian paradigm (Caporaso, 1996; Häberle 2002), the main actors in the creation processes of the primary law of the European Union are still the states. Thus, even if the creation and transfer of powers to supranational institutions points towards the transformation of the traditional concept of sovereignty, it is still sovereign states who agree to transfer powers to the European Union through means of international law. As Bruno de Witte (2009: 267) said, '[T]he main instrument of constitutional change in the European Union has been, during the last 25 years, the revision treaty, that is, an international agreement between the member states'.

Given that reforms of European Union primary law are made through the ratification of international treaties, national constitutional law becomes extremely relevant, as it determines how such treaties may be validly ratified (Grimm, 1995). This means that it is each internal legal system which determines the procedure and requisites that the state will need to comply with in order to manifest and commit its will (Maduro, 2003). This is precisely what has permitted national NHCs to intervene in the processes of ratification. Subject to the differences and peculiarities of each internal legal system, a number of actors (see Closa and Castillo, 2012) were entitled to consult these courts and to ask them whether the treaty contained rules contrary to the constitution or whether the process of ratification was being correctly carried out. The European Union claims to be vested with an autonomous legitimacy derived from the treaties and to be 'an independent legal order' (MacCormick, 1995: 261) whose validity should not be assessed from the perspective of national constitutions (see Sørensen, 1983; Weiler, 1999). But even if one accepts the doctrine of the autonomy of European Union law once the founding treaties are ratified, it is clear that during their process of ratification they are subject to the requirements of internal constitutional law.

Procedures for the transfer of powers in the current constitutions of the EU member states are very diverse. Some of them explicitly mention the European Union, and others refer more generally to international organizations, obviously including implicitly supranational organizations like the EU (Arnold, 2003: 88). Some constitutions require parliamentary super-majorities to grant consent to the ratification of the treaty, and others simply require an ordinary law. This question will be further explored in Chapter 5. But for now, suffice it to underline that in every case national constitutions establish the procedure for the transfer of powers to international organizations. This is relevant for NHCs for two reasons. On the one hand, these constitutional provisions provide courts with an *object* of control, thus making possible their participation in the processes of treaty ratification, since the manifestation of the state was made through a formal act of the state authorities – usually an act of the parliament – which could be controlled by the court. On the other hand, constitutional rules about treaty ratification provided courts with a *parameter* of control, since it could be assessed whether the formalities followed by the state authorities when ratifying the treaty were consistent with the procedures constitutionally established.

(b) From the viewpoint of the internal legal systems, everything seems to be clear. Things, however, look somewhat more complex when analyzed from the viewpoint of European law. From this perspective, the distinction between *ex ante* and *ex post* review (see Closa, 2013a) becomes crucial, due to the different political involvements of a ruling issued in the first or the second context. In her detailed doctrinal work, 'National Courts Mandate in the European Union', Monica Claes explicitly said that '[t]here is nothing in European law to preclude national courts from reviewing the constitutionality of Treaties *before* their ratification' (Claes, 2006: 465). However, it must be noted that after the treaty has been ratified, especially after it has entered into force, it is, in principle, binding upon the signing states (MacCormick, 1997: 333). The question whether courts still have the capacity to review European treaties once in force becomes crucial. Although from the viewpoint of internal constitutional law the question may be debated, from the viewpoint of European law, states having ratified European treaties ought to respect their commitment; as Claes (2006: 496) put it

> once ratified, the European Treaties must enjoy full immunity from judicial review (. . .) Already under the rules of classic international law, immunity from constitutional review follows from the principle that *pacta sunt servanda* (. . .) In addition, the immunity from constitutional review is a direct consequence of the European principles of autonomy of the Community legal order, its supremacy and of the principle of loyalty as laid down in Article 10 of the Treaty.

Needless to say, the possible consequences of the review of a treaty in force are not only of a legal nature, but particularly of a political one. Imagine that a provision of a treaty in force is found unconstitutional. In such case, a constitutional amendment would become urgent, and still it probably could not solve retroactively all the legal and political problems deriving from the declaration of incompatibility. Moreover, if the constitutional amendment cannot be carried out, the concerned state would face a difficult situation in which it would have to opt between breaching its international obligations with other member states or violating its national constitution (Closa, 2013a: 116). Risky as it may be, the fact is that the history of European integration shows examples of NHCs asked to assess the constitutionality of European treaties already ratified and already in force. Suffice it to remind readers of the Maastricht decision of the Danish Supreme Court, issued in 1996, three years after the treaty was in force (Rasmussen, 1998; Harck and Olsen, 1999). In that case, the court found the treaty constitutional, so no further problems arose; but declaring it unconstitutional was another option theoretically available for the court. This possibility was also acknowledged by the Czech Constitutional Court, which in its Lisbon I decision stated that

> the Constitutional Court expressed the opinion that, even after ratification of the Accession Treaty, the normatively supreme position of the constitutional order was not rendered meaningless, and that, in exceptional cases, one can conclude that a treaty is inconsistent with the constitutional order even ex post, subsequently, after it has been ratified.[2]

Focusing on the practical dimension of the distinction between *ex ante* and *ex post* review, it is important to remark that if courts have a chance to declare treaties unconstitutional without such declaration having deep practical involvement, it is only before the treaty has entered into force.

Finally, the distinction between *ex ante* and *ex post* review of treaties can become, however, relatively blurred, since a third scenario exists: the scenario in which the court is asked to assess the constitutionality of the treaty before it has been ratified but the ratification procedure is completed – or the treaty even enters into force – before the court reaches a final decision. Similar is the situation in which the court is asked to review the treaty after it has been ratified in the country but before it has entered into force. Although apparently few possibilities exist for cases like these to happen, the fact is that this was exactly the scenario for two rulings: the ruling on the Lisbon Treaty by the Polish Constitutional Court, and the second ruling on the same treaty by the Austrian Constitutional Court. For the sake of comprehensiveness, these cases will also be included in the object of study of this research.

Judicial Decisions on the Merits: Three Possible Outcomes

Constitutional review of European Union treaties may have three types of outcomes: it may well be that the proceedings end without a decision on the merits, that the court finds the treaty constitutional, or that it finds it unconstitutional.

A case may end without a substantive decision on the merits for different reasons. It may happen that the claimant withdraws the claim, thus depriving the court from the chance to make a final pronouncement, as happened in Germany with the claim against the European Defense Community (EDC) Treaty brought by the president of the republic (see Loewestein, 1955; Closa, 2013a). It may also happen that the object of the claim (the treaty) ceases existing as a legally valid object of review due to certain events taking place during its process of ratification. Again in Germany, the Federal Constitutional Court never decided on the claim against the Constitutional Treaty given the failed process of ratification after the French and Dutch referendums (Kiiver, 2010; Closa, 2013a: 110). Courts may also refuse to enter into the merits of the question due to different procedural reasons; for instance, when the interest of the claimant is not sufficiently well founded (see Chapter 5).

In these cases, academics (Loewestein, 1955; Closa, 2013a) have sometimes discussed whether the rejection of the petition on formal grounds simply followed, as stressed by the courts, from the mandates of the legal system, or if such decision may be explained as the result of a strategic move by the court. These authors have suggested that in some cases the absence of a decision on the merits may avoid delicate situations, such as the creation of political costs. Additionally, it has to be taken into account that with the lodging of a claim, petitioners may not only seek a declaration of unconstitutionality, but also, as a secondary goal, the delay in ratification (Closa and Castillo, 2012). This was apparently the case, for instance, with the Czech Republic in the process of ratification of the Lisbon Treaty.[3] Such strategy may fail if courts quickly reject the petition on formal grounds. In these cases, claimants would receive as an answer to their judicialization strategy only disappointing judicial inaction.

The second possible outcome of constitutional review of a treaty is its declaration of constitutionality. By declaring treaties constitutional, NHCs give green light to their process of ratification (Closa and Castillo, 2012), stating that no serious breaches of the national constitution have been found. Most of the cases covered by this research have this type of outcome: the French Constitutional Council in its second decision for the Maastricht Treaty; the German Federal Constitutional Court in its Maastricht and Lisbon cases; the Spanish Constitutional Court in its 'Declaración' on the Constitutional Treaty; the Slovak Constitutional Court in its untimely decision on the Constitutional Treaty; the Polish, Latvian and Czech constitutional courts – the Czech one on two occasions – in the cases for the Lisbon Treaty or the Belgian Constitutional Court in two out of three cases for the same treaty (see Closa, 2013a).

Framings of the rulings by political actors were quite common after declarations of constitutionality. When the German Constitutional Court declared the constitutionality of the Lisbon treaty, the president of the European Commission, Jose Manuel Durao Barroso, 'welcomed' the ruling, and said that 'I am confident we can complete the process of ratification of the Treaty of Lisbon in all countries by autumn'.[4] Chancellor Merkel went further by saying that it was 'a good day for the Lisbon Treaty' and that the treaty had passed 'another important hurdle'.[5] Klaus Hänsch, member of the German Social Democratic Party, interpreted it as a 'good day for Germany'.[6] Similar was the response to the Czech Constitutional Court's decision in its second review of the Lisbon Treaty.[7] Of course, the declaration of constitutionality is usually celebrated as a victory by the supporters of the treaty, to the point that the judicial decision can be understood by them as a political weapon, as a new political argument in their favor and, of course, against those opposing the ratification. At the same time, however, opponents of the treaty – sometimes the petitioners – may be tempted to frame declarations of constitutionality as a partial victory. For instance, despite the fact that the Lisbon case before the German Constitutional Court ended up in a declaration of constitutionality, one of the politicians behind the suit, the Christlich-Soziale Union (CSU) member of the parliament Peter Gauweiler, interpreted the ruling as 'a huge success', since the court ruled that the accompanying legislation should be reformed in order to empower the Bundestag, or since Karlsruhe had insisted on its capacity to defend the rights of the German citizens, 'even against EU regulations'[8].

The third and last possible outcome is the declaration of unconstitutionality of the treaty. Despite the fact that processes of ratification of European Union treaties were never brought to a dead end by a judicial decision (see Closa, 2013b), a large number of rulings ending up in a declaration of unconstitutionality of the treaty exist: the *Crotty* ruling of the Irish Supreme Court in its decision on the European Single Act; the Maastricht declaration of the Spanish Constitutional Court; the first Maastricht decision of the French Constitutional Council; and the rest of the decision by this institution on the Amsterdam, Constitutional and Lisbon Treaty cases (Closa, 2013a). The political framings of this kind of ruling vary widely according to the argumentative tone of the court and the features of the political scenario in which the ruling takes place. In principle, a decision of this kind could be easily recycled by actors opposing the treaty as a political argument. However, things are not that simple. Baquero's (2008) description of the declarations of unconstitutionality of the Maastricht Treaty in Spain and France as essentially harmless rituals was confirmed by the reactions of some pro-ratification ministers of parliament (MPs). In Spain, members of the centre-right Partido Popular (PP) considered the declaration of the court to be 'fully consistent with the constitution and the only which strictly fitted it'.[9] These actors not only did not seem to fear the consequences of the judicial decision, but in fact they seemed to back it. The reason is that, as will be defended in this book, despite the ruling they did not lose control of the overall process of ratification of the treaty.

These three scenarios do not only exhaust the number of empirically observed outcomes in the cases covered by this book, but also the list of theoretically possible outcomes. As has been justified in this section, every type of ruling had different types of political implications. The premise of this book is that courts took these implications into account. Of course, this is not to say that the legal dimension of the rulings is irrelevant (see Chapter 5), but just to say that, in addition to it, political explanations are considered necessary in order to understand judicial behaviour.

Description of Decisions on the Merits by Court and by Treaty

This section will provide empirical information regarding courts' decisions on the merits. The aim is to underline, describe and explain the strong variation in these decisions, as the three 'theoretically possible' outcomes which were mentioned in the previous section were empirically observed. In particular, this section aims to show that variation existed within treaties (Figure 3.1) as well as within institutions (Figure 3.2), and to describe the evolution of these decisions over time. As it will be shown,

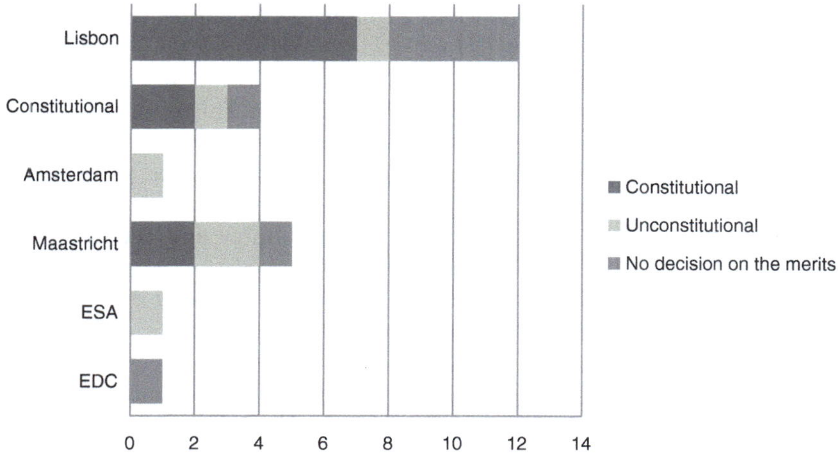

Figure 3.1 Judicial decisions on the merits by treaty

Source: Primary sources, Closa and Castillo (2012), Closa (2013a). Author's own elaboration.

the analysis reveals that idiosyncratic explanations based on the 'special' nature of one treaty or of one concrete institution are not sufficient to explain any of the outcomes.

In analyzing courts' decisions by treaties (see Figure 3.1), it is observed that the evolution of the participation of NHCs in the processes of ratification seems to follow a number of patterns. Most notably, a certain increase in the overall number of rulings has taken place over time, even if the path is irregular. After the EDC and the Single European Act (SEA) treaties, five complaints were filed against the Maastricht Treaty. Then, for the Amsterdam Treaty only one petition for review was presented, but the number increased again to four for the Constitutional Treaty, and up to twelve for the Lisbon Treaty. In previous studies, the number of cases per treaty has been explained as the result of the impact of two variables (Closa, 2013a: 100; Closa and Castillo, 2012: 132): the increase in the number of member states over time, and the trend towards a higher number of judicial cases for the most relevant treaties of the European Union, as the Maastricht, Constitutional and Lisbon treaties indisputable are. However, do these two variables also explain treaties for which no rulings were issued? Actually, there were a number of cases like these: the European Coal and Steel Community (ECSC) Treaty, the EEC Treaty, the Euratom Treaty and the Treaty of Nice. The case of the ECSC and EEC treaties is particularly striking. These treaties were at least as important as the EDC Treaty, and the number of signing states and the historic context of ratification were similar. However, whereas the process of ratification of the EDC Treaty was judicialized, the ratifications of the former treaties were not. The key factor to explain this variation seems to be the *Sozialdemokratische Partei Deutschlands* (SPD), which opposed the EDC Treaty but not the rest of treaties, thus judicializing only the process of ratification of the former (see Egle, 2011: 27 ff.). This points, thus, at the need for one additional variable when analyzing the degree of judicialization of each process of treaty ratification: the degree of political contestation of the treaty. Political contestation may vary according to the political traditions and cleavages of each country and according to the content of the treaty. Although it is not the only relevant variable, political (and social) contestation must be regarded as one of the essential variables in order to understand the participation of NHCs in the processes analyzed.

Figure 3.1 also shows the evolution in the types of decisions. The most judicialized treaties (Maastricht, Constitutional and Lisbon) reveal a clear pattern of decrease in the percentage of declarations of unconstitutionality. These accounted for 40 per cent of the cases during the process of ratification of the Maastricht Treaty, 25 per cent in the process of ratification of the Constitutional Treaty, and for only 8.3 per cent in the process of ratification of the Lisbon Treaty. Thus, declarations of unconstitutionality were increasingly avoided by courts. Rejections of the petitions on formal grounds only slightly increased: 20 per cent of cases for the Maastricht Treaty, 25 per cent for the Constitutional Treaty and 33 per cent for the Lisbon Treaty. And finally, declarations of constitutionality experienced a clear increase: 40 per cent of cases for the Maastricht Treaty, 50 per cent for the Constitutional Treaty, and 58 per cent for the Lisbon Treaty. Less judicialized treaties (EDC Treaty, Single Act and Amsterdam Treaty) are not included in this analysis, as only one case existed for each, and thus percentages are less significant. It is important to remark that for each of the three most judicialized treaties, each of the possible outcomes took place, and so idiosyncratic explanations of judicial activity based on the content of the treaty have to be discarded. The trends explained, however, might point at structural and cross-national patterns of evolution over time derived from processes of learning by courts and political elites. These background tendencies can be said to complement the more case-oriented and deterministic explanations that will be offered in the next chapters.

Variation in decisions on the merits existed among treaties, and also among institutions. Many of the NHCs issued decisions of different types, sometimes even for the same treaty.

As can be seen in Figure 3.2, the description of outcomes by courts does not provide in principle clear trends. As said, a high variation existed regarding decisions on the merits. For five out of eleven NHCs, only one complaint was presented, whereas for the remaining six institutions, two or more petitions were presented. The institution with the largest share of

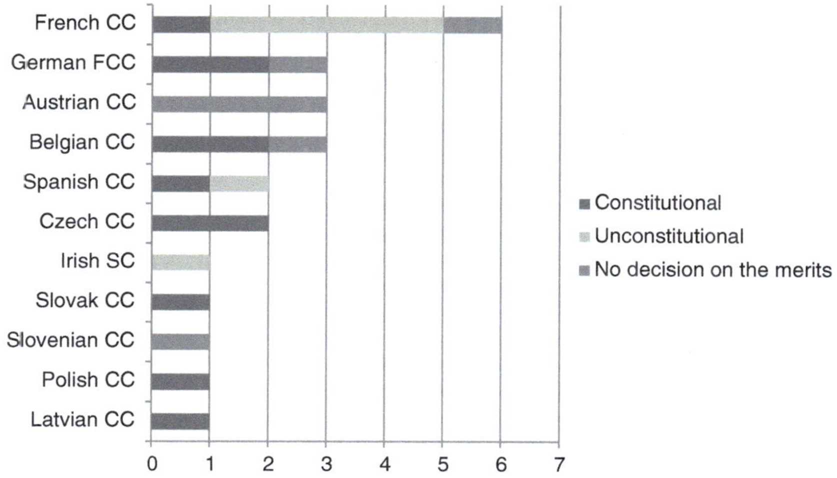

Figure 3.2 Judicial decisions on the merits by courts

Source: Primary sources, Closa and Castillo (2012), Closa (2013a). Author's own elaboration.

declarations of unconstitutionality is the French Constitutional Council: 66 per cent of its decisions were declarations of unconstitutionality. This is exactly the opposite of the Belgian Constitutional Court: 66 per cent of its decisions were declarations of constitutionality. In the case of the Spanish court, 50 per cent of its decisions were declarations of unconstitutionality (one out of two decisions). Although the only decision of the Irish Supreme Court was a declaration of unconstitutionality, it is worth noting that in none of the courts that issued more than one decision did declarations of unconstitutionality account for 100 per cent of them. However, it was different for rejections of the petitions on formal grounds, which were 100 per cent of the decisions of the Austrian Constitutional Court. Additionally, 100 per cent of the decisions of the Czech Constitutional Court were declarations of constitutionality. Thus, declarations of unconstitutionality seemed to be the option to which courts were less 'loyal', and even those institutions that dared make such decisions were not prone to repeating them often.

Conclusions

In this chapter I have shown that NHCs have become significant actors in the processes of ratification of European Union treaties. Law and politics intertwine in a phenomenon of increasing importance. Although NHCs are only allowed to speak the language of law (see Shapiro, 2002: 175), they make decisions with clear political implications. Courts' increased visibility will likely lead to a similar increase in political pressures on them. Whether they want it or not, because courts have turned into important actors, it may be rational for politicians to have an eye on their national courts, not only when trying to ratify European Union treaties, but also in the very process of agreeing to their content and wording.

Judicial review of European Union treaties is possible because of the very nature of the processes of ratification (see Maduro, 2003). In a scenario in which almost every member state of the European Union has at the moment a judicial-type organ empowered with the capacity to review international treaties, the multiplication of rulings is more than expected (see Closa, 2013a). Meanwhile, political actors have learnt how to strategically frame the outcomes of judicial decision making and how to integrate them into their political narratives. Future revisions of European Union treaties will likely come with more judicial decisions as actors learn that activating courts may be an intelligent strategy in episodes of so-called 'judicialization' (see Vallinder, 1994 for information on the concept). The recent rulings of some NHCs on the European Stability Mechanism (ESM) (see Schmidt, 2013; Wendel, 2013) confirm this impression. Once again, episodes of judicialization could be observed. And once again, political actors quickly reacted and integrated the judicial decision into their narrative. For instance, Chancellor Merkel declared after a decision of the German court on the ESM that '[t]oday, Germany is once again sending a strong signal to Europe and beyond: Germany is assuming with determination its responsibility as the biggest economy and as a reliable partner in Europe'.[10]

This research will focus on the cases in which courts made a substantive decision on the merits and declared either the constitutionality or the unconstitutionality of the treaty. Such rulings will be analyzed in their constitutional context, and the legal argumentation of the courts will be assessed. But this book will also try to understand the political and institutional constraints faced by courts and how these affected courts' decisions on the merits. As will be seen, the obstinate empirical reality seems to refute the old expectation of the French *École de l'Exégèse*: the impartial and apolitical application of law by the courts (Siltala, 2011:138).

Notes

1 *Marbury v. Madison*, 5 U.S. 137 [1803].
2 Czech Constitutional Court, decision Pl. ÚS 19/08 (*Lisbon I*), headnotes.
3 'Legal experts noted that the Czech Parliament had already approved the Lisbon treaty and that the court was unlikely to reverse its previous decision to reject an earlier legal challenge to the treaty. But they added that a new legal case would invariably delay the signing of the treaty, possibly for several months, if not longer' *The New York Times/International Herald Tribune*, 21 September 2009 www.nytimes.com/2009/09/22/world/europe/22iht-czech.html (14.02.2015).

4 *Der Spiegel*, 30 June 2009 www.spiegel.de/international/europe/0,1518,633414,00.html (09.02.2011).
5 *Der Spiegel*, 30 June 2009 www.spiegel.de/international/europe/0,1518,633414,00.html (10.02.2011).
6 *Der Spiegel*, 1 July 2009 www.spiegel.de/international/europe/0,1518,633691,00.html (01.04.2012).
7 *Der Spiegel*, 3 November 2009 www.spiegel.de/international/europe/0,1518,659038,00.html (01.04.2012).
8 *Der Spiegel*, 1 January 2009 www.spiegel.de/international/europe/0,1518,633702,00.html (19.04.2012).
9 ABC, 2 July 1992. http://hemeroteca.abc.es/nav/Navigate.exe/hemeroteca/madrid/abc/1992/07/02/023.html (31.08.2013).
10 BBC, 12 September 2012 www.bbc.co.uk/news/world-europe-19567867 (31.08.2012).

References

Ackerman, B. (1989) 'Constitutional politics/constitutional law', *Faculty Scholarship Series. Paper 140* at http://digitalcommons.law.yale.edu/cgi/viewcontent.cgi?article=1139&context=fss_papers (19.07.2013).

Ackerman, B. (1997) 'The rise of world constitutionalism', *Virginia Law Review* 83(4): 771–97.

Arnold, R. (2003) 'Peut-on définir le phénomène d'européanisation des droits constitutionnels nationaux?', in Ziller, J. (ed.), *The Europeanisation of Constitutional Law in the Light of the Constitution for Europe*, Paris: L'Harmattan, pp. 85–96.

Baquero, J. (2008) 'The legacy of the Maastricht-Urteil and the pluralist movement', *European Law Journal* 14(4): 389–422.

Bickel, A. (1986) *The Least Dangerous Branch: The Supreme Court at the Bar of Politics*, New Haven: Yale University Press.

Blichner, L., and Molander, A. (2005) 'What is juridification', *Arena Working Paper* 14, at www.sv.uio.no/arena/english/research/publications/arena-publications/workingpapers/working-papers2005/wp05_14.pdf (21.04.2012).

Caporaso, J. (1996) 'The European Union and forms of state: Westphalian, regulatory or post-modern?', *Journal of Common Market Studies* 34(1): 29–52.

Claes, M. (2006) *The National Courts Mandate in the European Constitution*, Oxford: Oxford University Press.

Claes, M. (2007) 'The Europeanisation of national constitutions in the constitutionalisation of Europe: Some observations against the background of the constitutional experience of the EU-15', *Croatian Yearbook of European Law and Policy* 3: 1–38.

Closa, C. (2013a) 'National higher courts and the ratification of European Union treaties', *West European Politics* 36(1): 97–121.

Closa, C. (2013b) *The Politics of Ratification of European Union Treaties*, London: Routledge.

Closa, C. and Castillo, P. (2012) 'National Courts and Ratification of European Union Treaties', in Evas, T., Lord, C., and Liebert, U. *Multilayered Representation in the European Union. Parliaments, Courts and the Public Sphere*, Berlin: Nomos, pp. 129–57.

Cole, T. (1959) 'Three constitutional courts: A comparison', *The American Political Science Review* 53(4): 936–84.
De Búrca, G. (1996) 'The quest for legitimacy in the European Union', *The Modern Law Review* 59(3): 349–76.
De Witte, B. (2009) 'International law as a tool for the European Union', *European Constitutional Law Review* 5(2): 265–83.
Egle, C. (2011) 'The SPD's Preferences on European Integration: Always One Step Behind?' in Demitrakopoulos, D., *Social Democracy and European Integration. The Politics of Preference Formation*, London: Routledge, pp. 23–51.
Ferrajoli, L. (2010) *Derechos y Garantías*, Madrid: Trotta.
Ferreres, V. (2004) 'The European model of constitutional review of legislation: Toward decentralization?', *International Journal of Constitutional Law* 2(3): 461491.
Friedman, B. (1998) 'The history of the countermajoritarian difficulty, part one', *New York University Law Review* 73(2): 334–433.
Garlicki, L. (2007) 'Constitutional courts versus supreme courts', *International Journal of Constitutional Law* 5(1): 44–68.
Grimm, D. (1995) 'Does Europe need a constitution?', *European Law Journal* 1(3): 282–302.
Häberle, P. (2002) *Pluralismo y Constitutión: Estudios Sobre Teoría Constitucional de la Sociedad Abierta*, Madrid: Tecnos.
Habermas, J. (2001) 'Constitutional democracy: A paradoxical union of contradictory principles?' *Political Theory* 29(6): 776–81.
Harck, S. and Parlmer Olsen, H. (1999) 'Decision concerning the Maastricht Treaty. 1998 Ugeskrift for Retsvaesen, H 800', *The American Journal of International Law* 93(1): 209–14.
Kelsen, H., (2009 [1931]), '¿Quién debe ser el defensor de la Constitución?' in Lombardi, G., (ed.), *La polémica Schmitt-Kelsen sobre justicia constitucional*, Tecnos: Madrid.
Kiiver, P. (2010) 'The Lisbon Judgment of the German Constitutional Court: A Court-Ordered Strengthening of the National Legislature in the EU', *European Law Journal* 16(5): 578–88.
Kommers, D.P. (1975) 'The value of comparative constitutional law', *John Marshall Journal of Practice and Procedure* 9: 685–96.
Kyritsis, D. (2012) 'Constitutional review in representative democracy', *Oxford Journal of Legal Studies* 32(2): 297–324.
Lijphart, A. (1999) *Patterns of Democracy – Government Forms and Performance in Thirty-Six Countries*, New Haven: Yale University Press.
MacCormick, N. (1995) 'The Maastricht-Urteil: Sovereignty now', *European Law Journal* 1(3): 259–66.
MacCormick, N. (1997) 'Democracy, subsidiarity, and citizenship in the "European Commonwealth"', *Law and Philosophy* 16(4): 331–56.
MacCormick, N. (1999) *Questioning Sovereignty*, Oxford: Oxford University Press.
Maduro, M. (2003) 'Las formas del poder constitucional de la Unión Europea', *Revista de Estudios Políticos* 119: 11–55.
Martinico, G. (2013) *The Tangled Complexity of the EU Constitutional Process. The Frustrating Knot of Europe*, London: Routledge.
Porras, A. (1981) 'Notas sobre la teoría del poder constituyente y la experiencia española', *Revista de Estudios Políticos* 24: 175–200.

Posch, A. (2008) 'Community law and Austrian constitutional law', *International Constitutional Law Journal* 2(4): 272–28.

Rasmussen, H. (1998) 'Denmark's Maastricht ratification case: Some serious questions about constitutionality', *Journal of European Integration* 21(1): 1–35.

Rose, W. (2003) '*Marbury v. Madison*: How John Marshall changed history by misquoting the Constitution', *PS Political Science and Politics* 36(2): 209–14.

Schmidt, S. (2013) 'A sense of déjà vu? The FCC's preliminary European Stability Mechanism verdict', *German Law Journal* 14(1): 1–20.

Schmitt, C. (2009 [1931]) 'El Defensor de la Constitución', in Lombardi, G., (ed.), *La Polémica Schmitt/Kelsen Sobre Justicia Constitucional*, Madrid: Tecnos.

Schwartz, H. (1999) 'A Brief History of Judicial Review', in Schedler, A., Diamond, L. and Plattner, M., *The Self-Restraining State. Power and Accountability in New Democracies*, Boulder: Lynne Rienner Publishers, pp. 145–50.

Shapiro, M. (2002) 'The Success of Judicial Review and Democracy', in Shapiro, M. and Stone Sweet, A., *On Law Politics and Judicialization*, Oxford: Oxford University Press, pp. 149–208.

Siltala, R. (2011) *Law, Truth, and Reason. A Treatise on Legal Argumentation*, New York: Springer.

Sørensen, M. (1983) 'Autonomous legal orders: Some considerations relating to a systems analysis of international organisations in the world legal order', *The International and Comparative Law Quarterly* 32(3): 559–76.

Stone, A. (1990) 'The birth and development of abstract review: Constitutional courts and policymaking in Western Europe', *Policy Studies Journal* 19(1):81–95.

Stone Sweet, A. (2002) 'Constitutional Courts and Parliamentary Democracy', *West European Politics* 25(1): 77–100.

Stone Sweet, A. (2007) 'The politics of constitutional review in France and Europe', *International Journal of Constitutional Law* 5(1): 69–92.

Stone, A. (2008) 'Judicial review without rights: Some problems for the democratic legitimacy of structural judicial review', *Oxford Journal of Legal Studies* 28(1): 1–32.

Vallinder, T. (1994) 'The judicialization of politics – A world-wide phenomenon: Introduction', *International Political Science Review* 15(2): 91–9.

Weiler, J. H. H. (1996) 'European neo-constitutionalism: In search of foundations for the European constitutional order', *Political Studies* 44(3): 517–33.

Weiler, J. H. H. (1999) *The Constitution of Europe. "Do the New Clothes Have an Emperor?" and Other Essays on European Integration*, Cambridge: Cambridge University Press.

Wendel, M. (2013) 'Judicial restraint and the return to openness: The decision of the German Federal Constitutional Court on the ESM and the Fiscal Treaty of 12 September 2012', *German Law Journal* 14(1): 21–52.

Whittington, K. (2002) 'An "indispensable feature"? Constitutionalism and judicial review', *Legislation and Public Policy* 6: 21–33.

Zarka, Y.-C. (2008), *Un Detalle Nazi en el Pensamiento de Carl Schmitt*, Barcelona: Anthropos.

Zurn, C. (2002) 'Deliberative democracy and constitutional review', *Law and Philosophy* 21(4–5): 467–542.

4 *Kompetenz-Kompetenz*—The Doctrine of the Last Say

The Interpretative Decisions of Courts

Introduction: Constitutional Review in Post-Kelsenian Legal Systems

The process of European integration has given rise to an exceptional situation. Now, each member state of the European Union is under the simultaneous influence of two overlapping legal systems: the European one and the national one. Pluralist conceptions of law have become frequent (see Maduro, 2003: 12). Both of these two legal systems claim that their rules should be ultimately applied by national courts, which are also European courts from the viewpoint of European law (Maher, 1994; Kumm, 2005; Barber, 2006). The phenomenon of legal systems in which the hierarchy of norms culminates in *a single apex* now seems antiquated (see Röben, 2003; Rosenfeld, 2008; Rossi, 2008). On the one hand, the traditional apex of the internal legal system is still based on the constitution of each member state. But on the other hand, the apex of the new European legal system is based on the treaties of European primary law (see Walker, 2011: 364). In principle, rules that allocate powers between members states and the European Union should prevent this situation from becoming problematic. The rules of each of these overlapping and interrelated legal system should be applied to the cases in which their respective competences are at stake. However, it is not always easy to delineate the competences of each legal system accurately. Thus, there is a question of which system possesses the competence to determine the scope of competences. Two types of actors claim to provide a legitimate response to this question, and both claim that their response is an authoritative interpretation of the law: the European Court of Justice (ECJ) and some national higher courts (NHCs) (see MacCormick, 1995; Weiler, 1999).

The question of *Kompetenz-Kompetenz* addresses this conflict (see Beck, 2011). Although *Kompetenz-Kompetenz* is a complex doctrine, its core idea could be summarized as suggesting that in clashes between core constitutional provisions and European secondary law, NHCs are vested with the power to declare that the constitutional provision should be applied (Lock, 2009; Bieber, 2009). The doctrine *Kompetenz-Kompetenz* has often been reproduced by NHCs in their rulings on European Union treaties, most likely because the assessment of these treaties provides a good opportunity to approach it. From a legal perspective, the assessment of a European Union treaty that is about to enter into force is the most adequate occasion to analyze how such a treaty, and the European legal system in general, will interact with the national legal system and the national constitution. From a political perspective, statements of *Kompetenz-Kompetenz* can allow NHCs to seek at least one of their institutional goals: self-empowerment.

In the previous chapter, one type of decision by courts was described: decisions on the merits. The salience of decisions on the merits and their immediate implications for the ratification of the treaty should not make anyone forget that courts also make other types of decisions: interpretative decisions in the legal argumentation of their rulings. Judicial behaviour is a complex phenomenon. It is expressed through decisions on the merits, but also through interpretative decisions. Thus, in order to improve the understanding of judicial behaviour in the analyzed cases and to provide for a more sophisticated description of its subtleties, statements of *Kompetenz-Kompetenz* will also be studied.

In this chapter, thus, the doctrine of *Kompetenz-Kompetenz* and its associated problems are analyzed. After this introduction, a brief explanation of the *Maastricht Urteil* ruling issued by the German Federal Constitutional Court will be provided, together with a definition of the doctrine *Kompetenz-Kompetenz*. The next section will describe how other NHCs approached the question of *Kompetenz-Kompetenz* in their rulings on European Union treaties. In the fourth section, the focus will be on the general evolution of declarations of *Kompetenz-Kompetenz* over time in different waves of treaty ratification. Next, the relation between the doctrine of *Kompetenz-Kompetenz* and the approach of NHCs to principles such as democracy or sovereignty will be scrutinized. The last section concludes.

The Last Say: Towards a Definition of *Kompetenz-Kompetenz*

A good definition of *Kompetenz-Kompetenz* should focus on the conflict between NHCs and the European Court of Justice. Generally, NHCs have based the application of European law – even the principles of primacy and direct effect – on their own constitutional law (Posch, 2008: 274). This tendency is not surprising, since institutions such as constitutional courts exist precisely to guarantee the enforcement of national constitutions. However, with the *Kompetenz-Kompetenz* doctrine, courts took a hard line to their commitment to defend their constitutional system. According to this doctrine, a national court could make exceptions, if necessary, to the homogeneous application of European Union law and to the interpretative authority of the Court of Justice (Maher, 1994: 227 ff.). As suggested by Neil MacCormick (1999:199), the *Kompetenz-Kompetenz* is about the power to mark the limits of EU law:

> It followed therefore that the competence to determine the competence of European organs must lie somewhere other than in these organs. From a German point of view, the Court effectively held that it itself had this competence. The Court itself would have the final power of decision over any future question concerning the outer limit of European competence in respect of matters concerning Germany, or concerning any of the fundamental constitutional rights or powers of the German federation.

From this viewpoint, the doctrine of *Kompetenz-Kompetenz* thus comprises the power of NHCs to have a final say regarding the applicability of EU law and regarding its compatibility with the national constitution. In some cases, according to NHCs, *Kompetenz-Kompetenz* is about their capacity to assess whether EU institutions have passed EU secondary law beyond the powers conferred upon them by the treaties (the narrowest and strictest expression of the doctrine). Complementarily, NHCs have also sometimes stated their last say regarding the applicability of EU law in conflict with the constitutional rights of citizens or with core constitutional provisions.

To fully understand this doctrine, one must analyze its history as part of the European judicial dialogue, and particularly its process of creation. Foreshadowed in German case law, particularly the *Solange* saga (Reich, 1996: 104; Rosenfeld, 2008: 419), the doctrine of *Kompetenz-Kompetenz* was ultimately outlined in the *Maastricht-Urteil* ruling of the German Federal Constitutional Court (see *inter alia* Herdegen, 1994; Everling, 1994; Weiler, 1995a; MacCormick, 1995; Baquero, 2008). To illustrate the content of this doctrine, it is worth reproducing the most important passages of the ruling:

> The Federal Constitutional Court by its jurisdiction guarantees that an effective protection of basic rights for the inhabitants of Germany will also generally be maintained as against the sovereign powers of the Communities and will be accorded the same respect as the protection of basic rights required unconditionally by the Constitution, and in particular the Court provides a general safeguard of the essential content of the basic rights. The Court thus guarantees this essential content as against the sovereign powers of the Community as well. Acts done under a special power, separate from national powers of the member-States, exercised by a supra-national organisation also affect the holders of basic rights in Germany. They therefore affect the guarantees of the Constitution and the duties of the Constitutional

> Court, the object of which is the protection of constitutional rights in Germany – in this respect not merely as against German state bodies. However, the Court exercises its jurisdiction on the applicability of secondary Community legislation in Germany in a 'relationship of co-operation' with the European Court, under which that Court guarantees protection of basic rights in any particular case for the whole area of the European Communities, and the Constitutional Court can therefore restrict itself to a general guarantee of the constitutional standards that cannot be dispensed with.[1]

Thus, the principles of primacy and direct effect, which were developed by the European Court of Justice in cases such as *Costa v. ENEL*[2] and *Van Gend and Loos*,[3] had a limit: the fundamental rights of German citizens, whose protection is the main task of the German Federal Constitutional Court (Everling, 1994). The same ruling continues as follows:

> If European institutions or agencies were to treat or develop the Union Treaty in a way that was no longer covered by the Treaty in the form that is the basis for the Act of Accession, the resultant legislative instruments would not be legally binding within the sphere of German sovereignty. The German state organs would be prevented for constitutional reasons from applying them in Germany. Accordingly the Federal Constitutional Court will review legal instruments of European institutions and agencies to see whether they remain within the limits of the sovereign rights conferred on them or transgress them.[4]

The *Maastricht-Urteil* case produced an abundant literature. It was a salient topic, particularly because of the open challenge that it posed to the case law of the European Court of Justice. The European Court of Justice had claimed for decades to be the ultimate authority of community law because

> any weakening (. . .) of the uniform application and interpretation of Community law throughout the Union would be liable to give rise to distortions of competition and discriminations (. . .) thus jeopardising (. . .) the proper functioning of the internal market.
>
> (Komarek, 2005)

As Maduro (2003: 13–14) recalls, in its case *Internationale Hadelgessesischaft*,[5] the Court of Justice stated that if the rules of national legal systems prevailed over the law of the European Union, the latter would lose its community nature; therefore, the legal foundations of the very community would be questioned. However, in its *Kompetenz-Kompetenz* doctrine, the German court contraposed its own arguments to this need for uniform interpretation of European Union law by declaring that in exceptional circumstances the interpretation of a national court based on its national constitution could prevail, and thus that the application of European Union law could lose its immunity from national constitutional assessments (see Everling, 1994; MacCormick, 1995; Kumm and Ferreres, 2005). With its *Kompetenz-Kompetenz* doctrine, the German Federal Constitutional Court reserved to itself the right to make an exception to the application of European Union law in Germany (Boom, 1995: 177). Until that moment, assessments of the validity of European Union law had been considered the exclusive competence of the European Court of Justice. The German court suggested it could review European Union law in two different scenarios: cases in which European Union law violated the constitutional rights of German citizens (Wieland, 1994: 261) – see also the *Solange* I case[6] – and cases in which the European Union adopted rules of secondary law beyond the powers transferred to it by member states (Wieland, 1994: 263). According to Karlsruhe, it was its right and duty to assess whether any of these circumstances took place.

From an inter-court competition perspective (Alter, 1997), *Kompetenz-Kompetenz* can be interpreted as an attempt by the German court to redefine and enlarge the scope of its power at the expense of the European Court of Justice. According to Wieland (1994: 264), the German court's emphasis on its own power could be explained either by a natural rivalry between the two courts or as a reaction to the activism of the Court of Justice. Although the Maastricht decision issued by the German Federal Constitutional Court refers to a cooperative relationship with the Court of Luxembourg (Stein, 2011: 223), this was perceived as insincere by some scholars (Claes and de Visser, 2012: 106). Subtle violence underlies this invitation to cooperate, particularly because cooperation was offered after a threat. This will of collaboration had already been voiced in the *Solange* saga with regard to questions of fundamental rights. But instead of enhancing cooperation, the *Maastricht-Urteil* ruling could be deemed as broadening the scope of NHCs' powers of review, which would also include the determination of whether the European Union laws are passed *ultra-vires*, that is, the competence to determine the extent of European Union competence.

Approaches to *Kompetenz-Kompetenz* in NHCs' Rulings on European Union Treaties: A Classification

Although it is perhaps the most famous instance, the *Maastricht-Urteil* ruling has not been the only challenge to the Court of Justice. Several rulings by other NHCs have also reproduced in some form the main basic claim of the doctrine (see *inter alia* Bříza, 2009: 154; Craig and de Burca, 2008: 373; Kruma, 2009: 149). This section describes the approaches to the *Kompetenz-Kompetenz* doctrine in all rulings on European Union treaties.

One way of representing NHCs' stances towards the question of *Kompetenz-Kompetenz* would be a dichotomous approach: either courts declared their *Kompetenz-Kompetenz* or they did not. Although this is an acceptable way of approaching the topic, it runs the risk of hiding a number of important questions. For example, such an approach misses the considerable differences in courts' phrasing of the doctrine, in the way it is located in the wider context of their legal narrative, in the emphasis utilized, etc. In simpler terms, although Karlsruhe was not the only court declaring its right to a 'last say' on the constitutionality of European Union law, the way in which this court worded it was clearly different from that of other NHCs.

Table 4.1 summarizes the information about this doctrine in all NHCs' rulings on EU treaties. Only in six of seventeen rulings were references to the *Kompetenz-Kompetenz* doctrine observed. Additionally, only the two German cases included a full statement of *Kompetenz-Kompetenz*. The German rulings clearly stated the court's *Kompetenz-Kompetenz* in an aggressive and explicit manner (see Baquero, 2009). Other NHCs followed the German path, but with a less challenging tone and declaring their openness to collaboration with the European Court of Justice; these were the first ruling on the Lisbon Treaty by the Czech Constitutional Court (Přibáň, 2009) and the Spanish Constitutional Treaty declaration (Schutte, 2005). These two rulings declared that exercising their *Kompetenz-Kompetenz* was hardly thinkable, although possible under extreme circumstances. Other NHCs, such as the Polish and Latvian

Table 4.1 Courts' statements of *Kompetenz-Kompetenz*

	Not stated	*Possible*	*Suggested*	*Stated*
Belgium	Lisbon I Lisbon II			
Czech Republic	Lisbon II		Lisbon I	
France	Maastricht I Maastricht II Amsterdam Constitutional T. Lisbon			
Germany				Maastricht Lisbon
Ireland	Single European Act			
Latvia		Lisbon		
Poland		Lisbon		
Slovak Republic	Constitutional T.			
Spain	Maastricht		Constitutional T.	

Source: Author's own elaboration from primary sources

constitutional tribunals, considered the question but avoided providing an explicit answer; they noted that any possible conflict between European law and their constitution would need to be resolved on a case-by-case basis. Finally, the remaining rulings did not declare their *Kompetenz-Kompetenz*. Approaches to *Kompetenz-Kompetenz* thus occur on a continuum.

Of course, Table 4.1 includes only rulings in which courts entered into the merits of the cases, so some rulings are excluded. For example, the Austrian and Slovenian courts always rejected on formal grounds the claims presented before them (Closa, 2013a) and consequently could not elaborate on their approach to the *Kompetenz-Kompetenz* doctrine. However, in the Austrian case, the general case law of the institution is at odds with such a doctrine: not only does the court not review European Union secondary law, but it even has declared the immunity of any internal law transposing EU legislation (Dutheillet, 2004: 30).

Harsh Statements of Kompetenz-Kompetenz: *The German Federal Constitutional Court*

The German Maastricht and Lisbon rulings are the cases in which *Kompetenz-Kompetenz* was stated in a most clear and radical way. The German court warned that it would make exceptions to the application of EU secondary law that was *ultra-vires*, that violated the fundamental rights of German citizens (see Grimm, 2009), or that violated the constitutional core of the German constitution. The previous subsection notes how Karlsruhe phrased the *Kompetenz-Kompetenz* doctrine in its Maastricht decision. In the Lisbon decision, it followed the path of the *Maastricht-Urteil* by declaring

> it must be possible within the German jurisdiction to assert the responsibility for integration if obvious transgressions of the boundaries occur when the European Union claims competences (. . .) and to preserve the inviolable core content of the Basic Law's constitutional identity by means of an identity review (. . .) The Federal Constitutional Court has already opened up the way of the ultra vires review for this, which applies where Community and Union institutions transgress the boundaries of their competences. If legal protection cannot be obtained at the Union level, the Federal Constitutional Court examines whether legal instruments of the European institutions and bodies keep within the boundaries of the sovereign powers accorded to them by way of conferral.[7]

The Lisbon ruling of the German Federal Constitutional Court was a continuation of the Maastricht decision (Häberle, 2009) but longer, more detailed and probably more critical. In this ruling, the idea of constitutional identity gained special salience (see Castillo, 2013a). This statement of *Kompetenz-Kompetenz* was celebrated as a victory by opponents of the treaty. As the member of parliament (MP) of the Christlich-Soziale Union (CSU) and claimant in the Lisbon case said, '[T]hen German citizens have the right to legal protection by the Federal Constitutional court – even against EU regulations. Karlsruhe can rule that EU laws that go too far cannot be applied in Germany. For the citizens of Germany, that is a huge success'.[8] The German cases, Maastricht and Lisbon, are thus located at one end of the continuum.

Statements of Kompetenz-Kompetenz *in Europhile Rulings: The Spanish and Czech Constitutional Courts*

A second group of more moderate stances includes the Spanish Constitutional Court and Czech Constitutional Court. Regarding the former, the declaration on the Constitutional Treaty was the first time in which it made a *Kompetenz-Kompetenz* declaration. The court argued that the supremacy of the constitution and primacy of EU law were of a different nature and therefore not contradictory (Alonso García, 2005: 1020; Rossi, 2008: 68) – a doctrine against which three of twelve magistrates issued dissenting opinions (Castillo, 2013b). Unlike in the Maastricht ruling, in this case the Spanish court considered the question of its own *Kompetenz-Kompetenz* (Teruel, 2006: 348); however, this doctrine was stated less aggressively than in the German court decision:

> In the unlikely case where, in the ulterior dynamics of the legislation of the European Union, said law is considered irreconcilable with the Spanish Constitution, without the hypothetical excesses of the European legislation with regard to the European Constitution itself being remedied by the ordinary channels set forth therein, in a final instance, the conservation of the sovereignty of the Spanish people and the given supremacy of the Constitution could lead this Court to approach the problems which, in such a case, would arise.[9]

Thus, although the phrasing of the Spanish court was far softer than that of its German counterpart, the *Tribunal Constitucional* 'did not want to rule out that, under special circumstances and notwithstanding other international remedies, it may intervene if the European institutions do not effectively repair the excesses of European law' (Schutte, 2005: 289).

The Spanish approach was followed during the next wave of rulings by the Czech Constitutional Court's Lisbon I decision (Vaičaitis. 2010: 79). The Czech court unambiguously declared its *Kompetenz-Kompetenz*, following the German doctrine (Přibáň, 2009: 357):

> The Constitutional Court remains the supreme protector of Czech constitutionality, including against possible excesses by Union bodies or European law, which also clearly answers the contested issue of

> the sovereignty of the Czech Republic; if the Constitutional Court is the supreme interpreter of the constitutional regulations of the Czech Republic, which have the highest legal force on Czech territory, it is obvious that Art. 1 par. 1 of the Constitution cannot be violated. If European bodies interpreted or developed EU law in a manner that would jeopardise the foundations of materially understood constitutionality and the essential requirements of a democratic, law-based state that are, under the Constitution of the Czech Republic, seen as inviolable (Art. 9 par. 2 of the Constitution), such legal acts could not be binding in the Czech Republic. In accordance with this, the Czech Constitutional Court also intends to review, as ultima ratio, whether the legal acts of European bodies remain within the bounds of the powers that were provided to them. In this regard the Constitutional Court basically agreed with certain conclusions of the German Federal Constitutional Court, stated in its Maastricht decision.[10]

The Czech court argued that the competences of the European Union had been defined in a sufficiently clear manner and that it was for the Court of Justice of the European Union to determine the division of competences within the European Union. However, the Czech Constitutional Court also admitted that in exceptional cases, it could operate as *ultima ratio* and review whether a European Union rule exceeded the scope of competences conferred to the European Union (Nemeckova, 2009: 243). The Czech court explicitly quoted the *Solange* II and *Maastricht-Urteil* decisions issued by the German Federal Constitutional Court, as well as the Polish Constitutional Court decision on the Accession Treaty. However, it took a slightly softer approach by arguing that the idea of the 'final say' of NHCs should be understood as a warning that did not necessarily have to be employed (Bříza, 2009: 154). Finally, although the Czech Constitutional Court was clear in its position regarding the *Kompetenz-Kompetenz* doctrine, unlike the German court, it did not make overly critical commentaries about sovereignty or democracy (see later in this chapter).

Curiously, when the court issued a second ruling on the treaty, its tone radically changed. For this second ruling, the claimants explicitly asked the court to reflect on the possible superiority of the Court of Justice vis-à-vis the national constitutional court, which provided the Czech court with an excuse to present an in-depth analysis of *Kompetenz-Kompetenz*. However, the Czech court did not react as the claimants expected (Castillo, 2013a). First, it emphasized its willingness to collaborate with the ECJ rather than challenge it. Second, it stated that potential contradictions between European Union law and national constitutions could be removed not only through priority application of the former, but also through constitutional amendments.[11] However, this was not a sign of change in the approach of the Czech court in the long run. Recently, its warnings were acted on when it decided to declare a previous decision of the ECJ *ultra vires*[12] (Martinico, 2013: 145).

Leaving the Question Unresolved: The Approach Taken by the Latvian and Polish Constitutional Courts

Between rulings declaring NHCs' *Kompetenz-Kompetenz* in a harsh or soft way and rulings not declaring such a doctrine, two exceptional cases can be identified: the Polish and Latvian rulings on the Lisbon Treaty. In these cases, the courts addressed the issue of *Kompetenz-Kompetenz*, but unlike in the rulings described in the previous subsections, they did not provide a definitive answer to the question of whether they would exercise the powers of review with which Karlsruhe had threatened the Court of Justice (Castillo, 2013a). In the Latvian case, which could be described as Europhile, the court considered the scenario of an eventual clash between different systems of protection of fundamental rights – particularly with regard to the Charter of Rights of the European Union: '[T]he Court cannot assess in abstracto the claim regarding the eventual conflict of the different systems of protection of Fundamental Rights. Such conflicts have to be solved on the base of the individual cases'.[13]

Does the Latvian Constitutional Court reserve to itself the right to use its judicial *Kompetenz-Kompetenz* in the future? Although the court does not explicitly say that it will enforce constitutional rights against European Union rules in cases of conflict, it says that it could need to solve such individual conflicts. The court suggests that, in the event of a clash, the enforcement of constitutional rules could prevail. The Polish court seems equally deliberately ambiguous in this regard. The court begins by making the following statement:

> The allegations of the applicant regard the possibility of applying the provisions of the Treaty in a way that broadens the scope of competences that have already been conferred, and therefore they refer to the ideas of the applicants concerning the way of applying the Treaty in the future. The Constitutional Tribunal is not competent to assess hypothetical ways of applying the Treaty of Lisbon. Such practice remains outside the jurisdiction of the constitutional court as long as it does not take the form of concrete regulations subject to review by the Constitutional Tribunal, pursuant to Article 188 of the Constitution. The conclusions concerning the potential application of the Treaty, in a way which would be inconsistent with the Treaty, fall outside the jurisdiction of the Constitutional Tribunal.[14]

The court considered the issue of *Kompetenz-Kompetenz* but did not provide a definitive answer to the question of whether it could declare European Union secondary law inapplicable. The Polish court argued that it is not tasked with providing legal solutions to hypothetical cases but to actual ones. It also warned that if concrete cases, 'concrete regulations subject to review by the Constitutional Tribunal', arise, it could consider the possibility of declaring European Union law inapplicable. Furthermore, the full reasoning of the ruling must be considered in light of its previous case law on the European Arrest Warrant and the Accession Treaty in which the court displayed a controversial attitude towards the question of the supremacy of EU law (Kowalik- Bańczyk, 2005; Vaičaitis, 2010: 79). According to various authors, Polish courts regard themselves as possessing the ultimate *Kompetenz-Kompetenz* (Craig and de Burca, 2008: 373; Kruma, 2009:149).

No Statement of Kompetenz-Kompetenz: *The French Council and Others*

Finally, in a large group of rulings the *Kompetenz-Kompetenz* doctrine is absent, including those of the French Constitutional Council. However, the assessment of the French rulings deserves some comment, because the absence of the *Kompetenz-Kompetenz* doctrine in these rulings is not as clear as in the rulings of other NHCs. It has been suggested that in some of the French rulings *Kompetenz-Kompetenz* was stated indirectly or tacitly. MacCormick (1995: 260), in particular, suggested that parts of the Council's Maastricht ruling could be understood as tacit statements of *Kompetenz-Kompetenz*. It is true that, in this ruling, the Council made a statement that could be interpreted as pointing in that direction, particularly where it affirms that the rights and freedoms of citizens are guaranteed by the European Court of Justice 'taken in conjunction with the intervention of national courts rendering decisions in the exercise of their jurisdiction'.[15] However, the conclusion that *Kompetenz-Kompetenz* was present in that ruling is forced. In this passage, the Council most likely refers to the systems that protect the constitutional rights established by national constitutions without implying that national catalogues of rights could be enforced by national courts against European law. Claes (2006: 629) seems to agree that *Kompetenz-Kompetenz* was absent in the aforementioned ruling and notes that 'the *Conseil constitutionnel* did not make any pronouncements as to its own jurisdiction in the matter, nor that of the ordinary courts'.

To clarify this question, the case law of the French Constitutional Council beyond its rulings on European Union treaties can be looked at. Commentators have been divided in this regard. Plötner (2003: 53) said that 'as far as the CC [Constitutional Council] is concerned, the *Kompetenz-Kompetenz* problem is solved: this competence finally remains with each Member State' (see also Reestman, 2009: 386). However, many academics seemed to disagree with that interpretation. Although the Council had, on some occasions, reviewed the constitutionality of European Union directives, it had done so only indirectly when reviewing a rule of internal law transposing them, being such internal rule the only object of a declaration of unconstitutionality (Protière and Blacher 2007: 140; see also a similar reasoning by the *conseiller* Olivier Dutheillet, 2004: 28). Supporting the view that the Council had never declared its *Kompetenz-Kompetenz*, Alberton (2008: 195) acknowledged that the Council's review of EU secondary law could be necessary, although the institution had declined so far to conduct such a review. Dupéré (2005: 154) clearly stated that the Constitutional Council ruled out any possibility of indirect control of EU secondary law through its doctrine of the 'essential conditions of national sovereignty', which can only be used for the *ex ante* control of treaties transferring powers to the EU; according to the author, once the treaty is ratified, the exercise of the transferred powers cannot be an object of review under such a doctrine. This opinion, according to which the *Kompetenz-Kompetenz* doctrine was absent from French rulings, will be followed in this book.

Finally, some institutions, such as the Irish Supreme Court, the Belgian Constitutional Court and the Slovakian Constitutional Court, simply do not approach the question of *Kompetenz-Kompetenz*, which is absent from their rulings on EU treaties. In its Lisbon cases, the Belgian Constitutional Court said nothing on the question of *Kompetenz-Kompetenz*. This was actually consistent with the Belgian court's Europhile case law (see Vandamme, 2008; Bossut and Verrijdt, 2011). There is a particular tradition of collaboration between the Belgian court and EU institutions, especially the CJEU. According to Claes (2006: 641):

> [T]he Cour d'arbitrage [now Constitutional Court] may well be the least protective and most communautaire of all constitutional courts: it refers questions for preliminary ruling; it has obviously shied away from obstructing the Belgian membership of the European Union which seemed defective for a direct conflict with a constitutional provision. The same prudence may be expected where the constitutionality of secondary law is at issue.

In the Slovakian case, a general doctrine on EU matters is less developed (Bobek and Kühn, 2009). In the decision on the Constitutional Treaty of the Slovakian court, a statement of *Kompetenz-Kompetenz* is also absent. Most likely, the claimants' petition, which was limited to the violation of their fundamental right to participate in public affairs due to the lack of participation in the ratification, did not allow the court to make such a statement. Still, it must be taken into account that other courts, particularly the German court, opted for a flexible approach to the petitions of the claimants in which claims were used as an excuse for further doctrinal comments on various matters (see Wendel, 2011: 114).

The Increasing Salience of *Kompetenz-Kompetenz*: Description of Its Evolution by Treaties

Kompetenz-Kompetenz was not, after all, the sole creation of the German Constitutional Court. Instead, the *Kompetenz-Kompetenz* doctrine must be understood as a process of collaboration, imitation and flexible coordination among NHCs. This section will describe the evolution of *Kompetenz-Kompetenz* statements in rulings on European Union treaties issued during the process of ratification.

Table 4.2 indicates the growing importance of statements of *Kompetenz-Kompetenz* over time. Only rulings in which NHCs entered into the merits of the cases are considered in it, although some comments will be also devoted to episodes in which petitions were rejected on formal grounds.

During the first processes of ratification of EU treaties, not a single ruling by an NHC included a statement of *Kompetenz-Kompetenz* or a similar doctrine, either for the European Defense Community Treaty or for the European Single Act. At this time, *Kompetenz-Kompetenz* seemed simply off the agenda. For the European Defense Community Treaty, the principles of primacy or direct effect had not been established. At the time of the *Crotty* ruling on the European Single Act, European Union law had already reached a certain level of development, but opposition by NHCs

Table 4.2 Evolution of statements of *Kompetenz-Kompetenz*

Treaty	*Case*	*Kompetenz-Kompetenz*	*% rulings*	*% institutions*
ESA	Irish S.C.	No	0%	0%
Maastricht	French C.C. I	No	25%	25%
	French C.C. II	No		
	Spanish C.C.	No		
	German F.C.C.	Yes (stated)		
Amsterdam	French C.C.	No	0%	0%
Constitutional	French C.C.	No	33%	33%
	SCC	Yes (suggested)		
	SkCC	No		
Lisbon	GFCC: Lisbon	Yes (stated)	50%	66%
	CZCC: Lisbon I	Yes (suggested)		
	CZCC: Lisbon II	No		
	FCC: Lisbon	No		
	PCC: Lisbon	Yes (possible)		
	LCC: Lisbon	Yes (possible)		
	BCC: Lisbon I	No		
	BCC: Lisbon II	No		
Total			35%	55%

Source: Author's own elaboration based on primary sources.

was not as vocal as it would become after the Maastricht treaty (see Weiler, 1999). It is precisely from that moment that *Kompetenz-Kompetenz* is increasingly echoed in rulings.

The first observation of a declaration of *Kompetenz-Kompetenz* can be found in the *Maastricht-Urteil* ruling issued by the German Federal Constitutional Court. Three NHCs intervened during the process of ratification of the treaty: the Spanish, French and German ones. The Spanish Constitutional Court intervened in one case, the French Constitutional Council intervened in three cases – although the third petition was rejected on formal grounds – and the German Federal Constitutional Court intervened in one case. The German court was the last to intervene, and its ruling included a statement of *Kompetenz-Kompetenz* for the first time with a complete wording (see MacCormick, 1995; Herdegen, 1994). The Spanish Constitutional Court and French Constitutional Council, however, clearly did not consider the question in their rulings. Therefore, the *Maastricht-Urteil* ruling issued by the German court represents one fourth of the rulings that entered into the merits of the case for that treaty.

The next process of treaty ratification for which a ruling existed is the Amsterdam Treaty. Only the French Constitutional Council issued a ruling on this treaty, which did not declare the *Kompetenz-Kompetenz* doctrine. Meanwhile, the Danish Supreme Court assessed the constitutionality of the Maastricht Treaty after its ratification was completed. In its ruling, the Danish court reproduced the *Kompetenz-Kompetenz* doctrine of the German court with similar wording and implications. The ruling even allowed lower courts to assess the compatibility of European Union law with the national constitution (Lachmann, 1998; Harck and Olsen, 1999).

In the next wave of rulings on the Constitutional Treaty, four courts were asked to make pronouncements: the Slovak Constitutional Court, the Spanish Constitutional Court, the French Constitutional Council and the Austrian Constitutional Court. Neither the French Constitutional Council nor the Slovak Constitutional Court made any reference to their *Kompetenz-Kompetenz* in their rulings, whereas the Austrian Constitutional Court did not even enter into the merits of the case. However, in the *Declaración 1/2004* issued by the Spanish Constitutional Court, a soft statement of *Kompetenz-Kompetenz* is found (Schutte, 2005). This statement by the Spanish court represented one third of the total of courts issuing a decision on the merits. Compared to the Maastricht Treaty, the ruling of the Spanish court meant that the question of *Kompetenz-Kompetenz* remained on NHCs' agendas.

Finally, during the process of ratification of the Lisbon Treaty, the share of declarations of *Kompetenz-Kompetenz* dramatically increases. The Czech Constitutional Court, explicitly quoting the *Maastricht-Urteil* ruling, reclaimed its last word on the applicability of European Union law (Pribán, 2009; Nemeckova, 2009). This is also the position of the German Federal Constitutional Court, which not only reiterated its

Maastricht-Urteil doctrine, but also extended it. However, the German court toned down its approach in one regard: whereas in *Maastricht-Urteil* the court had suggested the capacity of lower courts to exercise their *Kompetenz-Kompetenz*, according to the Lisbon ruling, only the German Federal Constitutional Court is empowered to do that (Baquero, 2009). For this treaty, two more NHCs issued rulings reminiscent of the *Kompetenz-Kompetenz* doctrine: the Latvian Constitutional Court and the Polish Constitutional Court. Although these courts did not explicitly declare their capacity to review European Union secondary law, the possibility of clashes between European Union and national constitutional law plays a role in their rulings. The courts leave unanswered the question regarding the actions they would take in cases of actual clashes. *Kompetenz-Kompetenz* is present in 50 per cent of rulings and 66 per cent of courts in this wave if cases without a substantive decision on the merits are excluded. In general, decisions of *Kompetenz-Kompetenz* played an increasing role in NHCs' rulings throughout the process of integration, and it was during the process of ratifying the Lisbon Treaty that they attained the highest prominence. Given this trend, it would be no surprise that declarations of *Kompetenz-Kompetenz* were important in future waves of treaty ratification.

On Constitutional Principles, Democracy, Sovereignty . . . and *Kompetenz-Kompetenz*

The *Kompetenz-Kompetenz* doctrine has not, however, been the only polemic question addressed by NHCs with powers of constitutional review in their rulings. Other topics with deep political involvements were also discussed by NHCs (see Wendel, 2011; Castillo, 2013a). Some rulings, such as the *Crotty* ruling or those of the French Constitutional Council, maintain a legalistic approach and are defined by a laconic style. However, over time, particularly during the wave of rulings assessing the Lisbon Treaty, other topics beyond the legalistic assessment of the constitutionality of the treaty were addressed. On the one hand, courts reflected on whether certain legislation accompanying the treaties should be reformed (Lock, 2009; Wendel, 2011). On the other hand, these rulings discussed principles of a more political – perhaps philosophical – nature regarding the democratic functioning of the European Union, its respect for national sovereignty or the need to safeguard a constitutional core (see *inter alia* Wendel, 2011; Beck, 2011).

Requiring Modification of Statutes: The Assessment of Accompanying Legislation

A declaration of constitutionality of the treaty, together with a declaration of unconstitutionality of accompanying legislation, can be illustrated with the case law of the court of Karlsruhe. The German Federal Constitutional Court, in its Lisbon decision, affirmed the need for a statutory reform in Germany despite the constitutionality of the treaty (Wendel, 2011). The court solemnly stated that the Act Extending and Strengthening the Rights of the *Bundestag* and the *Bundesrat* in European Union Matters did not comply with the constitutional requirements of Articles 38.1 and 23.1 of the Basic Law and should 'be re-drafted in accordance with constitutional requirements before the ratification of the treaty'[16] in so far as 'the *Bundestag* and the *Bundesrat* have not yet been accorded sufficient rights of participation in European lawmaking and treaty amendment procedures'[17] (see Castillo, 2013a). In one interpretation of this episode, the court could be depicted as a recalcitrant actor that indirectly tried to obstruct the process of ratification of the treaty. An alternative interpretation, however, suggests that the court made the least costly decision when assessing the constitutionality of the treaty. According to Lock (2009), 'either it could declare the Lisbon Treaty to be incompatible with the Basic Law, which would have created a major political crisis, or it could introduce a hurdle at the national level in order to prevent the erosion of national competences' (see also the similar arguments by Closa, 2013a: 113). The request of the court was immediately attended by the coalition government, which amended the legislation by September 2009, before the general elections took place (Kiiver, 2009: 579). Similar questions were raised in other cases, such as the Czech Republic's ratification of the Lisbon Treaty. However, this court, unlike the German one, argued that it was for the legislative chamber to decide how to regulate the rights of the national parliament under the new treaty (Wendel, 2011: 120).

Limits: The Idea of a Constitutional Core

The concept of a 'constitutional core' was mentioned in the case law of different courts, although it was phrased differently, depending on national traditions and idiosyncratic factors. In particular, during the recent ratification of the Lisbon Treaty, this issue gained a prominent role (Castillo, 2013a). According to the idea of 'constitutional core', the transfer of powers to the European Union is limited by core elements of national constitutions. However, in most of the cases in which NHCs referred to such a constitutional core, they pointed at general principles rather than concrete areas of power.

In the German Constitutional Court's Lisbon decision, this constitutional core is referred to as a constitutional identity, which is protected under the 'eternity clause' of Article 79.3 of the German Basic Law (Wendel, 2011: 125; Castillo, 2013a). In this ruling, the court enumerated an exceptionally concrete list of fields which it deemed to be essential state functions: criminal law and procedure, fiscal decisions on public revenue and public expenditure, the internal and external use of force, social policy, education, culture, language, media, family law and the regulation of religious communities[18] (see also Wendel, 2011: 125). According to Baquero (2009: 5), the Lisbon decision is concrete in the enunciation of powers to be preserved by the German state 'where the Maastricht decision had been vague'. According to Krämer (2010: 18), however, such an approach was 'too rigid'.

In the case law of other courts, the concept remains relatively flexible. Lists of powers included in the constitutional core are not provided, and only general principles are enumerated. In the case of the Czech rulings (Kruma, 2010: 43), the concept used is that of a 'material core' of the constitution. The idea of 'material core' was used by President Václav Klaus to argue that a contradiction between the Lisbon Treaty and the Czech constitution that 'cannot be removed even by a possible amendment to the Constitution'[19] existed. In this case, the idea of a material core of the constitution is based on concrete mandates in Articles 9(2) and 9(3) of the constitution, which state the inadmissibility of any change of fundamental attributes of the democratic, law-observing state and of interpretations of legal norms warranting the removal or threatening the foundations of the democratic state, respectively. In addition, the Czech court went further than any other court and declared the natural-law origin of certain principles, such as 'democracy, the sovereignty of the people, and separation of powers' which could not be altered even by an amendment to the constitution.[20] Still, the court refused to list explicitly an abstract catalogue of non-transferrable rights, as requested by the petitioners (Wendel, 2011: 127). In the Polish Lisbon ruling, the idea of 'constitutional identity' includes values upon which the constitution is based and powers which cannot be transferred, including the fundamental principles of the constitution, the rights of individuals, the principle of rule of law, the principles of statehood and democratic governance and the principles of social justice and subsidiarity, among others[21] (Czapliňski, 2011: 201).

Finally, some courts only mention the issue without clearly defining the concept, simply suggesting that transfers of powers are limited by certain constitutional principles. In the case law of the Spanish Constitutional Court, a certain evolution can be observed. In its Maastricht ruling, the court did not enter into detailed considerations on this matter, but only mentioned limits to the transfer of powers regarding the basic principles of social and democratic state based on the rule of law, the higher values of the legal system and the constitutional rights of citizens.[22] However, in its Constitutional Treaty declaration, it considered that a basic core of the constitutional identity of the member states – 'their existence and basic structures, as well as their values, principles and fundamental rights' – is acknowledged by the very treaty in Article I-5.1, which in the view of the court satisfied the requirements established by NHCs[23] (Teruel, 2006; Castillo de la Torre, 2005). Finally, the Latvian ruling on the Lisbon Treaty lists a number of principles that the transfer of competences should respect (Kruma, 2010: 43): rule of law and the basis of an independent, sovereign and democratic republic, as well as the rights of citizens to decide upon issues that are essential to a democratic state.[24]

Sovereignty: Classical Approaches versus Pooled Sovereignty

The discussions about the notion of sovereignty with reference to the European Union and its member states have been salient in academic writings (see MacCormick, 1997). However, the debate to which the question has given rise is so relevant that it has been echoed by the rulings of the NHCs. In the French Constitutional Council's decisions, the idea of sovereignty appears repeatedly and seems to be a slightly different French equivalent of other notions of a constitutional core.[25] In the doctrine of the Council, the 'conditions essentielles d'exercise de la souveraineté national' is the parameter used to assess the constitutionality of the provisions of the treaties. Michelle Troper (2008) argues that this concept includes a set of competences (such as the national defense, the currency, the justice system or the citizenship) that may be transferred to supranational institutions only after a constitutional amendment has been passed. Thus, the idea refers to a core of constitutional powers, which, unlike ordinary powers, the French constitution attributes solely to French political organs. However, unlike other more strict conceptions of the idea of constitutional core, the French case does not prevent the transfer of those powers to supranational institutions if the constitution is reformed (Wendel, 2011: 123). The French doctrine, thus, is more flexible and open to European integration than the constructions of other European NHCs.

The idea of sovereignty played also a role in the case law of other courts. The Spanish Constitutional Court, for instance, noted in its Constitutional Treaty declaration that sovereignty remains an attribute of the Spanish people[26] (Castillo de la Torre, 2005). However, if the concept had a protagonist role in any court's doctrine, it was in that of the German Federal Constitutional Court. In its Maastricht decision, Karlsruhe took a restrictive approach to the concept: in its view, the European Union could not be conceived as a state, but as an association of states that all remain sovereign, thus retaining the right to withdraw from the organization (Claes, 2006: 483). Following the path created by its former ruling, the Lisbon decision of the German court appears to be a treatise on the principle of sovereignty, which includes doctrinal and academic quotations. The importance of the issue can be illustrated by the titles that some law scholars gave to their pieces about the ruling, such as 'Why the European Union Is Not a State' (Lock, 2009) or 'The European Union as an Association of Sovereign States: Karlsruhe's Ruling on the Treaty of Lisbon' (Schorkopf, 2009). In Lisbon, Karlsruhe started by interpreting the principle of sovereignty incorporated into the national constitution and by acknowledging that '[t]he German constitution is directed towards opening the sovereign state order to peaceful cooperation of the nations and towards European integration'.[27] However, the court immediately countered this assertion by noting that the constitution is far from granting supranational institutions powers to act on behalf of Germany and that it does not allow the abandonment of the rights of self-determination or German sovereignty.[28] Indeed, 'if however, the threshold were crossed to a federal state and to the giving up of national sovereignty, this would require a free decision of the people in Germany beyond the present applicability of the Basic Law'.[29] Some scholars clearly disagreed with the approach taken by the German court. Lock (2009: 408), for instance, went as far as to say that the '*Bundesverfassungsgericht's* formalistic approach to sovereignty as an absolute concept is worth re-considering'.

Not every court draws on such a narrow concept of sovereignty. Other NHCs developed more Europhile doctrines, which seemed sympathetic towards the idea of pooled sovereignty. It is the case of the doctrine of the Czech Court (Krämer, 2010: 14; Komarek and editors, 2009). The court declared that

> the transfer of certain state competences, that arises from the free will of the sovereign, and will continue to be exercised with the sovereign's participation in a manner that is agreed on in advance and that is reviewable, is not a conceptual weakening of the sovereignty of a state, but, on the contrary, can lead to strengthening it within the joint actions of an integrated whole.[30]
>
> (Kruma, 2010: 44)

A similar approach is taken by the Polish Constitutional Court (Czaplinski, 2011: 200), which asserts that in its view 'the concept of sovereignty as the supreme and unlimited power (. . .) is subject to changes corresponding to developments that have been taken place in the world in the last few centuries' and understood the international liabilities of the state, not as a loss of sovereignty, but as its confirmation and manifestation.[31]

Finally, the case law of two courts addresses the question of sovereignty in relation to the controversial issue of the nature of the European Union. The Slovak court, in its Constitutional Treaty ruling, does not discuss the question of sovereignty explicitly. However, it does reflect on the statehood of the European Union and argues that, although the European Union has developed towards the state form, it is not possible to know at which precise moment the process will culminate, if it ever does.[32] The Latvian court also addresses this question by declaring that the Lisbon Treaty 'does not provide for any norm that would confirm that the European Union claims to become a state'. It additionally quotes Weiler and other scholars to note that the treaty explicitly provides for respect for the identity and sovereignty of the member states and that 'the exercise of powers by the Union appears not as the will of a single sovereign, but rather as the common exercise of public power by various actors'.[33]

Democracy: Assessing the Democratic Deficit of the European Union

Democracy, especially the question of a democratic deficit, has been at the core of discussion about integration for decades (see *inter alia* Norris, 1997; Moravsik, 2002). However, this topic can also be found in the discourses of NHCs (see Wendel, 2011). In some rulings, deep theoretical discussions of the nature and functioning of democracy in the context of the integration process may be found, and the well-known European democratic deficit is often referred to. In addition, a number of rulings discuss the idea of democracy with regard to a potential right of citizens to pass in referendum the ratification of treaties (Castillo, 2013a). This topic will be discussed later in this book. In this subsection, the focus will be on the discourse of courts regarding the functioning of democracy at the level of the European Union.

The approach of the *Maastricht-Urteil* ruling to democracy is widely known. In this ruling, the German Constitutional Court argued that democracy at the level of the European Union was insufficiently developed (MacCormick, 1997: 340). In the view of the court, the European Union Parliament performed only minor functions compared to those performed by parliaments in national democracies. Therefore, according to the court, national parliaments were to have an important role in the European Union policy-making process, to the point that they could be essential to the legitimacy of the very process of European Union integration (see in this regard Claes, 2006: 484). Academics disagreed on the question of whether the German court in this ruling left open the possibility that the European Union could develop a true democracy. In Weiland's view (1994: 263), the court accepted the idea that the European Union Parliament could confer more democratic legitimacy to the European Union if public opinion was created, transparency of political aims of the European Union was increased and, 'somewhat surprisingly', every citizen of the European Union had the ability to communicate with the European Union institutions in his or her native language. However, in a clearly critical assessment of the ruling, Weiler (1995b) stated that the court had embraced an organic, Schmittian concept of democracy in which the absence of a demos (see also MacCormick, 1997) in a traditional sense – that is, linked to the nation-state – would prevent democracy from properly functioning at the European Union level. The democratic principle appears again in the Lisbon ruling with a clear substantive meaning: the individual's right to take part in the elections of members of the *Bundestag* according to Articles 38.1 and 38.2 of the constitution. In addition, the court argued that the principle 'would lose its meaning if the elected state body did not have a sufficient degree of responsibilities and competences in which the legitimised power to act can be realised',[34] which includes respect for people's constituent power.[35] According to Wendel (2011: 1129), the German court's position was that the necessary level of democratic legitimacy of the European Union could only derive from the national 'state people'. The court's concept of democracy was deemed to be archaic: in the view of some authors, the courts' understanding of democracy would be limited to a state with a people and a territory (Halberstam and Möllers, 2009: 1247). This view would imply that the European Union is not in a position of developing a true democracy.

The rest of the courts were not as pessimistic about democracy (Kruma, 2010: 46). The Czech and Polish courts were the most explicit (van den Brink, 2010). In its Lisbon decision, the Czech court stated that member states retained a regulating role for their own democratic institutions – that is, national parliaments – in European affairs[36] and recognized that the Lisbon Treaty reinforced their role in the decision-making process at the European Union level.[37] Drawing on Advocate General Maduro, the court stated that 'the democratic process on the Union and domestic level mutually supplement and are dependent on each other'. Contrary to the Lisbon doctrine of the German Constitutional Court, the Czech court rejected the idea that representative democracy can exist only within states[38] (see Wendel, 2011: 117). In the Polish ruling on the Lisbon Treaty, democratic concerns were raised by the claimants, but the court stated that 'generally, the process of European integration meets the standards of constitutionality as well as the requirements related to the democratic legitimacy of such actions'.[39]

Questioning the Construction of the European Union Legal System: Kompetenz-Kompetenz *and Its Relation with the Rest of Interpretative Reasoning of the Courts*

As has been shown, *Kompetenz-Kompetenz* was not the only relevant question in the legal argumentation of the rulings. Indeed, such statements were accompanied by declarations and reflections on other important principles, including decisions concerning the accompanying legislation.

Table 4.3 identifies the topics on which courts reflected in their rulings. The cases in which rulings declared a court's own *Kompetenz-Kompetenz* were also, generally, rulings in which discussions of principles such as democracy and sovereignty had a core role. However, the approach used in the table hides the different stances towards these principles that may be identified in the rulings. On the one hand, the German Federal Constitutional Court opted for an aggressive approach and provided a critical

Table 4.3 Topics addressed by the courts in their rulings

Court	*Case*	Kompetenz-Kompetenz	*Statutory reforms*	*Constitutional core*	*Sovereignty*	*Democracy*
Irish S.C.	ESA	No	No	No	No	No
French C.C.	Maastricht I	No	No	No	Yes	No
Spanish C.C.	Maastricht	No	No	Yes	No	No
French C.C.	Maastricht II	No	No	No	No	No
German F.C.C.	Maastricht	Stated	No	Yes	Yes	Yes
French C.C.	Amsterdam	No	No	No	Yes	No
French C.C.	Constitutional T.	No	No	No	Yes	No
Spanish C.C.	Constitutional T.	Suggested	No	Yes	Yes	Yes
French C.C.	Lisbon	No	No	No	Yes	No
Slovak C.C.	Constitutional T	No	No	No	Yes	No
Czech C.C.	Lisbon	Suggested	Yes	Yes	Yes	Yes
Belgian C.C.	Lisbon I	No	No	No	No	No
Latvian C.C.	Lisbon	Open to	No	Yes	Yes	No
German F.C.C.	Lisbon	Stated	Yes	Yes	Yes	Yes
Belgian C.C.	Lisbon II	No	No	No	No	No
Czech C.C.	Lisbon II	Avoided	Yes	Yes	Yes	Yes
Polish C.C.	Lisbon	Open to	No	Yes	Yes	Yes

Source: Author's own elaboration based on primary sources.

analysis of the functioning of democracy at the European Union level and of respect for national sovereignty (see MacCormick, 1997). On the other hand, the other NHCs framed the principles of democracy and sovereignty in much more Europhile narratives. These concerns were usually raised by the litigants, and the role of the courts was essentially a defensive justification of European institutions (see, for instance, Krämer, 2010: 11).

Two questions arise after this description. The first is whether there was an internal relation among these elements – *Kompetenz-Kompetenz*, democracy, sovereignty and constitutional core – in the narrative of the courts. The second refers to the need for clarifying whether this relation is causal one.

Regarding the first question, the answer is yes. Rulings were constructed as narratives in which reflections on different principles and political concepts were interrelated. The best example is that of the German case law. In its Maastricht ruling, for instance, a clear link between democratic deficit and the issue of transfers of power could be observed. The court argued that the insufficient development of democracy at the European Union level imposed limits to the extension of powers of the European Union. This idea was again emphasized in the Lisbon ruling in which democracy, sovereignty and transfers of power are linked in the discourse of the court: '[F]rom the perspective of the principle of democracy, the violation of the constitutional identity codified in Article 79.3 of the Basic Law is at the same time an encroachment upon the constituent power of the people'.[40] These elements were related to questions about the 'last say' because the court understood sovereignty as implying that Germany must retain its *Kompetenz-Kompetenz* (Lock, 2009: 409). The very core of the idea of sovereignty is that the state ultimately decides the scope of powers conferred to supranational institutions. There is thus a relation between the idea of constitutional identity and *Kompetenz-Kompetenz*. As the court states

> the Act approving an international agreement and the national accompanying laws must therefore be capable of permitting European integration continuing to take place according to the principle of conferral without the possibility for the European Union of taking possession of Kompetenz-Kompetenz or to violate the Member States' constitutional identity, which is not open to integration, in this case, that of the Basic Law.[41]

The link between these concepts is also clear in the case law of other less critical courts. In the Polish Lisbon ruling, for instance, the court made a clear link among these elements: core constitutional competences cannot be transferred to international organizations to the point that they 'prevent the Republic of Poland from functioning as a sovereign and democratic state'.[42] Thus, following a relatively simple reasoning, courts interpret democracy as an expression of sovereignty: the people's sovereignty is expressed through democratic forms of participation in the management of public issues. In this sense, the transfer of powers to the European Union could not deprive the country of basic elements of sovereignty: a fundamental core of constitutional elements had to be respected by the process of integration. Here is where the question of *Kompetenz-Kompetenz* arises because courts in many cases declare themselves to be the ultimate safeguards of those elements.

Therefore, the different topics addressed by courts are discursively interrelated. One may then wonder whether declarations of *Kompetenz-Kompetenz* were the cause or the consequence of discussions on principles such as democracy or sovereignty. Two explanations may be offered. The first is inspired by Karen Alter's inter-court competition theory (Alter, 1997) – the idea that courts seek empowerment – and by realist and sceptical theories of law. According to this explanation, critical legal argumentations are the result of a strategic behaviour, statements of *Kompetenz-Kompetenz* being the actual core elements of the rulings. Through statements of *Kompetenz-Kompetenz*, national courts seek empowerment; however, such doctrinal stances must be justified in a legalistic way with reference to constitutional principles. For this reason, the clearer the statement by the court of its 'last say', the more critical towards the European Union the overall ruling should be. This would be the reason why the German court was the most aggressive in its narrative, even if reflections about core constitutional elements, democracy and sovereignty play a role in many rulings. Thus, at the core of the critical rulings of the German court one would find the will to self-empower; as suggested by one commentator, 'the judgment coming out of Karlsruhe must be seen as an expression of the Federal Constitutional Court Justices' fear of subjecting themselves to the European Court of Justice. Indeed, the judgment raises questions about Germany's commitment to Europe' (Grosser, 2009).

The second explanation, however, inverts the causal link. This interpretation is largely legalistic. Precisely because NHCs honestly considered European Union law to be a threat to certain core constitutional principles – democracy, sovereignty and constitutional rights – they decided to challenge the European Court of Justice and declare their right and duty as the ultimate defenders of the constitution with varying degrees of enthusiasm. Far from being faithfully legalistic, this explanation is consistent with sociological neoinstitutionalism in which values and the ethos of the institution modulate the behaviour of actors. From this perspective, NHCs would feel obliged to enforce constitutional provisions against European Union secondary law. In this sense, Fossum and Menendez (2011) considered

> the unease with which national constitutional courts have confronted the conflict between Community and national norms does indeed derive from the obvious fact that the norms that are supposed to prevail (Community norms) do not obviously have a higher democratic legitimacy than the national ones with which they are in conflict.

Indeed, both explanations are compatible. Statements of *Kompetenz-Kompetenz* made by NHCs could simultaneously express both interest in empowerment and concern for the respect of constitutional principles. Both questions could simply have converged.

Conclusions: The Doctrine of *Kompetenz-Kompetenz* as a Political Conflict

The incorporation of interpretative decisions such as *Kompetenz-Kompetenz* and statements on principles such as democracy and sovereignty is not a minor question. Baquero (2009) recently accused the Lisbon ruling issued by the German Federal Constitutional Court of being 'a brake to integration', and Peter Häberle (2009) called the decision 'regressive' and 'ankylosed'. Scholars have devoted their attention to national courts' rulings on European Union treaties, not only for their decisions on the merits of the cases, but also for their interpretative decisions and the way in which the legal reasoning approached the connection between European Union and constitutional law. In fact, the latter question, with the doctrine of *Kompetenz-Kompetenz* at its core, has been one of the main concerns addressed in doctrinal analyses.

This attention may be explained by the political considerations underlying legal reasoning in rulings such as *Maastricht-Urteil* and *Lissabon-Urteil*. In the history of European integration, it is difficult to find another example of an actor able to manage its power as efficiently as the German Federal Constitutional Court. In the *Solange* saga, after all, the German court achieved the far-reaching goal of modifying the agenda of the ECJ (see Davies, 2012), incorporating into it a stronger protection of fundamental rights (Rosenfeld, 2008: 419). Following the most basic logic of behaviourist psychology, Karlsruhe used a threat of punishment in *Solange* I and a reward in *Solange* II. The German court easily imposed its doctrinal preferences on the Court of Justice, thus conditioning the subsequent evolution of the case law of Luxembourg. Checkmate in two moves. The *Solange* saga not only constituted a successful first utilization – almost an experiment – of a strategy followed subsequently by Karlsruhe, but also fostered the legitimacy of the court. Given the object of the conflict, the protection of fundamental rights, even those who considered it inappropriate for the German Federal Constitutional Court to try to modify the agenda of the Court of Justice had to acknowledge the indisputable legitimacy of the concrete claim for human rights.

Andreas Voßkuhle (2010: 189), president of the German Federal Constitutional Court at the time of its Lisbon ruling, in a comprehensive but perhaps excessively optimistic analysis, recently asserted the following:

> There is not, nor has there been, a question of a struggle for power or of a rivalry between the Federal Constitutional Court and the Court of Justice. Those who talk all the same about 'imminent judicial conflicts', a 'war of the judges' or 'complete supervision by Karlsruhe' basically fail to see that the relationship between the Court of Justice and the Federal Constitutional Court is not about superiority or subordination but about appropriately sharing and assigning responsibilities in a complex multilevel system.

Voßkuhle was right in one issue: there is no pretension of hierarchical superiority by either actor. However, his analysis fails precisely by implying that every conflict must be linked to hierarchy and takes place vertically. The conflict between Karlsruhe and Luxembourg, however, is horizontal; it is not a fight for hierarchy but for competence. Moreover, beyond rhetorical invitations to cooperation, subtle conflict is undeniable. In this conflict, *Kompetenz-Kompetenz* has been the main tool utilized by NHCs. However, its utilization over time and across space has not been homogeneous. As it has been shown, not all the courts declared their *Kompetenz-Kompetenz*, and differences in emphasis and phrasing existed among those courts that did. In the following chapters, the factors underlying this variation will be accounted for.

Notes

1 German Federal Constitutional Court, Cases 2BvR 2134/92 and 2 BvR 2159/92 (*Maastricht*), part III.B.2.
2 *Costa v. Ente Nazionale per L'Energia Elettrica (ENEL)*, ECJ Case 6/64 (1964).
3 *NV Algemene transport: en expeditie onderneming Van Gend & Loos v. Nederlandse administratie der belastingen*, ECJ case 26/62.
4 German Federal Constitutional Court, Cases 2BvR 2134/92 and 2 BvR 2159/92 (*Maastricht*), Part C.I.
5 Case 11–70, *Internationale Handelgesselschaft v. Eifuhr- und Vorratssetelle für Getreide und Futtermittel* [1970] ECR 1125, paragraph 3.
6 German Constitutional Court, decision of 29 May 1974, Internationale Handelsgesellschaft (*Solange I*).
7 German Federal Constitutional Court, Cases 2 BvE 2/08 et al. (*Lisbon*), paragraph 240.
8 Der Spiegel, 1 July 2009, www.spiegel.de/international/europe/0,1518,633702,00.html (19.04.2012).
9 Spanish Constitutional Court, Declaration 001/2004 (*Constitutional Treaty*), part II.4.
10 Czech Constitutional Court, decision PL. ÚS 19/08 (*Lisbon I*), paragraph 216.
11 Czech Constitutional Court, decision Pl. ÚS 29/09 (*Lisbon II*), paragraph 172.

12 Czech Constitutional Court, decision Pl. ÚS 5/12 (*Slovak Pensions XVII*) of 31 January 2012.
13 Latvian Constitutional Court, case 2008–35–01 (*Lisbon*), part III, 18.8.
14 Polish Constitutional Court, case K32/09 (*Lisbon*), part III, 2.6.
15 French Constitutional Council, decision 92–308 DC (*Maastricht I*), paragraphs 17 and 18.
16 German Federal Constitutional Court, Cases 2 BvE 2/08 et al. (*Lisbon*), paragraph 273.
17 German Federal Constitutional Court, Cases 2 BvE 2/08 et al. (*Lisbon*), paragraph 409.
18 German Federal Constitutional Court, Cases 2 BvE 2/08 et al. (*Lisbon*), paragraph 253.
19 Czech Constitutional Court, decision Pl. ÚS 19/08 (*Lisbon I*), headnotes.
20 Czech Constitutional Court, decision Pl. ÚS 19/08 (*Lisbon I*), paragraph 93.
21 Polish Constitutional Court, decision K32/09 (*Lisbon*), part III, 2.1.
22 Spanish Constitutional Court, declaration 1/1992 (*Maastricht*), part I.3.
23 Spanish Constitutional Court, declaration 1/2004 (*Constitutional Treaty*), part II.3.
24 Latvian Constitutional Court, decision 2008–35–01 (*Lisbon*), part. III, 17.
25 The concept of the 'essential conditions of the exercise of national sovereignty' may be understood as an expression of the idea of a constitutional core, of the principle of sovereignty or both.
26 Spanish Constitutional Court, declaration 1/2004 (*Constitutional Treaty*), part III.4.
27 German Federal Constitutional Court, Cases 2 BvE 2/08 et al. (*Lisbon*), paragraph 220.
28 German Federal Constitutional Court, Cases 2 BvE 2/08 et al. (*Lisbon*), paragraph 228.
29 German Federal Constitutional Court, Cases 2 BvE 2/08 et al. (*Lisbon*), paragraph 263.
30 Czech Constitutional Court, decision Pl. ÚS 19/08 (*Lisbon I*), paragraph 108.
31 Polish Constitutional Court, decision K 32/09 (*Lisbon*), part III, 2.1.
32 Slovak Constitutional Court, decision II.U.S. 171/05–175 (*Constitutional Treaty*), part III, first section.
33 Latvian Constitutional Court, decision 2008–35–01 (*Lisbon*), part III, 16.3.
34 German Federal Constitutional Court, Cases 2 BvE 2/08 et al. (*Lisbon*), paragraph 175.
35 German Federal Constitutional Court, Cases 2 BvE 2/08 et al. (*Lisbon*), paragraph 208.
36 Czech Constitutional Court, decision Pl. ÚS 29/09 (*Lisbon II*), paragraph 124.
37 Czech Constitutional Court, decision Pl. ÚS 29/09 (*Lisbon II*), paragraph 135.
38 Czech Constitutional Court, decision Pl. ÚS 29/09 (*Lisbon II*), paragraph 138.
39 Polish Constitutional Court, decision K32/09 (*Lisbon*), part III, 2.2.
40 German Federal Constitutional Court, Cases 2 BvE 2/08 et al. (*Lisbon*), paragraph 218.
41 German Federal Constitutional Court, Cases 2 BvE 2/08 et al. (*Lisbon*), paragraph 239.
42 Polish Constitutional Court, decision K 32/09 (*Lisbon*), part III, 2.6.

References

Alberton, G. (2008) 'L'apprésension du système communautaire par la Constitution française du 4 octobre 1958: Etat des lieux avant et après le referendum du

29 mai 2005', in Tajadura, J and De Miguel, J. *Justicia constitucional y Unión Europea. Un estudio comparado de las experiencias de España, Francia, Italia y Portugal*, Madrid: CEPC, pp.179–215.

Alonso García, R. (2005) 'The Spanish constitution and the European constitution: The script for a virtual collision and other observations on the principle of primacy', *German Law Journal* 6(6): 1002–24.

Alter, K. (1997) 'Explaining National Courts Acceptance of European Court Jurisprudence: A Critical Evaluation of Theories of Legal Integration', in Slaughter, A-M, Stone Sweet, A., and Weiler, J. H. H., *The European Court and National Courts – Doctrine and Jurisprudence. Legal Change in Its Social Context*, Oxford: Hart, pp. 227–52

Baquero, J. (2008) 'The legacy of the Maastricht-Urteil and the pluralist movement', *European Law Journal* 14(4): 389–422.

Baquero, J. (2009) 'A Judicial Götterdämmerung. The Lisbon Decision of the German Constitutional Court', in Auel, K. and Baquero, J., *Karlruhe's Europe*, Notre Europe Studies and Research 78, at: www.notreeurope.eu/uploads/tx_publication/Etud78-Karlsruhe_sEurope-en_01.pdf (15.08.2010).

Barber, N. W. (2006) 'Legal pluralism and the European Union', *European Law Journal* 12(3): 306–29.

Beck, G. (2011) 'The Lisbon judgement of the German Constitutional Court, the primacy of EU law and the problem of *Kompetenz-Kompetenz*: A conflict between right and right in which there is no praetor', *European Law Journal* 17(4): 470–94.

Bieber, R., (2009) ' "An association of sovereign states" ': Comments on the German Constitutional Court's decision on the Lisbon Treaty', *European Constitutional Law Review* 5(3): 391–406.

Bobek, M., and Kühn, Z., (2009) 'Europe Yet to Come: The Application of EU Law in Slovakia', in Lazowski, A., (ed.) *The Application of EU Law in the New Member States – Brave New World*. The Hague: T. M. C. Asser Press and Cambridge University Press, pp. 357–87.

Boom, S. (1995) 'The European Union after the Maastricht decision: Will Germany be the "Virginia of Europe"?', *The American Journal of Comparative Law* 43(2): 177–226.

Bossuyt, M., and Verrijdt, W., (2011) 'The full effect of EU law and constitutional review in Belgium and France after the Melki judgement', *European Constitutional Law Review* 7(3): 355–91.

Bříza, P. (2009) 'The Czech Republic. The constitutional court on the Lisbon Treaty. Decision of 26 November 2008', *European Constitutional Law Review* 5(1): 143–64.

Castillo, P. (2013a) 'Playing the judicial card. Litigation strategies during the process of ratification of the Lisbon Treaty', *European Law Journal* 20(5): 630–48.

Castillo, P. (2013b) 'La política judicial del tribunal constitucional en los procesos de ratificación de tratados de la Unión Europea: aproximación desde un nuevo realismo jurídico', *Revista de Estudios Políticos* 159: 107–38.

Castillo de la Torre, F., (2005), 'Tribunal Constitucional (Spanish Constitutional Court), opinion 1/2004 of 13 December 2004, on the treaty establishing a constitution for Europe', *Common Market Law Review* 42(4): 1169–1202.

Claes, M. (2006) *The National Courts Mandate in the European Constitution*, Oxford: Oxford University Press.

Claes, M. and de Visser, M. (2012) 'Are you networked yet? On dialogues in European judicial networks', *Utrech Law Review* 8(1): 100–14.

Closa, C. (2013a) 'National higher courts and the ratification of European Union treaties', *West European Politics* 36(1): 97–121.

Craig, P., and de Burca, G. (2008) *EU Law. Text, Cases and Materials*, Oxford: Oxford University Press.

Czaplinski, W. (2011) 'Recent constitutional jurisprudence concerning the European Union: some remarks on 2010 judgements of the Polish Constitutional Court', *ERA-FORUM* 12(1): 197–204.

Davies, B. (2012) 'Pushing back: What happens when member states resist the European Court of Justice? A multi-modal approach to the history of European law', *Contemporary European History* 21(3): 417–435.

Dupéré, O. (2005) 'Jurisprudence constitutionnelle, Le contrôle de constitutionnalité du droit dérivé de l'Union Européenne. Lectures croisées par le Conseil d'état et le Conseil Constitutionnel', *Revue Française de Droit Constitutionnel* 61: 147–69.

Dutheillet de Lamothe, O. (2004) 'Le conseil constitutionnel et le droit européen', *Revue Française de Droit Constitutionnel* 57: 23–35.

Everling, U. (1994) 'The Maastricht judgement of the German Federal Constitutional Court and its significance for the development of the European Union', *Yearbook of European Law* 14(1): 1–19.

Fossum, J. E. and Menéndez A. J. (2011) *The Constitution's Gift*, Lanham: Rowman & Littlefield Publishers.

Grimm, D. (2009) 'Defending sovereign statehood against transforming the European Union. Comments on the German Constitutional Court's decision on the Lisbon Treaty', *European Constitutional Law Review* 5(3): 353–73.

Grosser, A. (2009) 'The Federal Constitutional Court's Lisbon case: Germany's "Sonderweg": An outsider's perspective', *German Law Journal* 10(8): 1263–66.

Häberle, P. (2009) 'La regresiva "sentencia Lisboa" como "Maastricht-II" anquilosada', *Revista de Derecho Constitucional Europeo* 12: 397–429.

Halberstam, D. and Möllers, C. (2009) 'The German Constitutional Court says "Ja zu Deutschland!"', *German Law Journal* 10(8): 1241–58.

Harck, S. and Parlmer Olsen, H. (1999) 'Decision concerning the Maastricht Treaty. 1998 Ugeskrift for Retsvaesen, H 800', *The American Journal of International Law* 93(1): 209–14.

Herdegen, M., (1994) 'Maastricht and the German Constitutional Court: Constitutional restraints for an ever closer union', *Common Market Law Review* 31(2): 235.

Kiiver, P. (2010) 'The Lisbon judgment of the German Constitutional Court: A court-ordered strengthening of the national legislature in the EU', *European Law Journal* 16(5): 578–88.

Komarek, J. (2005) 'Federal Elements in the Community Judicial System: Building Coherency in the Community Legal Order', at http://mosquito-net.eu/documents/Komarek_Federal_Elements-CMLRev-final.pdf (21.04.2012).

Komarek, J. and editors (2009) 'The Czech Constitutional Court's second decision on the Lisbon Treaty of 3 November 2009', *European Constitutional Law Review* 5(3): 345–52.

Kowalik-Bańczyk, K. (2005) 'Should we polish it up? The Polish Constitutional Tribunal and the idea of supremacy of EU law', *German Law Journal* 6 (10): 1355–66.

Krämer, R. (2010) 'Looking through Different Glasses at the Lisbon Treaty: The German Constitutional Court and the Czech Constitutional Court', in Fischer-Lescano, A., Joerges, C. and Wonka, A. *The German Constitutional Court's Lisbon Ruling: Legal and Political Science Perspectives*, ZERP Diskussionapapier 1/2010, at www.mpifg.de/people/mh/paper/ZERP%20Discussion%20Paper%201.2010.pdf (12.06.2012).

Kruma, K. (2009) 'Constitutional Courts in the Europeanisation of National Constitutions', in Closa, Carlos (ed.) *The Lisbon Treaty and National Constitutions. Europeanisation and Democratic Implications*, at www.astrid-online.it/Riforma-de/Studi-e-ri/Archivio-25/ARENA-Report-3_2009.pdf#page=145 (12.06.2012).

Kruma, K. (2010) 'Constitutional Courts and the Lisbon Treaty. The Future Based on Mutual Trust', Centre for European Policy Studies, at www.isn.ethz.ch/isn/Digital-Library/Publications/Detail/?ots591=0c54e3b3-1e9c-be1e-2c24-a6a8c7060233&lng=en&id=117517 (12.06.2012).

Kumm, M. (2005) 'The jurisprudence of constitutional conflict: Constitutional supremacy in Europe before and after the Constitutional Treaty', *European Law Journal* 11(3): 262–307.

Kumm, M. and Ferreres, V. (2005) 'The primacy clause of the Constitutional Treaty and the future of constitutional conflict in the European Union', *International Journal of Constitutional Law* 3(2–3): 473–92.

Lachmann, P. (1998) 'The Treaty of Maastricht vs. the Danish Constitution', *Nordic Journal of International Law* 68: 365–68.

Lock, T. (2009) 'Why the European Union is not a state. Some critical remarks. Comments on the German Constitutional Court's decision on the Lisbon Treaty', *European Constitutional Law Review* 5(3): 407–20.

MacCormick, N. (1995) 'The Maastricht-Urteil: Sovereignty now', *European Law Journal* 1(3): 259–66.

MacCormick, N. (1997) 'Democracy, subsidiarity, and citizenship in the 'European commonwealth', *Law and Philosophy* 16(4): 331–56.

MacCormick, N. (1999) *Questioning Sovereignty*, Oxford: Oxford University Press.

Maduro, M. (2003) 'Las formas del poder constitucional de la Unión Europea', *Revista de Estudios Políticos* 119: 11–55.

Maher, I., (1994) 'National courts as European community courts', *Legal Studies* 14(2): 226–43.

Martinico, G. (2013) *The Tangled Complexity of the EU Constitutional Process. The Frustrating Knot of Europe*, New York: Routledge.

Moravsik, A. (2002) 'In defence of the 'democratic deficit': Reassessing legitimacy in the European Union', *Journal of Common Market Studies* 40(4):603–24.

Nemeckova, P. (2009) 'La sentencia del Tribunal Constitucional Checo de 26.11.2008 sobre la compatibilidad del Tratado de Lisboa con la Constitución de la República Checa', *Revista de Derecho Comunitario Europeo* January/April: 239–58.

Norris, P. (1997) 'Special issue: Political representation in the European Parliament – Representation and the democratic deficit', *European Journal of Political Research* 32(2): 273–82.

Plötner, J., (2003) 'Report on France', in Slaughter, A. M., Stone Sweet, A., and Weiler, J. H. H., *The European Court and National Courts-Doctrine and Jurisprudence: Legal Change in Its Social Context*", Portland: Oxford-Hart Publishing, pp.41–76.

Posch, A. (2008) 'Community law and Austrian constitutional law', *International Constitutional Law Journal* 2(4): 272–28.

Přibáň, J. (2009) 'From "which rule of law?" to "the rule of which law"? Post-communist experiences of European legal integration', *The Hague Journal on the Rule of Law* 1(2):337–58.

Protière G., and Blachèr, P. (2007) 'Le Conseil Constitutionnel, gardien de la Constitution face aux directives communautaires', *Revue Française de Droit constitutionnel* 69:123–44.

Reich, N. (1996) 'Judge-made Europe á la carte: Some remarks on recent conflicts between European and German Constitutional law provoked by the banana litigation', *European Journal of International Law* 7(1):103–07.

Reestman, J.-H. (2009) 'The Franco-German constitutional divide. Reflections on national and constitutional identity', *European Constitutional Law Review* 5(3): 374–90.

Röben, V. (2003) 'Constitutionalism of the European Union after the draft Constitutional Treaty, How much hierarchy', *Columbia Journal of European Law* 10: 339–77.

Rosenfeld, M. (2008) 'Rethinking constitutional ordering in an era of legal and ideological pluralism', *International Journal of Constitutional Law* 6(3–4): 415–54.

Rossi, L. S. (2008) 'How fundamental are fundamental principles? Primacy and fundamental rights after Lisbon', *Yearbook of European Law* 27(1): 65–87.

Schorkopf, F. (2009) 'The European Union as an association of sovereign states: Karlsruhe's ruling on the Treaty of Lisbon', *German Law Journal* 10(8): 1219–40.

Schutte, C. (2005) 'Case note: Spain. Tribunal constitutional on the European constitution. Declaration of 13 December 2004', *European Constitutional Law Review* 1(2): 281–92.

Stein, T. (2011) 'Always steering a straight course? The German Federal Constitutional Court and European integration', *ERA Forum* 12(1): 219–28.

Teruel Lozano, G. (2006) 'El Tribunal Constitucional ante el principio de primacía del derecho comunitario (Análisis de la jurisprudencia constitucional respecto de la compatibilidad del principio de primacía con la constitución de la nación española de 1978)', *Anales de Derecho* 24: 319–52.

Troper, M. (2008) 'Comment la constitution de 1958 definit la suverainete nationale?', *Dossiers thématiques du Conseil Constitutionnel*, at www.conseil-constitutionnel.fr/conseil-constitutionnel/francais/documentation/dossiers-thematiques/2008-cinquantenaire-la-constitution-en-20-questions/la-constitution-en-20-questions-question-n-5.17354.html (25.04.2012).

Vaičaitis, V. (2010) 'European constitutionalism v. Reformed constitution for Europe', *Jurisprudence* 1(119): 69–83.

Van den Brink, T. (2010) 'The Czech Constitutional Court and the Treaty of Lisbon', *Tijdschrift voor Constitutioneel Recht* 3: 315–21.
Vandamme, T. (2008) 'Prochain arret: La Belgique! Explaining recent preliminary references of the Belgian Constitutional Court', *European Constitutional Law Review* 4(1): 127–48.
Voßkuhle, A. (2010) 'Multilevel cooperation of the European constitutional courts, Der Europäische Vergassungsgerichtsverbund', *European Constitutional Law Review* 6(2): 175–98.
Walker, N. (2011) 'Reconciling MacCormick: Constitutional pluralism and the unity of practical reason', *Ratio Juris* 24(4): 369–84.
Weiler, J. H. H. (1995a) *Europa, Fin de Siglo*, Madrid: Centro de Estudios Constitutionales.
Weiler, J. H. H. (1995b) 'Does Europe need a constitution? Demos, telos and the German Maastricht decision', *European Law Journal* 1(3): 219–58.
Weiler, J. H. H. (1999) *The Constitution of Europe. "Do the New Clothes Have an Emperor?" and Other Essays on European Integration*, Cambridge: Cambridge University Press.
Wendel, M. (2011) 'Lisbon before the courts: Comparative perspectives', *European Constitutional Law Review* 7(1): 96–137.
Wieland, J. (1994) 'Kaleidoscope. Germany in the European Union – The Maastricht decision of the Bundesverfassungsgericht', *European Journal of International Law* 5(1): 259–66.

5 The Legal Dimension

Assessing Judicial Behaviour from the Viewpoint of Legal Rules

Introduction: The Law and the Courts

The best tradition in socio-legal studies recommends taking the legal dimension of the cases seriously when doing empirical analysis of judicial behaviour (see, for instance, Carbonier, 2008 [1966]: 1232). Most recent approaches have also insisted on this. In their article on new legal realism, Nourse and Shaffer (2011: 120) asked the field to turn to 'mediating theories':

> [T]heory that does not simply seek to explain law through the eyes of another discipline. Rather, mediating theory mediates between the strong assumptions of self-referential disciplinarity – that only politics (or psychology) counts or only law counts – and seeks to account for both: that is, in terms of how law and politics (or psychology) interact.

If the emphasis is put on political aspects of the cases in other parts of this research, in this chapter, legal issues are the focus of attention, and thus the political understanding of the cases is complemented with a doctrinal analysis and a test of the impact of legal rules on judicial behaviour. In this sense, this work benefits from the medium-N size of its object of study. Usual econometric studies in judicial politics deal with a number of cases too large as to be able to make a doctrinal analysis of them. In this research, however, the population consists of seventeen cases, which all share the same object of judicial review: European Union treaties. For such a number of cases, a qualitative approach and a doctrinal comment of the rulings is possible.

To perform this task, after this short presentation, a doctrinal analysis of the rulings will be carried out; to do so, the rulings will be grouped by their outcome, and the legal argumentation of courts and the common structures of the rulings will be commented on and analyzed. Subsequently, the focus of attention will be on one type of rule that indisputably played a salient role in the rulings: European clauses in national constitutions.

The analysis of European clauses will be done through three different but overlapping strategies: a doctrinal analysis and classification of the European clauses and their role in the rulings, a political science qualitative analysis of their mobilization by litigants and their impact on the judicial decisions and a statistical bivariate analysis of the association between certain features of European clauses and the 'outcomes' of judicial decision making. To end this chapter, some final conclusions will be offered.

The Judicial Discourse: Courts' Legalistic Narratives

Although one of the goals of this research is to build a political model of judicial behaviour, the protagonists of the analysis, courts, only speak the language of law. Courts' legalistic discourse is worth analyzing for many reasons. First, it is interesting to see that common patterns and discourse structures underlie groups of rulings. Second, it is worth underlining that some elements contained in the treaties were particularly controversial, usually alleged by the claimants and discussed by courts. Third, as will be shown, in some cases the legal reasoning of the ruling seemed to be at odds with its final decision on the merits. Doctrinal analyses of the rulings will help to better understand all of these elements. Since the legal discourse of courts with reference to declarations of *Kompetenz-Kompetenz* was already discussed in Chapter 4, in this section the focus will be on legal argumentations regarding decisions on the merits.

Declarations of Constitutionality: Placating Political Concerns

Declarations of constitutionality were the most abundant decisions made by courts in the cases covered by this book. A closer look at them reveals that three main inter-related patterns are shared by most (although not all) of them:

1. The existence of a common structure for many of the rulings, in which the court first declares constitutional commitment to European integration and then goes on to dismiss the concrete points alleged by the claimants.
2. The allegation by the petitioners of evocative claims with deep political involvements, such as the protection of constitutional rights, the role of the national parliament and the need to hold a ratification referendum.
3. The exceptionality of the German court, which was by far the most critical of all national constitutional jurisdictions

In a recent article (Castillo, 2013a), some of these patterns – especially the second one – were analyzed with regard to rulings on the Lisbon Treaty. In this book, the analysis will assess to what extent these patterns also apply to cases on earlier treaties. By emphasizing the diachronic dimension of the cases, it will be shown how these patterns formed and consolidated over time in different waves of treaty ratification in processes of cross-case imitation, learning or contagion.

A Common Structure in the Rulings: Constitutional Commitments to European Integration

As said, many of the rulings shared the same structure. First, national higher courts (NHCs) expressed a solemn commitment to European integration, or at least provided for an explanation of the constitutional basis which served to justify ratification of the treaty. Second, courts went on to dismiss one by one the allegations of the claimants, even if with different styles and emphases.

The German court was one of the most categorical ones regarding constitutional openness to European integration. In the Maastricht ruling, the German court began its analysis of the merits of the case by accepting that the German constitution, according to its preamble and Article 23, allows for the membership of a 'community of States which is entitled to take sovereign action on its own right'.[1] This very idea was repeated in the Lisbon ruling, in which the court insisted in that '[t]he German Constitution is directed towards opening the sovereign state order to peaceful cooperation of the nations and towards European integration'.[2] According to the court, however, this does not imply that total freedom is given to the German authorities to validly ratify any kind of integration treaty, whatsoever its content could be.

The acknowledgement of a constitutional openness to integration is not exclusive of the German court. Indeed, before the German Maastricht ruling, the Irish Supreme Court had already acknowledged that '[Art. 29, s. 4, sub-s. 3] was enacted as the Third Amendment to the Constitution by virtue of a referendum held in 1972 and permitted the State to join the European Communities',[3] even though the court finally declared the unconstitutionality of the Single European Act. Also in the second decision of the French Constitutional Council for the Maastricht Treaty, the ruling based transfers of powers to the European Union in Article 88(2) of the French Constitution. In its *Declaración* on the Constitutional Treaty, the Spanish Constitutional Court stated that Article 93 of the constitution – even when it does not explicitly mention the European Union – was the basis for the ratification of the treaty and for Spanish membership in the European Union (Castillo, 2013b). Article 93, in the view of the court, constitutes the 'constitutional means for the country's integration in the European communities'.[4] In the Slovak ruling for the Constitutional Treaty, this role is fulfilled by Article 7.2 of the constitution, which serves to justify the ratification of the treaty in the parliamentary arena. In the process of ratification of the Lisbon Treaty, openness to integration was acknowledged, *inter alia*, in the Latvian ruling, based on Art. 68 of the constitution, or in the Czech one, based on Art. 10.a (see Castillo, 2013a).

A Legal Debate around Political Questions: Referendums, Constitutional Rights and National Parliaments

As said, the second element of the structure of the rulings was the review of the allegations of the claimants. Courts obviously performed their duty of assessing the compatibility of the treaty with the constitution regarding these allegations. Interestingly, some topics were dealt with in many of the rulings. They usually pointed at questions with deep political involvements, such as the need to consult the people about the ratification of the treaty, the protection of constitutional rights, the position of the national parliament or the eventual losses of sovereignty (Castillo, 2013a). However, although evidence is not conclusive, it seems to suggest that the way in which these allegations are phrased and framed by the actors is the result of processes of mutual observation and evolution along the waves of treaty ratification:

- *National parliaments*. Concerns regarding the loss of powers by the national institutions due to new transfers of powers, and particularly the loss of powers of the national legislature, were often discussed. These concerns seemed to begin in the very *Maastricht-Urteil* ruling of the German court, in which Karlsruhe constructed its discourse around the threat that the treaty posed for the national parliament, to the point that the petition of the claimant was admitted because of this (Meessen, 1993: 514–515). Although the German court finally considered the Maastricht Treaty to be constitutional also in this regard, the question soon found an echo in later rulings. Courts, however, always dismissed this type of allegation. In the French Maastricht II ruling, the Council assessed the alleged deprival of rights of the parliament due to the new transfer of powers. However, the Council found that such transfer of powers was still permitted under Article 88.2 of the constitution.[5] The allegation was put forward in France again for the Constitutional Treaty,[6] this time successfully (Claes, 2007: 25). In the process of ratification of the Lisbon Treaty, opponents of ratification insisted on this topic, although unsuccessfully: this issue had a prominent role, not only in the ruling by the German court, but also in those of the Latvian, Polish and Czech courts (Castillo, 2013a). Indeed, the German court took this question extremely seriously and even demanded statutory reform in order to better accommodate the rights of the German legislator in the frame of the new treaty (Wendel, 2011).

- *Referendums.* One of the most typical allegations by the claimants was the need to hold referendums in order to ratify the treaty. The first example of this type of strategy had been the *Crotty* ruling; however, although *Crotty* had been successful, subsequent petitions for referendum were dismissed by the courts. In the Slovak ruling for the Constitutional Treaty, the parties alleged that ratification of the treaty involved entering into a state union within the meaning of Article 7(1) of the constitution, which foresees referendum for this case, although the court dismissed this petition (see Faber and Wessels, 2006; Closa and Castillo, 2012). During the process of ratification of the Lisbon Treaty, the petition for referendum became one of the most widespread allegations: referendum was requested in the Czech Republic, Latvia and Belgium, and in two of the cases that were dismissed on formal grounds: the Slovenian and the first Austrian ones (Castillo, 2013a).
- *Constitutional rights.* The question of the compatibility of the new treaties with the constitutional rights enshrined in national constitutions was also discussed. It is worth noting how this topic evolved in the European judicial dialogue: from the *Solange* allegation that the EU did not have a sufficiently developed system for the protection of rights (see Reich, 1996; Rosenfeld, 2008) to the allegation during the process of ratification of the Lisbon Treaty that the protection of rights provided by the EU could be a threat to that provided at the national level (Castillo, 2013a). As was often the case with the rest of claims mentioned earlier, courts always dismissed rights-based complaints. In the Spanish Constitutional Treaty case, the court found that the Charter of Rights of the European Union was not incompatible with the catalogue contained in the Spanish Constitution and, indeed, it underlined that according to Article 10.2 of the Constitution international agreements on human rights ratified by Spain are a key interpretative criteria in defining the scope and content of the rights in the constitutional catalogue (Rodríguez, 2005).[7] In the process of ratification of the Lisbon Treaty, fears regarding the protection of constitutional rights were raised in Germany, Latvia and the Czech Republic; in these countries either the Charter of Rights or the ratification by the EU of the European Convention of Human Rights was alleged as a potential threat to the protection of the constitutional catalogue of rights (Castillo, 2013a).

The Exceptionality of the German Court

The German court has been discussed earlier, as the general structure in its rulings is similar to that of the rest of the declarations of constitutionality. However, it has also been pointed out that the German rulings were, to some extent, exceptional, given their critical tone. Curiously enough, the first declaration of constitutionality of a European Union treaty made by a constitutional court was the extremely critical *Maastricht-Urteil* ruling of the German Federal Constitutional Court. This surprising relation between critical legal argumentations and declarations of constitutionality on the merits of the case is indeed a common feature shared by the Maastricht and Lisbon rulings of the German court, which for this reason deserve a separate analysis. In these rulings, Karlsruhe seems to follow a pattern in which it first underlined the risks of conflict between the treaties and the national constitution, and then found a justification for the declaration of constitutionality despite these risks. From a cynical viewpoint, one could even argue that the German court tried to show itself as a benevolent court precisely by declaring the constitutionality of a treaty whose constitutional weaknesses it had previously emphasized.

In the two German rulings, the content of the petition is the thread running through the legal argumentation of the court, with Article 38.1 of the Basic Law – particularly its first sentence: 'Members of the German Bundestag shall be elected in general, direct, free, equal and secret elections' – having a core role. In the Maastricht case, the court only admitted the claim by Mamfred Brunner to the extent that it argued that the petitioner's right to vote would be affected by a transfer of competences by the German parliament to another institution (Meessen, 1993: 514–515). In this ruling, for the first time Karlsruhe interpreted this provision as not only referring to the right to vote, but also as a right to elect a parliament having the power to decide all questions of importance for the state (Wieland, 1994: 259). Moreover, the court discussed the content of Article 38 with a view to the constitutional principles of sovereignty and democracy, and built up a critical argument. As explained in the previous chapter, Karlsruhe considered that democracy was insufficiently developed at the European Union level (MacCormick, 1997) and made clear that in its view the European Union was no more than an association of sovereign states (Claes, 2006).

In the Lisbon decision, the discourse by the court was similar. In this ruling, again, Article 38 of the Basic Law played a central role in the reasoning of the court (Wendel, 2011: 109), which also reflected largely on Article 79 of the constitution – the 'eternity clause' – and, of course, the 'integration clause' of Article 23. The connection between Article 38 and Article 79 is at the core of the reasoning of the court (Wendel, 2011), which devoted a number paragraphs to the capacity of the European Union to develop a true democracy. As said by Niedobitek (2009: 1270), '[G]iven that the constitutional starting point of the Court's judgment is Article 38 of the Basic law (. . .) it is not surprising that the whole judgment centers on the democratic principle'. The court also insisted on its doctrine regarding the concept of sovereignty, which in its view fully remained with member states (Lock, 2009). The concept of 'constitutional identity' was also particularly salient in this ruling, with the court making clear that such identity could not be violated by organs or decisions of the European Union (Castillo, 2013a). And finally, in this ruling, the court found that the Act Extending and Strengthening the Rights of the Bundestag and the Bundesrat in European Union Matters had to be amended, in so far as the rights of the legislative chambers had not been sufficiently developed (Closa, 2013: 113). As had been the case for the Maastricht ruling, in its Lisbon ruling the court did not hesitate in developing a critical legal argumentation, in making explicit its concerns regarding the development of European integration and in setting limits to such development.

What matters now is that, despite its rhetoric, at the end of the day the court did not find a violation of the constitution by any of the treaties. In its Maastricht ruling, the court considered that the European Union respected member states' identities, that the functions and powers of the European Union were contained in the treaty in a manner sufficiently foreseeable and that further extension of powers could be controlled by the national parliament. The court also considered that the process of forming the political will in the European Union did not weaken the responsibilities and capacity of control of the German parliament, at least not in a manner in which the principle of democracy could be said to be infringed upon, thus removing the last obstacle for the ratification of the treaty (Wiegandt, 1995: 890). In the Lisbon case, after the court assessed numerous aspects of the Lisbon Treaty – from the involvement of the German legislature in EU decision making to the *passerelle* clause of the treaty, its 'flexibility clause', the 'emergency brakes clause' or the powers of the European Union in the criminal area (Kiiver, 2010) – it reached the conclusion that the treaty, interpreted as Karlsruhe did, did not contradict the German Basic Law. Doubtlessly, the German court's bark was worse than its bite.

Declarations of Unconstitutionality as Technical, Dispassionate Assessments of the Treaties

As has been shown, there were a large number of declarations of constitutionality and hence many different patterns could be identified in these rulings. Declarations of unconstitutionality, however, were fewer. And from a legalist viewpoint, only two different approaches seemed to underlie these cases. The first of them is that of the Maastricht Treaty declaration by the Spanish Constitutional Court, in which the grounds for the declaration of unconstitutionality seemed to be the conflict between the very wording of one specific constitutional provision and one specific treaty provision. The second approach, that of the Irish *Crotty* ruling and the French Constitutional Council in its frequent declarations of unconstitutionality, seemed to go beyond concrete provisions: these institutions apparently took the view that to make new transfers of powers to the European Union, a constitutional amendment was always necessary.

- *A concrete contradiction.* As was just said, one of the cases can be explained in the light of a contradiction between a single, specific and concrete constitutional provision and the text of the treaty. It is the decision of the Spanish Constitutional Court on the Maastricht Treaty, the 'Declaration 001/1992', which required constitutional amendment before treaty ratification. In this case, the relevant provision was Article 13.2 of the constitution, on the right to suffrage in local elections (see Aragon, 1993; Closa, 2013: 114). Article 13.2 granted entitlement of the right to stand as candidates in local elections only to Spanish citizens, and Article 8.B.1 of the EEC Treaty, as reformed by the Maastricht Treaty, granted entitlement to any national of a European Union member state. Following the recommendation of the Spanish Council of State and the petition of the government, the court assessed the compatibility between both provisions and found a contradiction, which could be solved only by means of a constitutional amendment (see Aragon, 1993; Kumm, 2005; Castillo, 2013b). The result was the first amendment to the Spanish Constitution of 1978.
- *A presumption of unconstitutionality.* The rest of the cases – the *Crotty* case in Ireland and the declarations of unconstitutionality by the French Constitutional Council – seemed to follow a different logic. In relation to European Union treaties, everything not explicitly foreseen in the constitution was deemed to be unconstitutional, so that constitutional amendment was mandatory before treaty ratification (in this regard see also Wendel, 2011: 123 ff.). In the case of the Irish Supreme Court's ruling on the Single European Act, it was paradoxically the European clause in Article 29 of the Irish Constitution that was the basis of the declaration of unconstitutionality (Barret, 2009). After declaring the constitutionality of the European Communities (Amendment) Act, the court agreed with a three-against-two vote that ratification of the Single European Act was impermissible under the constitution, since its Title III went beyond the constitutional habilitation of Article 29.4.3 of the constitution (Barret, 2009: 9). After this ruling, the pattern of constitutional amendments continued for every major treaty ratification. New transfers of powers or reforms of EU institutions were deemed not to be constitutionally allowed unless the constitution was explicitly amended (Wendel, 2011: 121: Closa, 2013: 114).

The same logic applied to the French decisions in the Maastricht I, Amsterdam, Constitutional and Lisbon Treaty rulings. However, in the French case it was not a particular rule that justified declarations of unconstitutionality, but generally a doctrinal construction: 'the essentials conditions of the exercise of national sovereignty'. In its first ruling for the Maastricht Treaty, the Council found that the right to suffrage in local elections for EU nationals conflicted with Article 3 of the French Constitution, which bestowed the entitlement of the right to vote, in the conditions determined by the law, to all French nationals, adults of both sexes, in the exercise of their political rights (see Closa, 2013: 114). But more importantly, together with the unconstitutionality of the provisions on electoral rights, and with a view on constitutional principles, the Council also found that certain provisions on the Economic and Monetary Union and free movement of persons affected the 'essential conditions of exercise of the sovereignty' of the constitution (Closa, 2013: 114). This doctrine became extraordinarily relevant in later decisions (see also Wendel, 2011: 123 ff.). Regarding the Amsterdam Treaty, the provisions concerning the free movement of persons were found unconstitutional on such grounds, given the new rules authorizing the Council to take decisions on that matter using the Qualified Majority Voting procedure. And regarding the Constitutional and Lisbon treaties, the incompatibilities were found in relation to the new powers conferred by the treaties to the European Union or the new procedures to exercise them, together with the simplified procedure of treaty reform (see Wendel, 2011; Closa, 2013). In all cases, it was the doctrine of the 'essential conditions of national sovereignty' that served to justify the declarations of unconstitutionality.

The legal argumentation in declarations of unconstitutionality contrasts with that in declarations of constitutionality. It is striking to see that the former was the result of a technical and dispassionate assessment of the treaties, whereas questions with deep political involvement, as those included in the latter, never drove courts to declare treaties unconstitutional. Declarations of unconstitutionality, paradoxically, were never grounded on questions of high political significance. In the Maastricht cases, although constitutional rights were involved, declarations of unconstitutionality were not issued on the grounds that the treaties could endanger them, but on the grounds that an enlargement of the entitlement of certain rights – the right to suffrage – had to be carried out before ratification. In addition, the French doctrine of the 'essential conditions of national sovereignty', despite its appearance, seemed to be simply a means to integrate further into the French Constitution transfer of powers to the European Union. Neuman (2012: 357) called these declarations of unconstitutionality in France and the subsequent amendments 'technocratic updates [of the constitution] rather than as changes of principle'. Declarations of unconstitutionality were never a reaction in defence of democratic elements or the constitutional identity of member states, but seemed to be merely a technical process to better accommodate the national and European legal orders.

Cases Rejected on Formal Grounds

Rejections of the petitions on formal grounds can be divided into two groups. First, there were some rulings in which part of the claims were rejected for procedural reasons, without this preventing the court from entering into the merits of the cases regarding other points of the complaints (like the *Maastricht-Urteil* or the Belgian Lisbon I case). Second, however, there were cases rejected on formal grounds in their entirety: those are the cases of the German Federal Constitutional Court for the European Defense Community (EDC) Treaty, the third case for the Maastricht Treaty before the French Constitutional Council and the third Lisbon Treaty case before the Belgian Constitutional Court, the case of the Slovenian Constitutional Court on the Lisbon Treaty and the three cases before the Austrian Constitutional Court. In this subsection, only this second type of case will be analyzed, showing that they can be classified into three groups according to the reason for the rejection of the petition:

- *Moments and deadlines.* Closa (2013) considered timing and delay as a strategy courts used to avoid deciding on the merits of controversial cases. However, from a legalist perspective, it could be argued that courts were in such cases constrained by rules of admissibility, and thus when they rejected the claims, it was because they *had to* do it. In the EDC Treaty case in Germany, the petition for a preventive injunction of the court was rejected on the grounds that judicial review applied only against statutes which had been formally enacted by parliamentary assemblies (Loewestein, 1955: 810). The first case before the Austrian Constitutional Court for the Lisbon Treaty of 30 September 2008 was rejected on similar grounds: the court insisted that under Article 140 of the Austrian Constitution a treaty still not officially published in the *Federal Law Gazette* could not be subject to the review of the court (see Wendel, 2011; Castillo, 2013a). And the Belgian Constitutional Court, in its third case for the Lisbon Treaty (decision 156/2009 of 13 October 2009), took into consideration Article 3(2) of its own regulatory statute – *loi spéciale du 6 janvier 1989* – which states that the claims based on Article 134 of the constitution for the annulment of laws – *d'une loi, d'un décret ou d'une règle* – have to be presented within sixty days after their publication. According to these deadlines, the claim could not be reviewed by the court (Castillo, 2013a).
- *Insufficient demonstration of violations of rights or interests of the petitioners.* A second cause for the absence of review on the merits was the lack of a sufficient demonstration of violation of fundamental

rights by the claimants. A good example is that of the case UI-49/08 on the Lisbon Treaty of the Slovenian Constitutional Court, which also ended without a substantive decision on the merits. In this case the court stated that the claimants had not showed a direct legal interest in the matter, and thus the merits of their petition could not be reviewed. The Austrian Constitutional Court also rejected some petitions on the grounds that an alleged violation of constitutional rights had not been sufficiently demonstrated in its case on the Constitutional Treaty and in its second decision for the Lisbon Treaty.

- *Referendum*. Finally, the rejection of the petition in the third French case for the Maastricht Treaty is explained by specific factors. In its decision no. 92–313 DC, the Council stated it had no competence to enter into the merits of the case, as the act authorizing ratification of the European Union Treaty had been passed in referendum (see Flauss, 1995). In this, the Council was following a doctrine dating back to 1962 (Neuman, 2012: 304). As the Council itself acknowledged, Articles 17 and 23 of its own regulatory organic law limit its powers of review to 'laws passed by the Parliament', whereas a referendum was 'a direct expression of popular sovereignty'. The solution given by the Council, however, did not satisfy everyone; Flauss (1995) considered that the Council's stance undermined not only the Council's authority, but also that of the French Constitution, and that laws passed in referendum should be subject to judicial review as much as those passed in the Parliament.

European Clauses: Legal Rules as 'Explanatory Variables'

Although 'law is difficult to measure' (Gilbert, 2011: 333), its impact on judicial behaviour can be tested when it is 'explicit, specific, determinate and coercive' (Whittington, 2000: 620). European clauses in national constitutions share at least the three first features of the aforesaid series, and in substantive terms their conceptual relevance for the assessment of European Union treaties is obvious. 'European' or 'integration' clauses are usually considered rules opening up the internal legal system towards the European one. Some authors have emphasized the legitimizing role for the legal integration of such clauses (Fossum and Menendez, 2011), their function in paving the way for the supranational character of EU institutions (De Witte, 2012: 26) or their usefulness in providing a constitutional grounding for the principles of primacy and direct effect of European law (Donnarumma, 2010: 719). Other authors, in addition to recognizing the commitment towards European integration that such clauses may incorporate, take into account that they sometimes impose limits and conditions on transfers of power to the EU (Mangas, 2005). Finally, another interpretation points at European clauses being a prominent tool used by pro- and anti-treaty actors in their judicial battles (Castillo, 2013a).

Claes (2007) has analyzed *inter alia* four dimensions or issues in 'European clauses': whether or not the EU is mentioned in the constitution, whether or not the constitution imposes substantive principles that the EU has to respect in the exercise of its powers, whether or not it establishes a specific procedure for the transfer of powers to international organizations and whether or not it recognizes the primacy of EU law. Although the starting point of this section is this excellent research made by Claes (2005, 2007) about these clauses, the aim of this book is to complement it by also analyzing European clauses in the Central and Eastern European countries covered by this book, as well as by analyzing the role of these clauses in rulings on European Union treaties – that is, their use by the litigants, their role in courts' reasoning and their impact in judicial behaviour. Table 5.1 summarizes the information in all these aspects.

Table 5.1 shows integration clauses for each ruling; it must be taken into account that integration clauses changed in some national constitutions over time, so different cases in the same country can display different clauses. As seen in the table, the most frequent feature of national constitutions is their mention to the European Union, in one way or another; provisions mentioning the EU were found in thirteen cases, with a higher frequency as the process of integration advanced. Another highly frequent feature is the establishment of a specific procedural requirement for the transfer of powers to the EU, although within this group two subgroups can be found: those countries requiring reinforced majorities in the national legislative chambers, and those requiring a referendum in certain cases (Claes, 2007). Conversely, the establishment of substantive conditions to the exercise of powers and the recognition of the primacy of EU law were found in just a few of the cases. The table also displays Spearman's rho correlation coefficients,[8] showing that the only significant association is found between the existence of substantive principles to be respected by EU law – such as Art. 23 of the German Constitution – and declarations of *Kompetenz-Kompetenz*. Qualitative analyses (later in this chapter) and configurational analyses (in Chapter 8) will provide further understanding about the causal impact of some of these variables/conditions.

European Clauses, Integration Clauses, International Law Clauses: The European Union in National Constitutions

In the older member states of the European Union, provisions opening up their internal legal system towards supranational organizations were rather vague at first and did not mention the European project; European Union law was simply included within the wider category of international law (Mabaka, 2003: 25; Claes, 2005: 89)

The Irish Constitution was the first one to explicitly mentioning the European clause (Claes, 2005: 90) after a constitutional reform in the

Table 5.1 European clauses by case and correlations with judicial decisions

	EU mentioned	*Substantive conditions or principles*	*Special procedure for transfer of powers to IO*	*Primacy of EU law*
Irish S.C.: European Single Act	Yes	No	No	Yes
French CC: Maastricht I	No	No	No	No
French CC: Maastricht II	Yes	No	No	No
Spanish CC: Maastricht	No	No	Yes	No
German FCC: Maastricht	Yes	Yes	No	No
French CC: Amsterdam	Yes	No	No	No
French CC: Constitutional T.	Yes	No	No	No
Spanish CC; Constitutional T.	No	No	Yes	No
Slovak CC: Constitutional T.	Yes	No	No	Yes
German FCC: Lisbon	Yes	Yes	No	No
Czech CC: Lisbon I	Yes	No	Yes	No
Czech CC: Lisbon II	Yes	No	Yes	No
French CC; Lisbon	Yes	No	No	No
Polish CC: Lisbon	No	No	Yes	No
Latvian CC: Lisbon	Yes	Yes	Yes	No
Belgian CC: Lisbon I	Yes	No	Yes	No
Belgian CC: Lisbon II	Yes	No	Yes	No
Totals	13/17	3/17	8/17	2/17
Correlation with decisions of unconstitutionality	-,171	-,342	-,450	,112
Correlation with statements of *Kompetenz-Kompetenz*	-,100	,684**	,169	-,262

** Correlation is significant at the 0.01 level (two-tailed).

Source: National constitutions. Author's own elaboration.

accession period: the Third Amendment passed by referendum in 1972, with a majority of 82.4 per cent of the votes cast (Fennelly, 2008: 448). Therefore, when the Supreme Court had to make its decision on the *Crotty* case, the constitution already stated in its Article 29.4.3 that

> [t]he State may become a member of the European Coal and Steel Community (established by Treaty signed at Paris on the 18th day of April, 1951), the European Economic Community (established by Treaty signed at Rome on the 25th day of March, 1957) and the European Atomic Energy Community (established by Treaty signed at Rome on the 25th day of March, 1957)

in addition to the regulation of the duties of the state towards the communities. This provision, opening the internal legal system to European Union law (Scannell, 2001: 65), became extremely important for the relation between Ireland and the process of European integration. According to Justice Finley and to paragraph 4 of the *Crotty v. An Taoiseach* decision, the main issue of the case was whether such provision authorized the ratification of the Single European Act (see Barret, 2009).

In many countries, constitutional reforms creating true European clauses were not carried out until the process of ratification of the Maastricht Treaty (Claes, 2007: 21 ff.). In France, the amendment was subsequent to the first Maastricht ruling of the Constitutional Council. After the constitutional amendment, a new 'European article' (Hoffmeister, 2007: 64) was created. This provision, Article 88, constitutes today the most genuine constitutional link between the French and the European Union legal systems. Indeed, from 2004,[9] the binding character of European Union law in France – and the obligation to transpose directives – is grounded in Article 88.1 (Luchaire, 2004: 466). In Germany, the European clause was also created with occasion of the Maastricht Treaty (Hoffmeister, 2007: 63), although in this case before the Federal Constitutional Court pronounced its famous *Maastricht-Urteil* ruling. The constitutional reform seemed to be, at least in part, a response to the previous case law of the court, and especially to its *Solange* saga (Claes, 2007). The first part of the new Article 23 of the constitution makes a solemn declaration linking Germany to the European Union project: 'With a view to establishing a united Europe, the Federal Republic of Germany shall participate in the development of the European Union . . .' and continues with a detailed regulation of the interplay between domestic and European institutions, particularly establishing the European role of the legislative chambers and the Länders. Article 23 was at the core of the complaints and of the rulings in the Maastricht and Lisbon cases of the German court. In the Maastricht case, for instance, the court held inadmissible a part of the claim that was based on such provision and stated that the role of the German Parliament – with reference to Art. 23 – was respected by the treaty.

Things were slightly different for Central and Eastern European countries. When, after the fall of the Iron Curtain, new constitutions were drafted for most of these countries, the European Union already existed and the transitions towards democracy were sometimes carried out keeping in mind the goal of integration, even if at the same time many of the new or reformed constitutions had a strongly 'souverainist' approach (Albi, 2003: 40). In the transition period, or before accession, many countries enacted European clauses which served as a normative basis for European Union membership (Wendel, 2011: 97; Hoffmeister, 2007), thus overcoming any possible obstacle for accession contained in the national constitution (Faber and Wessels, 2006: 2). In Slovakia, the European clause can be found essentially in Article 7 of its constitution, although read together with Article 120(1). Article 7(2), which was adopted after a constitutional reform in February 2001 (Hoffmeister, 2007: 71), establishes the procedure to 'transfer the exercise of a part of its powers to the European Communities and the European Union'. However, the first paragraph of this provision –Art. 7(1) – mentions the possibility of the entry into a state union with other states, or secession, requiring a referendum in these circumstances. The core of the ruling II. U.S. 171/05–175, in which the Slovakian court assessed the constitutionality of the Constitutional Treaty, was devoted to clarifying whether the treaty was included in the first paragraph – as was defended by the claimants – or the second paragraph of Article 7 (see Faber and Wessels, 2006: 8; Closa and Castillo, 2012). The claimants were apparently trying to avoid the European clause of Article 7(2), which easily opened up the internal legal system to European treaties, in order to gain the opportunity to block ratification through referendum. In the Czech Republic, the country's participation in the European Union is explicitly foreseen in Article 62, introduced in the constitution after the reform of 1 June 2002, according to which 'The President of the Republic shall . . . i) call a referendum on the accession of the Czech Republic to the European Union and announce its results'. Such a clause, however, did not seem to have a role in the two cases in which the Czech Constitutional Court had its say on the Lisbon Treaty. Article 87, which also mentions the EU and gives the constitutional court powers to assess the constitutionality of EU treaties was different: that clause was the legal base for both rulings of the Czech court.

Finally, in Latvia, membership in the EU is regulated in Article 68(3), introduced as a result of the accession period (Hoffmeister, 2007: 69): 'Membership of Latvia in the European Union shall be decided by a national referendum, which is proposed by the Saeima', and Article 68(4): 'Substantial changes in the terms regarding the membership of Latvia in the European Union shall be decided by a national referendum if such referendum is requested by at least one-half of the members of the Saeima'. In addition, Article 101 regulates the right to vote in Latvia, including that of EU citizens in local and European elections. These provisions were at the core of the claim against the Lisbon Treaty in 2009, with the claimants pushing for an interpretation of the European clause according to which the requirement of referendum also applied to the ratification of the new treaty (see Wendel, 2011: 112 ff.). The Constitutional Court of Latvia, however, did not follow that reading of the provision and considered that the principle of legal certainty would be offended if the sufficiently clear wording of Article 68(4) of the constitution was construed to imply an obligation of the parliament to submit to a referendum the approval of substantial changes in the conditions of Latvia's membership of the EU (see Castillo, 2013a).

In a final group of cases – Spain and Poland – the European Union was not mentioned at the time of the rulings, despite these countries' membership to the EU and even if certain general clauses regarding the transfer of powers to supranational institutions existed. In Spain, the constitutional provision grounding Spain's membership to the EU is Article 93, a provision generically regulating the transfer of powers to supranational institutions. The European Union, however, is now mentioned in Art. 135 after a constitutional amendment carried out in 2011 in the wake of the Euro-crisis to limit public deficit. In Poland, the constitution only mentioned the transfer of sovereign rights to international organizations in general, as was also true with the Slovenian case (Faber and Wessels, 2006: 3).

Regulating Ratification: European Clauses Imposing a Specific Procedure for the Transfer of Powers to the European Union

In some cases, national constitutions regulate a procedure for the transfer of powers to supranational organizations, sometimes explicitly intended at regulating ratification of European Union treaties. In these cases, the procedure for the transfer of powers sometimes involves special requirements, such as legislative supermajorities, previous consent by the parliament, referendum or several of them simultaneously, whereas in other cases following the regular legislative procedure is enough to carry out ratification (see Claes, 2007).

Clauses Which Impose Specific Requirements Regarding the Legislative Chambers

Some constitutions regulate the ratification of EU treaties by imposing additional requirements related to the legislative chambers. Such are the cases of Spain and Belgium. In Spain, Article 93 of the constitution foresaw that transfers of powers have to be carried out by means of an organic law – requiring absolute majority in the Congress of Deputies – as well as previous authorization by the parliament for the conclusion of treaties which attribute to an international organization the exercise of powers derived from the constitution. Article 93 has been relevant in the decisions of the Spanish Constitutional Court on the Maastricht and Constitutional treaties (see Burgorgue-Larsen, 2005; Castillo de la Torre, 2005; Castillo, 2013b), since the government asked in both cases whether such provision could be deemed opening the Spanish legal system towards the European one. In the government's view, Article 93 could serve as a presumption of constitutionality of European treaties. This approach, however, was rejected by the court.

In Belgium the procedure of treaty ratification is complex, since its different aspects are regulated by different constitutional provisions. According to Article 34, the exercise of certain powers can be attributed by a treaty or by a law to international public institutions, and Article 77.6 establishes the power of the legislative chambers to pass laws of ratification of treaties. In addition, Art.168 specifically states the need to inform the chambers of the parliament before any revision of the treaties establishing the European Community; this provision has to be read together with Article 167, establishing the procedure for ratification of international treaties, which imposes, among others, the need for consent of the regional parliaments prior to ratification. Indeed, Article 167 has been used in proceedings against EU treaties. In its decision 58/2009, the Belgian Constitutional Court used this provision in order to show the constitutionality of the procedure of ratification after the parties alleged a discriminatory difference of treatment between Belgian nationals and those of the countries in which ratification involved referendum (Castillo, 2013a). In this very decision, as well as in the later decision 125/2009 of 16 July 2009, the claimants also alleged violation of Article 77.6 of the constitution, with the court finding the claim to be unfounded.

Clauses Which Regulate the Possibility to Hold a Referendum

In some cases, the constitution regulates the possibility of holding a referendum for ratification. In Poland, the legal basis for membership to the European Union is found in Articles 9 and 90 of the constitution. Article 90 requires either a two-thirds majority vote in the parliament or a nation-wide referendum, thus offering two alternative possibilities when transferring powers to the European Union (Hoffmeister, 2007: 71; Castillo, 2013a). According to Article 68 of the Latvian Constitution, a referendum is also required not only for accession of the country to the European Union, but also in order to carry out 'substantial changes in the terms regarding membership' if such referendum is required by at least half of the members of the parliament (see Hoffmeister, 2007; Castillo,

2013a). In the Czech Republic, Article 10 and Article 39(4) require a supermajority of three-fifths of senators in order to transfer powers to international organizations unless a constitutional law requires a referendum (Castillo, 2013a).

Note that in all the cases mentioned referendum is not a necessary part of the procedure for treaty ratification, but simply an option whose utilization may be decided by political actors. These provisions, however, were activated by opponents of ratification, who tried to favour an expansive interpretation of them. As said in previous studies (Castillo, 2013a), this happened at least in the Latvian (Arts. 68 and 77 of the constitution) and the two Czech cases (Art. 10 of the constitution) for the Lisbon Treaty, where claimants alleged that referendum for ratification should be held according to the European clauses. In the first ruling in the Czech Republic, in addition, Article 10 was deemed by the court as a basis for its *Kompetenz-Kompetenz*:

> If, on the basis of a transfer of powers, an international organization could continue to change its powers at will, and independently of its members, i.e. if a constitutional competence (competence relating the competence) were transferred to it, this would be a transfer inconsistent with Art.1 par.1 and Art. 10a of the constitution.

Ratification Following the Regular Legislative Procedure

Finally in some cases the constitution does not regulate a specific and more demanding procedure for the transfer of powers to the European Union. In Slovakia, the European clause can be found essentially in Article 7 of its constitution, although read together with Article 120(1). According to Article 7(2),

> The Slovak Republic may, by an international treaty, which was ratified and promulgated in the way laid down by a law, or on the basis of such treaty, transfer the exercise of a part of its powers to the European Communities and the European Union.

Article 7(1) of the constitution also establishes a procedure to enter into a state union with other states by way of referendum, but this article in principle does not apply to the transfer of powers to the European Union – some authors have suggested that it refers at a closer relationship with the Czech Republic (Albi, 2003: 41). Still, the claimants in the Constitutional Treaty case tried to mobilize this provision against the ratification of the treaty, suggesting that it and not Article 7(2) should apply in order to conclude ratification (Bartovic, 2010: 53; Closa and Castillo, 2012). The court rejected such interpretation, but the case confirms again the pattern of resource to referendum clauses by litigants.

Article 23 of the German Constitution also regulates the procedure for the transfer of powers:

> To this end the Federation may transfer sovereign powers (Hoheitsrechte) by a law with the consent of the Bundesrat. The establishment of the European Union, as well as changes in its treaty foundations and comparable regulations that amend or supplement this Basic Law, or make such amendments or supplements possible, shall be subject to paragraphs (2) and (3) of Article 79.

The German constitution, thus, does not impose special requirements for the ratification of European Union treaties; it is true that Article 23 foresees a majority of two-thirds in case of treaties complementing or amending the Basic Law (Ziller, 2006: 9), but this is no more than a repetition of the regular procedure of constitutional reform. In the case of amendment of the constitution – whether or not due to a European treaty – this super-majority applies. This is confirmed by Article 24, according to which the federation may by a law transfer powers to international organizations. It is worth noting that regardless of the interpretation of the scope of Article 23, two-thirds majorities were always reached in ratification sessions in Germany, so this provision was not an obstacle for ratification in this country.

Which Europe Are We Committed to? European Clauses Imposing Substantive Conditions to the Exercise of Powers by the European Union

In two cases, national constitutions foresee a list of principles to which the European Union has to be committed, which have to be respected by the integration project or which at least serve to justify membership to the European Union (see also Claes, 2007). These are the cases of Germany and, to a lesser extent, Latvia.

The German case is the most significant one. Article 23 of its constitution, after the *Solange* case, refers to a

> European Union that is committed to democratic, social, and federal principles, to the rule of law, and to the principle of subsidiarity, and that guarantees a level of protection of basic rights essentially comparable to that afforded by this Basic Law.

Thus, the German constitution already included a large list of principles to be respected by the EU when the Maastricht and Lisbon decisions were issued; those principles bind the European Union to democratic requirements that had to be respected at the European and national level (Grimm, 2009: 261) and that are connected to the eternity clause of

Article 79.3 (Reestman,2009: 384–385). This aspect of Article 23 of the German Constitution was activated by opponents of ratification in their claims. In the *Maastricht-Urteil* decision of the German Federal Constitutional Court, the complaints stated that the 'structural principles of the European Union which are listed in the new version of Art.23, para.1, sentence 1 of the GG have not been realized', with the court finding such complaint inadmissible, even if later in that ruling it examined the treaty in the light of principles and notions such as democracy, now with a focus on Article 38 of the constitution. Again, in the Lisbon Treaty case, Article 23 was deemed by the claimants to be an obstacle for the constitutionality of the act passing the Lisbon Treaty since, for instance, the commitment towards free market competition and an 'open market economy' could lie outside the principle of social state or Article 23.1. Indeed, as Grimm (2009: 360 ff.) recalls, the very court found that Article 23.1 required legal compensation at a national level for the existence of procedures of treaty amendment without national treaty ratification, and that it served as a basis to assess the quality of democracy at the EU level (see also Castillo, 2013a). Still, in none of the cases did the court find Article 23 to be in opposition to the constitutionality of the treaties.

In Latvia, there is a weaker clause referring to substantive principles which have to be at the base of any transfer of powers to the EU. According to Article 68 of its constitution, 'upon entering into international agreements, Latvia, with the purpose of strengthening democracy, may delegate a part of its State institution competencies to international institutions'. However, in this country, although the democratic principle was widely discussed by the Lisbon Treaty ruling (Wendel, 2011; Kruma, 2010), the court opted for a Europhile approach according to which the development of the process of integration does not contradict democratic standards.

In addition to these two cases, two others are worth discussing. In the French Constitution, only a weak and general condition to the ratification of EU treaties has been imposed: reciprocity. The French condition of reciprocity is general and does not refer to substantive political principles, so it cannot be put on the same level as the provisions of the German or even Latvian constitution. In the Slovenian Constitution, a provision similar to the German one can be found. Article 3a of its constitution refers to the transfer of 'the exercise of part of its sovereign rights to international organizations which are based on respect for human rights and fundamental freedoms, democracy and the principles of the rule of law'. However, in the Slovenian case the petition was rejected on formal grounds, so the provision could not have an impact on the decision of the court.

In summary, although material principles were sometimes mobilized by the litigants, they never were successful in achieving declarations of unconstitutionality. This is not to say that they did not have a role in courts' behaviour. On the contrary, at least in the German case, Article 23 seemed to have played an important role in the courts' decisions of *Kompetenz-Kompetenz*. Indeed, the relation between Article 23.1 of the German Constitution and the doctrine of *Kompetenz-Kompetenz* can be traced back to the very history of European legal integration in this country. Article 23.1 of the German Constitution is the result of pressures by the German Federal Constitutional Court in its *Solange* saga (Claes, 2007: 21). The amendment introducing the European clause in Germany constitutionalized to a large extent the discourse by Karlsruhe regarding European Union law. It is not surprising then that the German court grounded its approach to European Union treaties and its relation with them in such provision. Indeed, legal literature seems to confirm this relation. For instance, Wohlfarht (2009: 1280 ff.) suggests the existence of a link between Article 23 of the German Constitution and the court's approach to *Kompetenz-Kompetenz* as

> the Court explains [in its Lisbon ruling] that Article 23(1) of the Basic Law underlines that the Federal Republic of Germany takes part in the development of a European Union which is designed as an association of sovereign national states (a so-called "Staatenverbund"). The concept of Staatenverdung was first mentioned in the Maastricht Case (. . .) the Federal Constitutional Court identifies European primary law as the Constitution of Europe, but with the constraint that it remains a derived fundamental order (. . .) With reference to the Maastricht Case the Federal Constitutional Court explains that the Basic Law prohibits the transfer of competence to decide in its own competences.

Additionally, the link between Article 23.1 and the doctrine of the 'ultimate say' is probably even clearer with regard to the question of basic rights. Article 23.1 states that the European Union must guarantee a level of protection of basic rights comparable to that of the Basic Law. In its case law, the German court can be deemed to have simply carried this provision to its logical conclusion by stating, for instance, that by its jurisdictions it guarantees an effective protection of basic rights of German citizens even against the powers of the Community.[10]

Solving the Question of the Clash of Legal Systems: Constitutional Provisions Declaring the Primacy of European Union Law

Constitutional provisions recognizing the primacy of EU law (see Claes, 2007) are particularly important, especially with regard to the question of *Kompetenz-Kompetenz*. Where a national constitution clearly establishes the primacy of European Union law over national law, it permits

European Union secondary rules to operate in the internal legal system 'as a self-evident consequence of the integration' (Faber and Wessels, 2006: 4), and fewer questions arise regarding which legal system has precedence in cases. Although the possibility of a restrictive interpretation of such clauses always exists, these provisions may prevent courts from considering the need to preserve their internal legal systems even against European Union secondary law.

In most European countries, the general primacy of EU law has been recognized by the case law of their NHCs even in the absence of explicit constitutional provisions. However, precisely for this reason, 'unlimited' primacy of European Union secondary law has not been acknowledged, with core constitutional provisions acting as an ultimate limit to it. In the constitutions of some other countries, provisions regarding the relation between international agreements in general and the internal legal system can be found. These provisions do not refer to European Union law, but only to acts and decisions of international organizations to which the country has transferred the exercise of part of its sovereign rights, which shall have precedence in the event of conflicts with internal law (Art. 91.3 of the Polish Constitution, Art.10 of the Czech Constitution). However, these provisions, which neither mention the European Union nor explicitly refer to the very idea of primacy, are deemed to be too weak as to prevent courts from declaring their *Kompetenz-Kompetenz*, as confirmed by some doctrinal comments (Pollicino, 2010: 78 and 79).

For a few cases, though, the more precise wording of the constitutional provisions may make a difference. These are cases in which the European Union is explicitly mentioned and in which the principle of primacy – with a phrasing resembling that of the case law of the Court of Justice – is stated. In Ireland, the constitution not only accepts the primacy of European Union law over national legislation, but also over the very constitution, thus fully echoing the doctrine of the European Court (Arnold, 2003: 83). Its Article 29.4.3 states that

> [n]o provision of this Constitution invalidates laws enacted, acts done or measures adopted by the State necessitated by the obligations of membership of the Communities, or prevents laws enacted, acts done or measures adopted by the Communities, or institutions thereof, from having the force of law in the State.

However, although it is true that the Irish Supreme Court did not declare its *Kompetenz-Kompetenz* in the *Crotty* ruling, it is unlikely that this was due to Article 29.4.3 of its constitution. When *Crotty* was issued the doctrine of *Kompetenz-Kompetenz* was not still in the agendas of NHCs, this being probably the reason behind the silence of the Irish court with regard to its 'ultimate word' on the applicability of European Union secondary law. In addition to this, it must be taken into account that in very exceptional cases the Irish Supreme Court has been willing to take a 'flexible' approach to Art. 29.4.3, as exemplified by the Grogan (see Colvin,1991).

The Slovak Constitution also states that acts of the European Communities and the European Union 'shall have precedence' over the internal laws of the country (Art. 7.2). This provision, which aimed to 'accommodate EC/EU legal norms within the domestic system' (Láštic, 2006: 539), may have had an impact on the Slovak Constitutional Treaty ruling, issued at a time in which the doctrine of *Kompetenz-Kompetenz* was already in the legal discourse of many other European courts. Finally, in Slovenia, Article 3a of the constitution provides for a similar regulation, but it could not have an impact on the case on the Lisbon Treaty, as the petition was rejected on formal grounds.

Conclusions: Context of Discovery and Context of Justification

In order to assess the importance of legal rules in judicial decision making, it may be good to remember once again the classical distinction between the context of justification and the context of discovery (Popper, 2004 [1935]) as it was explained by legal realism (Nettel, 1996; Portela, 1998). In the context of justification, the conclusion follows from logical patterns inferred from the legal system. The ruling offers an image of normative coherence. Legal rules seem to be the only thing that matters. The cases in this book do not differ greatly from this picture. Courts, in their narrative, grounded their decisions on their legal systems, reflecting on the compatibility between the treaty assessed and the provisions of their national constitutions. Indeed, some cross-case patterns that can be found in these 'legalistic' narratives have been pointed out: courts addressed similar concerns in their rulings, they tended to emphasize openness towards European law, they rejected claims on formal grounds for similar reasons, etc. Courts' responses to the petitions seemed to combine cross-national and idiosyncratic elements. On the one hand similarities across countries were found. These similarities may be explained with reference to two facts: most national constitutions had converged after undergoing similar processes of Europeanization, and treaties assessed were the same for the different courts. On the other hand, dissimilarities may be found in the style of the different courts, from the verbose rulings of the German Federal Constitutional Court to the more laconic ones of the Belgian Constitutional Court and the French Constitutional Council. Context of justification in each ruling may be seen as the result of the interplay of these elements in courts' discourses.

The context of discovery, however, refers to factors that actually are at the core of the decision making of the courts, beyond the narrative they articulated in their rulings. This chapter tried to assess the explanatory capacity of a certain kind of legal rule: European clauses. The evidence provided was asymmetrical, although some interesting information was found. For some of the specific rules in which, following Claes (2007), European clauses were dissected, associations with judicial behaviour going in the expected direction were found. A statistically significant association between clauses imposing substantive conditions on the exercise of powers by the European Union and declarations of *Kompetenz-Kompetenz* was found. Additionally, clauses declaring the primacy of EU law could have had an impact on statements of *Kompetenz-Kompetenz* in certain cases even if their correlation was not significant in statistical terms. Other rules seemed to have a lower impact on judicial outcomes, but they were largely discussed by courts. This was the case, in particular, of clauses imposing a referendum as a necessary or optional step for ratification, which were activated by the claimants in as many occasions as possible (Castillo, 2013a). Thus, in general, European clauses were one of the gravity points around which rulings moved. This contradicts one of the main assumptions of the old realist tradition in legal philosophy: that rules do not play a role in judicial decisions. This distrust in legal rules may be traced back to the very writings of Eugen Ehrlich (2005 [1913]) and are found everywhere in American legal realism, particularly in the expression 'paper rules' in Llewellyn's (1930) famous piece 'A Realistic Jurisprudence: The Next Step'. This research shows that such a dismissive attitude towards legal rules is not entirely justified. They served to justify judicial decisions, they were mobilized by the triggers as part of their strategies and they sometimes – when their meaning was precise enough – could have constrained judicial behaviour. However, it is true that in order to fully understand judicial behaviour political and judicial-institutional variables have to be analyzed. This will be done in the next chapters.

Notes

1 German Federal Constitutional Court, Cases 2BvR 2134/92 and 2 BvR 2159/92 (*Maastricht*), part C.I.
2 German Federal Constitutional Court, Cases 2 BvE 2/08 et al. (*Lisbon*), paragraph 219.
3 Irish Supreme Court, case *Crotty v. An Taoiseach* [1987] IESC 4; [1987 IR 713], paragraph 5.
4 Spanish Constitutional Court, declaration 1/2004 (*Constitutional Treaty*), part II.2.
5 French Constitutional Council, ruling 92–312 DC (*Maastricht II*), paragraph 35.
6 "[L]e traité soumis au Conseil Constitutionnel accroît la participation des parlements nationaux aux activités de l'Union européenne ; qu'il leur reconnaît, à cet effet, de nouvelles prerogatives". French Constitutional Council, case 2004–505 DC *(Constitutional Treaty)*, paragraph 37.
7 Spanish Constitutional Court, declaration 1/2004 (*Constitutional Treaty*), part II.6.

8 See the methodological appendix for specifications on operationalization.
9 French Constitutional Council, decisions 496 DC of 10 June 2004, 697 DC of 1 July 2004, and 499 DC of 29 July 2004.
10 German Federal Constitutional Court, Cases 2BvR 2134/92 and 2 BvR 2159/92 (*Maastricht*), part III.B.2.

References

Albi, A., (2003) 'EU Amendments of the Central and Eastern European Candidate Countries', in Ziller, J., *L'Européanisation des droits constitutionnels á la lumière de la Constitution pour l'Europe*, France: L'Harmattan, pp. 39–50.

Aragon, M. (1993) 'La Constitución Española y el Tratado de la Unión Europea: La reforma de la Constitución', *Revista Española de Derecho Constitucional* 14(42): 9–26.

Arnold, R. (2003) 'Peut-on définir le phénomène d'européanisation des droits constitutionnels nationaux?', in Ziller, J. (ed.), *The Europeanisation of Constitutional Law in the Light of the Constitution for Europe*, France: L'Harmattan, pp. 85–96.

Barret, G. (2009), 'Taking the Direct Route – The Irish Supreme Court Decision in Crotty, Coughlan and McKenna (No. 2)', *UCD Working Papers in Law, Criminology & Socio-Legal Studies Research Paper* 8/2009, at http://papers.ssrn.com/sol3/papers.cfm?abstract_id=1400029 (20.06.2012).

Bartovic, V. (2010) 'National Council of the Slovak Republic in the EU Agenda: Giant in Theory, Dwarf in Practice', in Král, D. and Bartovic, V., *The Czech and the Slovak Parliaments After the Lisbon Treaty*, Europeum Institute for European Policy, at www.europeum.org/doc/publications/Narodni_parlamenty_ENG_Web.pdf (02.03.2011).

Burgorgue-Larsen, L. (2005) 'La déclaration du 13 décembre 2004 (DTC 1/2004): Un Solange II à l'espagnole', *Les Cahiers du Conseil Constitutionnel* 18:154–61.

Carbonnier, J., (2008 [1966]) *Les Recherches de Logique Juridique*, Paris: PUF.

Castillo, P. (2013a) 'Playing the judicial card. Litigation strategies during the process of ratification of the Lisbon Treaty', *European Law Journal* 20(5): 630–48.

Castillo, P. (2013b) 'La Política Judicial del Tribunal Constitucional en los procesos de ratificación de tratados de la Unión Europea: Aproximación desde un nuevo realismo jurídico', *Revista de Estudios Políticos* 159:107–38.

Castillo de la Torre, F., (2005), 'Tribunal Constitucional (Spanish Constitutional Court), opinion 1/2004 of 13 December 2004, on the treaty establishing a constitution for Europe', *Common Market Law Review* 42(4):1169–1202.

Claes, M. (2005) 'Constitutionalizing Europe at its source: The "European" clauses in the national constitutions – Evolution and typology', *Yearbook of European Law* 24(1):81–125.

Claes, M. (2006) *The National Courts Mandate in the European Constitution*, Oxford: Oxford University Press.

Claes, M. (2007) 'The Europeanisation of national constitutions in the constitutionalisation of Europe: Some observations against the background of the constitutional experience of the EU-15', *Croatian Yearbook of European Law and Policy* 3: 1–38.

Closa, C. (2013) 'National higher courts and the ratification of European Union treaties', *West European Politics* 36(1): 97–121.

Closa, C. and Castillo, P. (2012), 'National Courts and Ratification of European Union Treaties', in Evas, T., Lord, C., and Liebert, U. *Multilayered Representation in the European Union. Parliaments, Courts and the Public Sphere*, Berlin: Nomos, pp. 129–57.

Colvin, C. (1991) 'Society for the Protection of Unborn Children (Ireland) Ltd. v. Grogan: Irish Abortion Law and the free movement of services in the European community', *Fordham International Law Journal* 15(2): 476–526.

De Witte, B. (2012) 'The European Union as an International Legal Experiment', in Weiler, J. H. H. and de Búrca, G. *The Worlds of European Constitutionalism*, Cambridge: Cambridge U.P, pp. 19–56.

Donnarumma, M.R. (2010), 'Intégration européene et sauvegarde de l'identité nationale dans la jurisprudence de la Cour de justice et des Cours constitutionnelles', *Revue Française de Droit Constitutionnel* 84: 719–50.

Ehrlich, E. (2005[1913]) *Escritos sobre sociología y jurisprudencia*, Madrid: Marcial Pons.

Faber, A. and Wessels, W. (2006) 'Wider Europe, Deeper Integration? Constructing Europe Network', *Annual State of Art Paper of Team 4*, at www.eu-consent.net/library/Deliverables/D15_Team4.pdf (11.01.2012).

Fennelly, N. (2008) 'The Effect of European Community Law on Irish Law and the Irish Constitution', in Arnull, A., Eeckhout P. and Tridimas T., *Continuity and Change in EU Law*, Oxford: Oxford University Press, pp. 446–62.

Flauss, J.-F., (1995) 'Introductory Address', in European Commission for Democracy Through Law, *Constitutional Justice and Democracy by Referendum*, Strasbourg, 23–24 June 1995, at www.venice.coe.int/docs/1995/CDL-STD%281995%29014-e.asp (18.06.2012).

Fossum, J. E. and Menéndez A. J. (2011) *The Constitution's Gift*, United Kingdom: Rowman & Littlefield Publishers.

Gilbert, M. (2011), 'Does law matter? Theory and evidence from single-subject adjudication', *The Journal of Legal Studies* 40(2): 333–65.

Grimm, D. (2009) 'Defending sovereign statehood against transforming the European Union. Comments on the German Constitutional Court's decision on the Lisbon Treaty', *European Constitutional Law Review* 5(3): 353–73.

Hoffmeister, F. (2007) 'Constitutional implications of EU membership: A view from the commission', *Croatian Yearbook of European Law and* Policy 3: 59–97.

Kiiver, P. (2010) 'The Lisbon judgment of the German Constitutional Court: A court-ordered strengthening of the national legislature in the EU', *European Law Journal* 16(5): 578–88.

Kruma, K. (2010) 'Constitutional Courts and the Lisbon Treaty. The future Based on Mutual Trust', Centre for European Policy Studies, at www.isn.ethz.ch/isn/Digital-Library/Publications/Detail/?ots591=0c54e3b3-1e9c-be1e-2c24-a6a8c7060233&lng=en&id=117517 (12.06.2012).

Kumm, M. (2005) 'The jurisprudence of constitutional conflict: Constitutional supremacy in Europe before and after the Constitutional Treaty', *European Law Journal* 11(3): 262–307.

Láštic, E. (2006), 'Get the balance right: Institutional change in Slovakia during EU accession and membership', *Slovak Sociological Review* 6: 533–45.

Llewellyn, K. (1930) 'A realistic jurisprudence – The next step', *Columbia Law Review* 30: 431–65.

Lock, Tobias, (2009) 'Why the European Union is not a state. Some critical remarks. Comments on the German Constitutional Court's decision on the Lisbon Treaty', *European Constitutional Law Review* 5(3): 407–20.

Loewestein, K. (1955) 'The Bonn Constitution and the European community treaties. A study on judicial frustration', *The Yale Law Journal* 64: 805–39.

Luchaire, F. (2004) 'Le Conseil Constitutionnel devant la Constitution pour l'Europe', *Revue Française de Droit Constitutionnel* 59: 465–71.

Mabaka, P. (2003) 'L'Europe dans le droit constitutionnel positif des États', in Ziller, J. (ed.) *L'Européanisation des droits constitutionnels á la lumière de la Constitution pour l'Europe*, Paris: L'Harmattan, pp. 25–39.

MacCormick, N. (1997) 'Democracy, subsidiarity, and citizenship in the "European Commonwealth"', *Law and Philosophy* 16(4): 331–56.

Mangas, A. (2005), 'Sobre la primacía del Tratado Constitucional ¿tensiones constitucionales a la vista?', in Closa Montero, C., and Fernández Sola, N., *La Constitución de la Unión Europea*, Madrid: CEPC, pp. 153–64.

Meessen, K.M. (1993) 'Hedging European integration: The Maastricht judgment of the Federal Constitutional Court of Germany', *Fordham International Law Journal* 17(3): 515–30.

Nettel, A.L. (1996) 'La distinción entre contexto de descubrimiento y de justificación y la racionalidad de la decisión judicial', *Isonomía* 5: 107–17.

Neuman, G. (2012) 'The brakes that failed: Constitutional restriction of international agreements in France', *Cornell International Law Journal* 45(2): 257–65.

Niedobitek, M. (2009) 'The Lisbon case of 30 June 2009 – A comment from the European law perspective', *German Law Journal* 10(8): 1267–76.

Nourse, V. and Shaffer, R. (2011) 'Varieties of new legal realism: Can a new world order prompt a new legal theory?', *Cornell Law Review* 95(1): 61–138.

Pollicino, O. (2010) 'The new relationship between national and the European courts after the enlargement of Europe: Towards a unitary theory of jurisprudential supranational law', *Yearbook of European Law* 29(1): 65–111.

Popper, K. (2004 [1935]) *Logik der Forschung*, Berlin: Akademie-Verlag.

Portela, M. A. (1998) 'Argumentación y sentencia', *Doxa* 21(II): 333–38.

Reestman, J.-H. (2009) 'The Franco-German constitutional divide. Reflections on national and constitutional identity', *European Constitutional Law Review* 5(3): 374–90.

Reich, N. (1996) 'Judge-made Europe á la carte: Some remarks on recent conflicts between European and German constitutional law provoked by the banana litigation', *European Journal of International Law* 7(1):103–07.

Rodríguez Díaz, Á. (2005) '¿Quién debe ser el defensor de la Constitución española? Comentario a la DTC 1/2004 de 13 de diciembre', *Revista de Derecho Constitucional Europeo* 3: 327–52.

Rosenfeld, M. (2008) 'Rethinking constitutional ordering in an era of legal and ideological pluralism', *International Journal of Constitutional Law* 6(3–4): 415–54.

Scannell, D. (2001) 'The influence of the general principles of community law on rules of procedure and rules of substance in Ireland', *Judicial Studies Institute Journal* 1(1): 64–125.

Wendel, M. (2011) 'Lisbon before the courts: Comparative perspectives', *European Constitutional Law Review* 7(1): 96–137.

Whittington, K. (2000) 'Once more unto the breach: Post-behavioralist approaches to judicial politics', *Law and Social Inquiry* 25(2): 601–34.

Wiegandt, M. (1995) 'Germany's International Integration: The Rulings of the German Federal Constitutional Court on the Maastricht Treaty and the Out-of-Area Deployment of German Troops', *American University International Law Review* 10(2), at http://digitalcommons.wcl.american.edu/cgi/viewcontent.cgi?article=1438&context=auilr (06.02.2015).

Wieland, J. (1994) 'Kaleidoscope. Germany in the European Union – The Maastricht decision of the Bundesverfassungsgericht', *European Journal of International Law* 5(1): 259–266.

Wohlfahrt, C. (2009), 'The Lisbon case: A critical summary', *German Law Journal* 10: 1277–86.

Ziller, J. (2006) 'Le processus des ratifications du traité établissant une Constitution pour l'Europe et la période de réflexion', *EUI Working Papers LAW*, 2006/29.

6 The Political Dimension

A Pro-ratification Context

Introduction: The Political Dimension of Rulings on European Union Treaties

Political explanations have been absent for a long time from the hegemonic approach to the study of judiciaries: that carried out by law scholars. However, at least from the birth of American legal realism (see Holmes, 1997 [1897]) socio-political considerations began to play a role, even if marginal, in law faculties. And when courts began to be studied by political scientists (Pritchett, 1948; Dahl, 1957), a true revolution took place and the focus of attention completely changed. Scholars began to wonder about the causes of judicial decisions, and they found in political variables an inexhaustible source of explanations. Courts began to be understood as political actors and not simply as neutral and unbiased legal institutions (see Shapiro and Stone Sweet, 2002). Some scholars started to suggest that judges' political attitudes and preferences mattered for their decisions, and some others acknowledged the constraints that their institutional frame posed to justices (*inter alia* Epstein and Knight, 2000; Barnes, 2007). Attention started to focus on the relations of the judicial branch with the other branches of government (Eskridge, 1991; Clayton, 2002). As a result, a whole body of literature grew and developed around the idea that the study of courts could not be complete without studying politics at the same time. That is one of the premises of this research.

In the next pages I will carry out a comprehensive review of the political dimension of rulings covered by this book, developing the existing contributions about such cases (Closa and Castillo, 2012; Closa, 2013a, 2013b; Castillo, 2013a). The thread of this chapter is the review of and the dialogue with these previous studies. After this introduction, I will explore the actors responsible for judicializing the processes of ratification of the treaties. To do so, I will analyze the variation in the judicialization rates during the processes of ratification of each treaty, and subsequently I will provide for a diachronic analysis of the different types of actors that judicialized such ratifications. After this, I will try to assess the political consequences of courts' decisions in order to understand how they interfered with political actors' preferences and goals. In so doing, the chapter provides for a qualitative description of actual political scenarios in all processes of ratification. The chapter finishes with some brief conclusions.

Politics at the Beginning of the Cases

The Claimants: Judicializing the Process of Treaty Ratification

The claimant is the actor initiating the proceedings, and thus the actor responsible for judicializing the process of ratification of a European Union treaty. Judicialization of politics has been defined as the spread of judicial decision-making methods outside the judicial province (Vallinder, 1994: 91) and as the mechanism through which judicial law making has an impact on the strategic behaviour of non-judicial agents of governance (Stone Sweet, 2010: 7). From the perspective of this book, when a court participated and had a binding say in a process of treaty ratification, it could be said that such a process was judicialized.

Table 6.1 shows the degree of judicialization of processes of ratification of the main European Union treaties, including cases in which petitions were rejected on formal grounds. The table provides for some interesting information. First, and very importantly, processes of treaty ratification were never judicialized in more than one third of member states; given that political opposition to the treaties was not a rare phenomenon, future research will have to try to understand the institutional mechanisms and constraints that prevented political contestation from becoming a source of judicialization across the EU. The second pattern that can be observed

Table 6.1 Judicialization of the processes of treaty ratification

Treaty (year)	*Number of contracting states*	*Countries in which judicialization takes place*	*Ratio*
ESCS (1951)	6	0	0
EDC (1952)	6	1: Ger	0.2
EEC (1957)	6	0	0
SEA (1986)	12	1: Irl	0.08
Maastricht (1992)	12	3: Fr, Sp, Ger	0.25
Amsterdam (1997)	15	1: Fr	0.06
Nice (2001)	15	0	0
Constitutional (2004)	25	4: Fr, Sp, Sk, Au	0.16
Lisbon (2010)	27	8: Fr, Au, Cz, Slv, Be, Ltv, Ger, Pol	0.3

Source: Author's own elaboration

is that judicialization was indeed a usual phenomenon in some countries in which the ratification of many of the treaties was judicialized – France, Spain or Germany, for instance – whereas in other countries not a single instance of judicialization was observed. Actually, judicialization has not still taken place in most European Union member states, although there is a clear pattern of slow extension of this phenomenon to new countries for every new treaty.

The Status of the Claimants: Evolution by Treaties

One very interesting finding of this research relates to the change in the dominant type of claimants over time. As this subsection will show, these underwent a dramatic evolution which might point at processes of learning by the actors. In a former study (Closa and Castillo, 2012), the claimants of each case were qualitatively described and classified according to their political status – executives, legislatives and citizens. As this information has already been therein provided, I will not repeat it here, although Table 6.2 summarizes it. Instead, what I want to underline now is the diachronic dimension of the cases and how these categories of claimants registered a variation in their frequency, treaty after treaty, showing differentiated patterns. The 'Actor' column in Table 6.2 refers to the 'status' that claimants mobilized before courts. For instance, in cases in which political actors used their privileged standing as members of parliament (MPs) and activated an abstract regulation control procedure, they were classified as members of the legislative chamber. But if the same political actors used constitutional complaints in defence of their constitutional rights instead, they were classified as 'citizens' because they were litigating as such.

The basic trend that can be observed in Table 6.2 is the increase in the share of petitions filed by citizens. In the processes of ratification of minor treaties – European Defense Community (EDC), Single European Act (SEA) and Amsterdam – only one petition was filed for each treaty, and hence the 100 per cent of 'claimants' were of the same type. But during the processes of ratification of the major treaties – Maastricht, Constitutional and Lisbon – many complaints were presented, so that patterns that are clearer can be observed. In the process of ratification of the Maastricht Treaty, only 20 per cent of petitions (one out of five complaints) were presented by citizens. In the process of ratification of the Constitutional Treaty, the share of petitions presented by citizens is 50 per cent (two out of four petitions). And in the process of ratification of the Lisbon Treaty, the share increased up to 66.6 per cent, with eight complaints presented by citizens. This shows an increasing involvement in processes of treaty ratification by this type of actor, and probably points towards a process of learning about judicialization and litigation strategies. This being said, it has to be recalled that in some cases it was

Table 6.2 Status and stance of the claimants

Treaty	*Case*	*Actor*	*Stance*	*Other relevant information*	*Share type of claimant*
EDC Treaty	German FCC	Legislative	Against	SPD (opposition party)	- 100% Legislative
SEA	Irish SC	Citizen	Against	Mr. Crotty	- 100% Citizens
Maastricht Treaty	French CC I	Executive	In favour	President of the republic	- 40% Executive - 40% Legislative - 20% Citizens
	French CC II	Legislative	Against	Group of senators	
	French CC III	Legislative	Against	Group of MPs	
	Spanish CC	Executive	In favour	President of the government	
	German FCC	Citizens	Against	Claimants were to a large extent political actors: Manfred Brunner (FPD), green Euro-MPs, etc.	
Amsterdam Treaty	French CC	Executive	In favour	President of the republic and president of the government	- 100% Executive
Const. Treaty	French CC	Executive	In favour	President of the republic	- 50% Executive - 50% Citizens
	Spanish CC	Executive	In favour	President of the government	
	Austrian CC	Citizen	Against		
	Slovak CC	Citizens	Against	Intellectuals gathered around the conservative Institute of Milan Rastislav Stefanik	
Lisbon Treaty	German FCC	Citizens	Against	Members of the party '*Die Linke*' (plus a deputy of CSU, whose claim referred just to the instrument of ratification)	- 8.3% Executive - 25% Legislative - 66.6% Citizens
	Czech CC I	Legislative	Neutral	The Senate as a whole	
	Czech CCII	Legislative	Against	Group of senators close to President Klaus	
	French CC	Executive	In favour	President of the republic	
	Polish CC	Legislative	Against	Sixty-one members of the party Law and Justice	
	Slovenian CC	Citizens	Against	Association of patriotic societies *Hervardi*	
	Austrian CC I	Citizen	Against		
	Austrian CCII	Citizens	Against	Movement *Heimat und Umwelt* and other associations	
	Latvian CC	Citizens	Against		
	Belgian CC I	Citizens	Against		
	Belgian CC II	Citizens	Against		
	Belgian CC III	Citizens	Against		

Source: Closa and Castillo (2012), Closa (2013a) and author's own elaboration.

actually political actors who filed constitutional complaints and litigated as ordinary citizens (see Closa and Castillo, 2012).

The rest of the types of claimants, though, also had an important role. The largest majority of cases initiated by executives took place in France, with 67 per cent of all petitions brought by executives, and the rest took place in Spain (see Closa, 2013a). In France, it has been suggested that the ritual of executives bringing treaties before the Council for their review is 'a classical move' that started in the 1980s, when François Mitterrand used this procedure for the ratification of protocol no. 6 to the European Convention of Human Rights on the abolition of the death penalty (Ziller, 2008: 323). Through waves of treaty ratification, petitions presented by executives account for 40 per cent of all petitions presented for the Maastricht Treaty, 50 per cent of all petitions for the Constitutional Treaty and only 8.3 per cent of petitions for the Lisbon Treaty. Hence, in the last wave of treaty ratification, petitions by executives seem to be a phenomenon of decreasing relevance.

Finally, legislative chambers were the protagonists of the first phenomenon of judicialization of processes of treaty ratification: the complaint presented in Germany against the EDC Treaty (Loewestein, 1955; Closa, 2013a). After this, 40 per cent of petitions for the Maastricht Treaty and 25 per cent of petitions for the Lisbon Treaty were brought about by parliaments or MPs. In the long run, thus, the general trend seems to be one of increasing importance of judicialization caused by citizens and of decreasing importance of judicialization provoked by parliaments and executives.

Claimants and Judicial Decisions on the Merits

Table 6.3 summarizes the information about claimants and outcomes of the proceedings for all the cases, including those in which petitions were rejected on formal grounds. Some interesting conclusions can be extracted.

Regarding the stance of the claimants, Table 6.3 shows that the majority of cases were initiated by anti-ratification actors: 71 per cent of cases were initiated by opponents of ratification, 25 per cent by actors in favour of ratification and only 4 per cent (one case) by neutral actors. This confirms the idea that judicialization was mainly a tool of political opposition (Hönnige, 2011) and that opponents of ratification had a special incentive to bring the treaties before the courts: unlike supporters of ratification, they had a lot to win and nothing to lose with this strategy.

Regarding the type of claimants, Table 6.3 also reveals some interesting patterns. Twenty-five per cent of cases were initiated by the legislative chambers or some of their members, 25 per cent were initiated by executives and 50 per cent of cases were initiated by citizens, and hence citizens' complaints were the preferred mechanism in order to activate

Table 6.3 Claimants and their stances by decisions on the merits

	Constitutional	*Unconstitutional*	*No decision on merits*	*Share*
Executive	Spain Const. T. (F)	France Maastricht I (F) Spain Maastricht (F) France Amsterdam (F) France Const. T. (F) France Lisbon (F)		6/24
Legislative	France Maastricht II (A) Czech R. Lisbon I (N) Czech R. Lisbon II (A) Poland Lisbon (A)		Germany EDC Treaty (A) France Maastricht III (A)	6/24
Citizen	Germany Maastricht (A) Slovakia Const. T. (A) Germany Lisbon (A) Latvia Lisbon (A) Belgium Lisbon I (A) Belgium Lisbon II (A)	Ireland SEA (A)	Austria Const. T. (A) Slovenia Lisbon (A) Austria Lisbon I (A) Austria Lisbon II (A) Belgium Lisbon III (A)	12/24
Share	11/24	6/24	7/24	24/24

(F) in favour of ratification; (A) against ratification; (N) neutral

Source: Primary sources, Closa and Castillc (2012) and Closa (2013a). Author' own elaboration.

procedures for review of treaties. Individuals, whether linked or not to a political party or civil society association, got involved in processes of treaty ratification and used judicialization in order to intervene in such processes where no other political tools were at their disposal (see Closa, 2013a). In previous research (Closa and Castillo, 2012; Closa, 2013a), a crucial pattern had already been put forward: the clear connection between declarations of unconstitutionality and cases initiated by members of the executive, as all cases initiated by executives ended in declarations of unconstitutionality with the only exception of the Constitutional Treaty case of the Spanish Constitutional Court. The paradox is that actors supporting the ratification of the treaty, as executives were, had theoretically no incentives to initiate a procedure which might end up in a declaration of unconstitutionality. The French case, with four declarations of unconstitutionality at the request of pro-treaty executives (Closa, 2013a), is particularly puzzling. First, because presidents of the republic should have learned from previous cases that the result of the review would be a declaration of unconstitutionality. Second, because as Stone Sweet (2002: 85) said, the French Council had, at least from the seventies, asserted a certain independence from executives, so a final decision contrary to their preference was at least possible.

The explanation typically offered for this paradox is that these were to some point 'controlled procedures' in which the possible outcome of the case was not an obstacle for the ratification of the treaty. In all these cases a costless procedure of constitutional reform was available to the actors and so the declaration of unconstitutionality did not involve high risks (Closa and Castillo, 2012; Closa, 2013b). However, this explanation alone is insufficient: being 'costless' is not reason enough for a court to declare a treaty unconstitutional, as other outcomes – like a declaration of constitutionality – were equally costless. Thus, the explanation for these decisions must also refer to national higher courts' (NHCs') institutional goal of 'making what they see as good law' (Baum, 1994: 751; see Chapter 2). Magistrates probably were sincerely convinced that certain treaty provisions were incompatible with their national constitution. From this perspective, declarations of unconstitutionality took place not only because they were politically harmless, but also because they were deemed by magistrates to be constitutionally sound. As a result, these rulings gave rise to amendments of the constitution which 'cleared the way to ratification', as Neuman (2012: 298) said regarding the first Maastricht decision in France.

Besides this link between executives and decisions of unconstitutionality, the relationship between type of claimants and decisions on the merits reveals a number of other interesting patterns. To begin with, petitions initiated by the other types of actors were scarcely successful. In general, in cases initiated by citizens, rulings did not declare treaties unconstitutional (as was shown for the Lisbon Treaty in Castillo, 2013b); an exception was the *Crotty* case which, according to Barret (2009: 11), showed 'the potential alacrity with which the judicial branch is capable of invalidating parliamentary ratification of European Treaties'. Furthermore, treaties were never found unconstitutional at the request of MPs. Hence, less than 10 per cent of cases initiated by citizens and 0 per cent of cases initiated by MPs had the desired result.

In addition, cases rejected on procedural grounds show a clear pattern: although not every case initiated by a citizen ended up without a decision on the merits, most of the cases rejected on procedural grounds had been initiated by a citizen (70 per cent). Various different hypotheses can be provided for this over-representation of citizens' complaints in cases rejected on procedural grounds. First, actors with high institutional power possess greater knowledge and resources on litigation matters, which allow them to initiate cases with higher possibilities of success (in line with Galanter 1974; Handler, 1978). Second, it may be easier for a court to reject a petition from an ordinary citizen than one from an actor with a high institutional and political profile. These two explanations could be indeed complementary, and they seemed to converge in the cases explored: the higher the institutional profile of the claimant, the fewer rejections of petitions on formal grounds (almost 50 per cent of those presented by citizens, 33 per cent of those filed by MPs and 0 per cent of petitions presented by executives). Finally, it is also worth noting that all the cases rejected on formal grounds had been initiated by actors who actually opposed ratification, whereas none of the cases initiated by supporters of ratification were rejected on formal grounds.

Claimants and Statements of Kompetenz-Kompetenz

It is more complicated to theorize about a possible relationship between the type of claimant and judicial statements of *Kompetenz-Kompetenz*. Indeed, the theory of this book is that claimants are essentially concerned with decisions on the merits, whereas statements of *Kompetenz-Kompetenz* are mainly a question of 'intra-branch' or 'inter-court' politics in which the interests of the litigants are less at stake.

Table 6.4 displays cases sorted by their approach to the question of *Kompetenz-Kompetenz* and the type of claimant (only for those cases that were not rejected on formal grounds). In principle, no clear patterns can be observed. Statements of *Kompetenz-Kompetenz* were made in cases initiated at the request of executives (the Spanish Constitutional

Table 6.4 Claimants and their stances by statement of *Kompetenz-Kompetenz*

	Presence of Kompetenz-Kompetenz	*Absence of* Kompetenz-Kompetenz	*Share*
Executive	Spain Const. T. (F)	France Maastricht I (F) Spain Maastricht (F) France Amsterdam (F) France Const. T. (F) France Lisbon (F)	6/17
Legislative	Czech R. Lisbon I (N) Poland Lisbon (A)	France Maastricht II (A) Czech R. Lisbon II (A)	4/17
Citizen	Germany Maastricht (A) Germany Lisbon (A) Latvia Lisbon (A)	Ireland SEA (A) Slovakia Const. T. (A) Belgium Lisbon I (A) Belgium Lisbon II (A)	7/17
Share	6/17	11/17	17/17

(F) in favour of ratification; (A) against ratification; (N) neutral

Sources: Primary sources and Closa (2013a). Author's own elaboration.

Treaty case), of MPs (the Lisbon I ruling of the Czech court and the Polish court) and of citizens (the two German cases and the Latvian one). Furthermore, statements of *Kompetenz-Kompetenz* were made in cases brought by supporters of ratification (as in the Spanish case), neutral actors (as in the first Czech case) and opponents of ratification. Despite this, claimants were not always indifferent to this kind of interpretative decisions by courts. The best example is that of the Lisbon case of the German court. One of the complainants to the case was Peter Gauweiler, a Christlich-Soziale Union (CSU) member who, precisely because of his opposition to the treaty, was considered an outsider in his party's parliamentary group. However, after Karlsruhe made its pronouncement, things turned more favourable for him; given the interpretative argumentation of the court, he was able to frame the ruling as a partial success, to the point that even Peter Ramsauer, the parliamentary leader of the CSU, welcomed the decision.[1]

Politics after the Rulings: The Consequences of Judicial Decisions

In her book on the French Constitutional Council, sociologist and former member of the institution Dominique Schnapper (2010: 210) writes that when the annulment of a piece of legislation was proposed, a president of the Council used to repeat ritually that it was important 'not to shake the columns of the temple'. This sentence summarizes a very important lesson about the relationship between judicial institutions and their wider political environment: whatsoever the decision a court may make, it is important that such decision 'does not shake the columns of the temple', that it does not threaten the general political status quo. This is particularly relevant in processes of treaty ratification since in this context NHCs may potentially operate as veto players. As Carlos Closa (2009) said,

> The rules for the ratification of EU Treaties have remained basically the same since its creation in 1951 (. . .) these rules combine two requirements: on the one hand, unanimity (i.e. entering into force of the treaties depends on the agreement of all Member States); on the other, the remission to national procedures which establish the organs intervening.

The requirement of unanimity multiplies the chances of an *accident de parcours* (De Witte, 2004: 1), that is, the possibility of one country failing in its ratification, thus endangering the entry into force of the treaty for the whole European Union. In addition, this core role of national legal systems and of the procedures of treaty ratification therein established becomes an empowering factor for national veto players (Closa, 2013b).

NHCs theoretically had the option of vetoing, or at least endangering, the process of treaty ratification. In this section, however, it will be shown that they opted to not do it. Instead, they took into account the hegemonic preferences in favour of costless treaty ratification (Closa, 2013a). This could be due to different reasons. In the first place, political actors had at their disposal sufficient mechanisms to control courts, particularly the procedure for appointment of justices (Volcansek, 2007: 367; Garoupa et al, 2008). Second, as recognized by Anne-Marie Slaughter and Walter Mattli (1997), courts often try to anticipate the retaliation of political actors by avoiding decisions that go against their preferences. It has to be taken into account that in cases on European Union treaties, such preferences were not only those of national political elites, but also those of European ones. During treaty ratifications, judicial decision-making deals with a continental-wide political process. This can be exemplified by the reactions to courts' rulings on the Lisbon Treaty: soon after the German ruling, *Der Spiegel* acknowledged that

> the political elite in Brussels are breathing a sigh of relief. The fact that Germany's highest court has set very strict conditions on the ratification of the Lisbon Treaty doesn't seem to be bothering anyone: The main thing is that the treaty doesn't have to be reworked again.[2]

When the Czech Constitutional Court issued its second ruling on the same treaty, the comments went in the same direction: 'In the wake of the court's decision in Prague, there has been widespread relief across the Continent (. . .) Even José Manuel Barroso, the president of the European Commission, seems to be happy with things'.[3]

Previous studies (Closa and Castillo, 2012; Closa, 2013a, 2013b; Castillo, 2013a) have already defended the idea that courts anticipate the consequences of their decisions and avoid those which may endanger the ratification of the treaty. From the perspective of these studies, declarations of unconstitutionality will only take place in the presence of a flexible procedure of constitutional amendment which allows countries to proceed with ratification. Although these previous contributions are the starting point of this section, my aim is to improve them in a double direction. First, I want to overcome a limitation shared by these studies: the assumption that in cases of declaration of unconstitutionality, a constitutional amendment is always necessary in order to proceed with ratification; indeed, this is only true when the *content* of the treaty is contested by the claim, but not when the *procedure* for ratification is questioned. In the latter case, subsequent to a declaration of unconstitutionality, not a constitutional amendment but an alternative procedure for ratification – usually in referendum – theoretically follows. Second, taking advantage of the larger extension of this book, I will carry out a qualitative analysis of the political scenarios to which a declaration of unconstitutionality may give rise, and I will assess whether actual vetoes (on this concept see Tsebelis, 2002; Dyevre, 2010: 304), and thus a real threat to ratification existed in each case.

Scenarios after a Declaration of Unconstitutionality

Rational-choice new institutionalism poses that 'institutions can facilitate judicial decisions by reducing the costs associated with uncertainty about the consequences of decisions. They can also constrain choices by imposing costs on some possible judicial actions' (Whittington, 2000: 612). That is the role carried out by procedures of constitutional amendment in the majority of the cases covered by this book – those in which courts reviewed the constitutionality of substantive provisions of treaties – as in a case of a declaration of unconstitutionality, they determine the route of treaty ratification (Closa and Castillo, 2012; Closa, 2013a).

As Table 6.5 shows, in case of a declaration of unconstitutionality, ratification can only continue after one of these three options: amendment of the constitution through an ordinary procedure of reform, amendment of the constitution through a rigid procedure of reform or ratification carried through an alternative procedure. The first two options follow from a declaration of unconstitutionality of *the substantive content* of the treaty, whereas the third option follows from a declaration of unconstitutionality of *the procedure* of ratification. Table 6.5 systematizes this information by providing a comprehensive review of all procedures of constitutional amendment with indication of the provision in which they can be found and by offering additional information regarding alternative procedures for ratification when these were alleged by the claimants.[4]

As has been said, the idea that procedures of amendment structure the choices of NHCs was developed in previous studies (Closa and Castillo, 2012; Closa, 2013a), which also considered that these could give rise to some different types of political scenarios. The least dangerous of such political scenarios is amendment of the constitution by the legislative chamber; in such cases, the responsibility for treaty ratification is given back to political elites, who regain control over the outcome of the process. The second type of political scenario foreseen by these studies consists of the need to hold a referendum. In this case, political elites lose control over the entire process and one more actor – the citizens – intervene; this scenario can take place in the event of a constitutional amendment which involves referendum, but also in the event of the request of an alternative procedure for treaty ratification. In a third situation, pro-ratification actors will have to deal with procedures of constitutional amendment involving approval of the amendment in two successive legislatures; in these cases, the cost is higher, since this type of constitutional amendment may involve not only referendum but also the

Table 6.5 Procedures of constitutional amendment and alternative procedures for ratification

Country	*Ordinary procedure*		*Rigid procedure*		*Alleged need for alternative ratification*	
	Arts.	*Requirements*	*Arts.*	*Requirements*	*Arts.*	*Content*
Austria	44.1/ 44.2	Two-thirds majorities in both chambers plus referendum if required by one third of any of the chambers	44.2	Two-thirds majorities in both chambers plus referendum		
Belgium	195	Approval by the legislative followed by general elections, and majority of two thirds in the new chambers			10/ 11	Principle of equality *(applicants alleged discrimination, as referendum was held in other countries)*
Czech Republic	9.1/ 39.4	Three-fifths majorities in both chambers			10a	International agreements for transfers of power to be approved by parliament unless a constitutional law requires referendum
France	89	Two-thirds majorities in Congress of both chambers *or* referendum				
Germany	79.2	Two-thirds majorities in both chambers	79.3	Eternity clause		
Ireland	46.2	Simple majorities in both chambers plus referendum				
Latvia	76	Two-thirds majority	77	Two-thirds majorities plus referendum	68.3	Membership to EU and substantial changes to be decided in referendum

(*Continued*)

Table 6.5 (Continued)

Country	*Ordinary procedure*		*Rigid procedure*		*Alleged need for alternative ratification*	
	Arts.	*Requirements*	*Arts.*	*Requirements*	*Arts.*	*Content*
Poland	235.4	Two-thirds majority in the lower chamber and absolute majority in the upper chamber	235.6	Two-thirds majority in the lower chamber and absolute majority in the upper chamber, plus referendum	90.3	Consent for ratification of treaties to delegate powers may be granted by referendum
Slovakia	84.3	Three-fifths majority			7.1	State union requires referendum
Slovenia	169/ 170	Two-thirds majority plus referendum if requested by at least thirty deputies				
Spain	167	Three-fifths majorities in both chambers plus referendum if required by 10 per cent of MPs	168	Two-thirds majorities in both chambers in two subsequent elections plus referendum		

Source: Constitutional regulation, text of the rulings and secondary literature (Closa and Castillo, 2012; Closa, 2013; Castillo, 2013b). Author's own elaboration.

need to dissolve the parliament and call for new elections. Finally, in a fourth scenario, constitutional amendment is simply not possible; that is the case of the 'eternity clause' in the German constitution. It has to be taken into account that it is the content of the petition that will determine which constitutional provisions are activated and thus which political scenario would follow from the judicial decision. In the next sections, I will qualitatively review all the rulings and asses in which of these four types of situations they fall into.

The Least Risky Scenarios: Amendment of the Constitution by the Legislatures

In case of constitutional amendment in the parliamentary arena, the possibility of successful ratification depends on two factors: the majority required to amend the constitution and the correlation of political forces in the parliament. Table 6.6 systematizes this question in the lower chambers of national parliaments for all processes of ratification covered by this book,[5] providing for information in two important aspects: first, a representative sample of the preferences of political actors and thus information about the political context in which judicial decision making took place; second, information regarding the feasibility of constitutional amendment in case the treaty was declared unconstitutional, and thus a qualitative analysis of actual political costs in each case.

Table 6.6 Positions towards the treaties in the lower chamber and threshold for amendment

Country	*Treaty*	*Vote*	*% In favour*	*% Against*	*Threshold for amendment*
Germany	EDC	Ratification in the Bundestag	56	44	Two thirds
Ireland	Single Act	Unanimity after referendum	–	–	Simple majority
France	Maastricht	Joint Session for Constitutional Reform	89	11	Two thirds
Spain	Maastricht	Ratification in Congress	99	1	Three fifths
Germany	Maastricht	Ratification in the Bundestag	97	3	Two thirds
France	Amsterdam	Ratification in the National Assembly	86	14	Two thirds
France	Constitutional	Ratification in Referendum – no vote in chamber	–	–	Two thirds

(*Continued*)

Table 6.6 (Continued)

Country	*Treaty*	*Vote*	*% In favour*	*% Against*	*Threshold for amendment*
Spain	Constitutional	Ratification in the Congress	95	5	Three fifths
Slovakia	Constitutional	Ratification in the National Council	81	19	Three fifths
Austria	Constitutional	Ratification in Nationalrat	99	1	Two thirds
France	Lisbon	Ratification in the National Assembly	85	15	Two thirds
Czech R.	Lisbon	Ratification in the Lower Chamber	67	33	Three fifths
Latvia	Lisbon	Ratification in the Saeima	96	4	Two thirds
Germany	Lisbon	Ratification in the Bundestag	90	10	Two thirds
Belgium	Lisbon	Ratification in the Chamber of Representatives	87	13	Two thirds
Austria	Lisbon	Ratification in the Nationalrat	85	15	Two thirds
Slovenia	Lisbon	Ratification in the National Assembly	93	7	Two thirds
Poland	Lisbon	Ratification in the Seijm	87	13	Two thirds

Source: Author's own elaboration from different sources (Loewestein, 1955; Torrablanca and Sorroza, 2005; Pérez-Bustamante, 2008; Gangas Peiró, 2000).

The table shows some clear patterns. First, in all cases there were more MPs in favour than against ratification. Indeed, in almost every case a very high pro-ratification consensus existed, so that ratification of the treaty was passed with the vote in favour of the great majority of the deputies. This reinforces the idea that the environment surrounding NHCs was clearly pro-ratification, which is relevant if the premise is assumed that courts take into account the positions of other relevant actors when making their decisions.

Second, NHCs' decisions were not directly correlated to the positions of MPs. On the one hand, the cases with the highest parliamentary opposition to the treaties did not end in declarations of unconstitutionality; the Czech process of ratification of the Lisbon Treaty showed strong opposition – more than 30 per cent of deputies voting – and the Czech Constitutional Court declared its constitutionality twice. On the other hand, cases with great support for the ratification in the lower chamber did not always end in declarations of constitutionality; in the Spanish Maastricht Treaty case, for instance, almost 99 per cent of MPs in the *Congreso de los Diputados* supported the ratification of the treaty and the Constitutional Court declared its unconstitutionality. The same holds true regarding statements of *Kompetenz-Kompetenz*, which do not seem to be correlated to higher rates of opposition to the treaty in the parliament, as illustrated by the example of the Spanish Constitutional Treaty ruling.

Finally, Table 6.6 also shows that majorities were high enough almost everywhere to secure a constitutional amendment (Closa and Castillo, 2012; Closa, 2013a). They were so in all the cases in which constitutional amendment in the parliamentary arena actually had to be carried out as a result of a declaration of unconstitutionality: 99 per cent of MPs in favour in the Maastricht case in Spain, and shares equal or higher than 85 per cent of MPs in favour in all French cases. In the few scenarios in which the majority in favour of ratification might have not secured constitutional amendment (the EDC Treaty in Germany with 56 per cent of the chamber in favour of ratification, and maybe the Lisbon Treaty in the Czech Republic with 67 per cent of deputies), declarations of unconstitutionality were not issued.

Following the Crotty *Strategy: Referendums as the Consequence of a Declaration of Unconstitutionality*

It may be true that no other subject 'has led to as many referendums as the process of European Integration' (Hug, 2002: 115). But paradoxically such referendums were almost never due to a judicial decision, despite the fact that petitioners often alleged the need to hold them (see Wendel, 2011; Castillo, 2013b). Among the rulings covered in this book, the only case in which a referendum had to be held subsequent to a declaration of unconstitutionality was the *Crotty* ruling (Closa and Castillo, 2012; Closa, 2013a), even if such ruling was so resounding that opponents of the treaties and Euro-sceptic actors in general seemed to follow an imitation strategy and claimed before their NHCs that a referendum had to be held in their countries as well (see Castillo, 2013b).

Potentially, referendums as a result of a declaration of unconstitutionality could have taken place in two different scenarios. As noted by previous studies (see *inter alia* Wendel, 2011; Closa and Castillo, 2012; Closa, 2013a: 107), the first scenario in which a referendum may become decisive is that of a declaration of unconstitutionality of substantive content of the treaty, as in some cases referendum for constitutional amendment could be needed (see Table 6.5). The cases in which referendum was foreseen in the procedure for constitutional amendment were those of France (but only as an alternative to parliamentary amendment at the choice of the president of the republic); Ireland; the rigid procedures for amendment in Austria, Latvia, Poland and Spain and in the ordinary procedures for amendment in Austria, Slovenia and Spain, if requested by a sufficient number of deputies.

Table 6.7 Positions of citizens regarding the treaties/the EU

Country	*Treaty*	*Question*	*Answers*		*Source*
			Positive	*Negative*	
Germany	EDC	*No information*			
Ireland	ESA	Referendum on amendment of the constitution in order to ratify the treaty	69.9	30.1	Official data
France	Maastricht	Referendum on amendment of the constitution in order to ratify the treaty	51.04	48.95	Official data
Spain	Maastricht	Which effects will the treaty have	72	1	Eurobarometer 32
Germany	Maastricht	Which effects will the treaty have?	70	4	Eurobarometer 37
France	Amsterdam	Support for EU membership	48	14	Eurobarometer 48
France	Constitutional	Referendum for ratification of the treaty	45.32	54.87	Official data
Spain	Constitutional	Referendum for ratification of the treaty	76.73	17.24	Official data
Austria	Constitutional	Support for the treaty	47	34	Eurobarometer 63
Slovakia	Constitutional	Support for the treaty	60	18	Eurobarometer 63
Germany	Lisbon	Support for the treaty	54	46	Emnid/N24
Czech R.	Lisbon	Do you want the parliament to ratify the treaty?	53	47	STEM
France	Lisbon	Support for the treaty	56	44	CSA/Le Parisien
Poland	Lisbon	Do you want the president to ratify the treaty?	52	14	CBOS
Slovenia	Lisbon	Membership to the EU is a good thing?	51	11	Eurobarometer 68
Austria	Lisbon	Membership to the EU is a good thing?	39	21	Eurobarometer 70
Latvia	Lisbon	Membership to the EU is a good thing?	25	22	Eurobarometer 71
Belgium	Lisbon	Membership to the EU is a good thing	66	11	Eurobarometer 71

Source: Author's own elaboration.

But there is a second scenario in which referendum may become decisive: when the constitutionality of parliamentary ratification is questioned and ratification in referendum is alleged by the claimants as the only constitutionally adequate manner to give consent to the treaty. As Table 6.5 shows, this happened in the first Lisbon case in Belgium, as well as in the Slovak ruling for the Constitutional Treaty and in the Polish, Latvian and Czech rulings for the Lisbon Treaty. Although the claimants tried often to allege that referendum for ratification had to be held (Castillo, 2013b), paradoxically courts always dismissed these claims even though in many cases a majority of the population, according to the polls, seemed to back treaty ratification (see Table 6.7).

Of course, referendums may pose a risk for ratification if the citizens show a negative attitude towards the treaty. Table 6.7 displays the preferences of citizens. The data, however, have to be taken cautiously, as unfortunately a homogeneous and reliable source of information on the positions of citizens towards each treaty was not available.[6]

Curiously enough, declarations of unconstitutionality requiring referendums only took place on rare occasions, with different commentators agreeing that courts tried to avoid them (Wendel, 2011: 122–123; Closa and Castillo, 2012; Closa, 2013a). The question left unresolved by these studies is why such avoidance took place, since a qualitative look at the cases in the table reveals that the citizens had in most occasions a clear pro-treaty or pro-EU stance. Given the positive attitude of citizens, a referendum was not necessarily a threat to ratification. Indeed, referendum could have been used as a source of legitimacy of ratification; for example, consider the positions of citizens in countries like Spain, Germany, Slovakia, Poland or Belgium. However, in these cases, neither NHCs nor political actors dared to activate such referendums.

The Most Rigid Procedures for Amendment: The Need for New Elections

In the case of two countries (Belgium and Spain), the procedure of constitutional amendment included the celebration of new elections, since the support of two consecutive and different legislatures was required (Closa and Castillo, 2012: 152). In these cases, the excessive rigidity of such a requirement would have engendered political costs (Closa, 2013a).

In Belgium, the procedure for constitutional amendment is probably the most rigid among the cases covered by this research (see Table 6.5). A super-majority in two subsequent legislatures is required for every aspect of the constitution, not only for special parts (Closa, 2013a: 106). In principle, there is a means to circumvent this procedure of constitutional amendment: the so-called 'Special Laws', enacted by a two-thirds majority vote in the parliament. These Special Laws are not, however, formal amendments of the constitution, and they are only intended to carry out minor reforms in public institutions (Delpérée, 1991: 22). The content of the petitions in the Lisbon cases seemed to go beyond what can be done with these Special Laws, with the parties in some cases explicitly claiming the need for a constitutional amendment. In the case 2009–058 (Lisbon I), constitutional amendment was deemed necessary by the claimants due to the fact that in their view the 'new hierarchy of norms' created by the treaty infringed on Article 195 of the constitution.

The excessive rigidity of the procedure of constitutional amendment becomes obvious when ratifications of European Union treaties are at stake. In this regard, a Belgian constitutional law scholar recently recommended the introduction

> of a more flexible procedure that would be used when Belgium intends to give assent to a European treaty that would be incompatible with the Constitution without a prior revision of the domestic Constitution. This specific procedure could avoid the (rather un-necessary) dissolution of the Houses of the Parliament.
>
> (Behendt, 2012:18)

Such a statement seems to imply two things. First, it confirms the impression that a Special Law would be insufficient if a constitutional amendment was necessary in order to ratify a European Union treaty. Second, it suggests that if constitutional amendments were necessary in Belgium to proceed with treaty ratification, they would involve excessive costs. Contextual factors seem to reinforce this impression: the process of ratification of the Lisbon Treaty was marked by high political instability in Belgium. Between the beginning of 2007 and the end of 2009, Belgium had five different governments. Guy Verhofstadt was in power for two consecutive legislatures, from 1999 to 2007; in December 2007, he obtained a third mandate, but his government collapsed in March 2008 and was substituted by the government of Yves Leterme. Leterme's first government lasted only nine months, and at the end of 2008 a government was formed by Herman Van Rompuy. But again, Van Rompuy's government lasted less than a year, and in November 2009 was replaced by a second government of Leterme. If the need for anticipated elections can often be a source of political instability, this is particularly true for Belgium during the process of ratification of the Lisbon Treaty.

Things were slightly different in Spain. In this country there are two different procedures for constitutional amendment, but only the rigid one, which implied the need for dissolution of the chambers, was systematically avoided (Closa, 2013a; Castillo, 2013a). In the case for the Maastricht Treaty, and after the recommendation of the Council of State, the president of the government constrained his petition to aspects related to the ordinary procedure for amendment; in particular, he asked the court whether the right of EU citizens to stand as candidates in local elections, established by the treaty in article 8B.1, was in conflict with Article

13.2 of the Spanish Constitution[7] (Aragon, 1993: 10–11; Kumm, 2005: 265), which at that time stated that only Spanish citizens were entitled to exercise that right. Article 23 of the constitution, which regulated the substantive content of the right to vote and which was protected under the rigid procedure of constitutional amendment, was not questioned (Castillo, 2013a). Whereas in the Maastricht declaration the strategy followed was the removal from the petition aspects covered by the rigid procedure for amendment, in the Constitutional Treaty case the same strategy could not be followed. Although the government again avoided a general review of the Lisbon Treaty (Castillo de la Torre, 2005; Closa, 2009: 507), the treaty contained the declaration of primacy of EU law, incorporated finally in a treaty after years of development in the case law of the European Court of Justice (Mayer, 2005: 1497; Castillo, 2013a). In this case, the Spanish Council of State recommended the government ask the Constitutional Court whether such provision conflicted with Article 9.3 of the Spanish Constitution (Schutte, 2005: 282), which stated the hierarchical supremacy of the Spanish Constitution in the internal legal system and was protected under the rigid procedure of constitutional amendment (Castillo, 2013a). When a top Spanish newspaper asked some of the 'fathers' of the constitution and some legal scholars to give their opinion on the compatibility between the Spanish Constitution and the Constitutional Treaty with regard to the principle of primacy, one of them was particularly explicit on the matter: '[T]he legally perfect' solution would be the reform of the preliminary title of the constitution, 'but that [could] be quite costly', since it would involve the dissolution of the chambers. Another one declared to be in favour of the utilization of Article 167 of the constitution in case of a need for constitutional amendment – 'the simplest one'; he suggested that using the rigid procedure of Article 168 'is not the most convenient solution' since a dissolution of the chambers was in his view a 'very grave' decision.[8]

The two cases reviewed by the Spanish court referred to different parts of the constitution and were protected under different procedures of constitutional amendment. Unsurprisingly, the outcomes of the proceedings also differed (Closa, 2013a, Castillo, 2013a). In the Maastricht case, the court declared the unconstitutionality of the treaty, giving rise to a reform of the constitution 'without excessive problems', as acknowledged by López Aguilar (1992: 81). In the Constitutional Treaty case, in which the rigid procedure of constitutional amendment was at stake and thus new elections would have been required, the court declared the treaty constitutional (Closa, 2013a; Castillo, 2013a).

Forbidden Amendments: The German 'Eternity Clause'

Finally, in the case of one country a declaration of unconstitutionality could have driven the process of treaty ratification to a dead end: the case of Germany, due to its 'eternity clause' (see Closa and Castillo, 2012:

152; Closa, 2013a). The clause contained in Article 79.3 of the German Constitution is deemed to be based on Carl Schmitt's distinction between constitution and constitutional provision, according to which individual provisions of a constitution can be amended, while the constitution as a whole cannot be changed, unless the constituent power intervenes (Heining, 2011: 1887). What matters regarding this clause was the possibility of clash with the treaties, since that scenario would have resulted in it being impossible for Germany to proceed with treaty ratification. A legal analysis reveals that this risk existed, although the German court circumvented it. It seems reasonable to argue that, in constitutional assessments of treaties transferring powers to supranational institutions, Art. 79.3 could be affected, since a core aspect of sovereignty – that is, the capacity to exercise core powers derived from it is at stake; with the eternity clause 'the Basic Law is seen not only to assume sovereign statehood but also to guarantee it' (Eriksen and Fossum, 2011: 164).

In both the Maastricht and Lisbon cases, although the petitions raised a large number of questions, the court took them as an excuse for a more general analysis of the treaties in which the contents of the 'eternity clause' were involved. In one of the sharpest analyses of rulings on the Lisbon Treaty, a law scholar criticized this attitude:

> The approach of the *Bundesverfassungsgericht* is even more dubitable if one takes into consideration that this court's former competence to deliver advisory opinions was abolished in the early years of the Basic law. Seen in the light, the *Bundesverfassungsgericht*'s approach of declaring the case admissibility comes close to an act of constitutional 'self-authorisation'.
>
> (Wendel, 2011: 114)

This approach by the court created the excuse for deeper legal reflections encompassing principles such as democracy or sovereignty, directly linked to the contents protected by the 'eternity clause'.

Furthermore, the need to analyze the compatibility between the treaties and the eternity clause was implicit in the petitions. The merits of Brunner's complaint in the Maastricht ruling were accepted for review to the extent that he had claimed a violation of the fundamental right to vote in the elections to the German *Bundestag*, since that right was potentially affected by the transfer of powers exercised by the parliament to another institution (Meessen, 1993: 514–515). It is not difficult to find a relation between such right and Article 79.3 of the constitution, which protects, among other things, the democratic principle enshrined in Article 20. However, in the ruling the court avoided declaring the violation of such principle, with the argument that the partial loss of influence of the German parliament had been compensated by a corresponding gain of influence by the directly elected European parliament (Meessen, 1993:

519–520), even when Karlsruhe exhibited a critical approach to the functioning of democracy at the EU level and elaborated a sharp discourse on the democratic deficit of the EU.

Regarding the Lisbon ruling, the potential link with the eternity clause was even clearer (see Wendel, 2011), with different academics agreeing that the court had used Article 79.3 of the Basic Law in order to set a limit on the transfer of powers to the European institutions (Lock, 2009; Häberle, 2009; Joerges, 2010). The court placed the national constitutional identity – according to the very ruling, the 'non-transferable identity of the Constitution (Article 79.3 of the Basic Law)' – at the core of its reasoning (Mayer, 2010: 35). Such a concept of national constitutional identity was construed to include a wide variety of values, such as shared economic, cultural and social circumstances of life, as well as a previous understanding with regard to culture, history and language (Möller, 2010: 87; see also Wendel, 2011). In this sense, the court made clear that the control of the German constitutional identity was rooted in Article 79.3 in conjunction with Article 23.1.3 and that

> the identity review makes it possible to examine whether due to the action of the European institutions, the principles under Article 1 and Article 20 of the Basic Law, which are declared inviolable in Article 79.3 of the Basic Law, are violated.[9]

Thus, Article 79.3 had in the Lisbon ruling a clear impact on the question of *Kompetenz-Kompetenz* (see Gārditz and Hillgruber, 2011). However, in its decision on the merits the court did not find a contradiction between the constitution and the Lisbon Treaty in these or other aspects. The clash with the eternity clause was avoided.

It is worth making a final comment on this issue. Given that Article 79.3 of the German Constitution has been linked in the reasoning of the court with the problems associated with treaty ratification and the question of *Kompetenz-Kompetenz*, any future decision of Karlsruhe might find an insurmountable problem. If the court's *Kompetenz-Kompetenz* is rooted in the 'eternity clause' of the constitution, then EU law violating such doctrine could never be valid in Germany, as even the option to amend the German Constitution would be blocked (see also Closa, 2013a).

Declarations of Unconstitutionality as Harmless Decisions?

As was said earlier, the main claim of existing literature (Closa and Castillo, 2012; Closa, 2013a, 2013b; Castillo, 2013a) regarding the cases covered by this book was that NHCs calculated the consequences of their decisions and behaved accordingly: the more grave the legal consequences of a declaration of unconstitutionality, the less prone were the courts to make such decisions. The analysis in this section has confirmed this finding even after two elements were added to the general theory: first, the possibility that the procedure of ratification of a treaty, and not only the content of the treaty, was declared unconstitutional; and second, the exhaustive qualitative analysis of all cases to assess whether any of the actors intervening in the different scenarios could actually veto the process. Table 6.8 summarizes this section by providing exhaustive information about three dimensions of the analysis: content of the claim, legal consequences of a declaration of unconstitutionality and actual political threats for ratification in each case.

Table 6.8 shows the consequences of an eventual declaration of unconstitutionality for each of the cases in which the court entered into the merits. Following previous research (Closa, 2013a; Closa and Castillo, 2012) cases were classified according to the consequences of a declaration of unconstitutionality into four scenarios: parliamentary amendment of the constitution required, referendum required, intervening elections required and forbidden amendment. In cases in which more than one procedure of constitutional amendment existed, the content of the petition was taken into account, and it was assessed whether the alleged conflict involved constitutional provisions protected under the ordinary or the rigid procedure of amendment. In cases where the petition was addressed to both of them, I opted for a conservative approach and classified the cases according to the most rigid procedure for amendment possible. For the French Constitutional Council, however, cases were classified into the category 'parliamentary amendment', as the two procedures for reform were alternatives, and executives could choose the least dangerous one (see Carcassone, 1999: 91). Finally, cases in which the procedure of ratification, and not the substantive content of the treaty, was contested were included in the group of cases in which the consequence of a declaration of unconstitutionality was the celebration of referendum, unless the consequences of constitutional amendment were more grave, as in the Belgian case.

Declarations of unconstitutionality occurred mainly when treaty ratification could proceed after parliamentary amendment of the constitution, thus confirming the core findings of previous studies (Closa and Castillo, 2012; Closa, 2013a, 2013b; Castillo, 2013a). The qualitative analysis in this section (see Table 6.6) also revealed that, in addition, for all the cases the number of MPs supporting ratification was always much higher than the number against it, with the share of votes in favour reaching in some cases 99 per cent (Austria for the Constitutional Treaty), 97 per cent (Germany for the Maastricht Treaty) or 96 per cent (Latvia for the Lisbon Treaty). It is thus difficult to say whether the causal mechanism explaining judicial decisions refers only to the constitutional dimension (the type of amendment) or also deals with the political dimension (the favourable political environment), as these two aspects always overlapped (see Closa

Table 6.8 Consequences of declarations of unconstitutionality and decisions on the merits

Case	*Content of the petition*	*Gravest consequence of a declaration of unconstitutionality*	*Political costs in case of declaration of unconstitutionality*	*Decision on the merits*
Spanish CC. Maastricht	Substantive provisions protected under flexible procedure for amendment	***Parliamentary amendment***	No: Only parliamentary amendment, with a secure majority in the chambers	Unconstitutional
French CC. Maastricht I	Substantive provisions protected under the alternative procedure for amendment			Unconstitutional
French CC. Maastricht II				Constitutional
French CC. Amsterdam				Unconstitutional
French CC. Constitutional T				Unconstitutional
French CC. Lisbon				Unconstitutional
Irish SC. European Single Act	Substantive provisions protected under the only procedure for amendment	***Referendum***	Not in the short term: citizens support ratification	Unconstitutional
Latvian CC. Lisbon	Both substantive provisions and procedure for ratification		Maybe: One of the most Euro-sceptic citizenries in the European Union	Constitutional
Polish CC. Lisbon			No: Citizens support ratification	Constitutional
Slovakian CC. Constitutional T				Constitutional
Czech CC. Lisbon I				Constitutional
Czech CC. Lisbon II				Constitutional
Spanish CC. Constitutional T.	Substantive provisions protected under rigid procedure for amendment	***Intervening elections***	Yes: Dissolution of the chambers and new elections required	Constitutional
Belgian CC. Lisbon I	Both substantive provisions and procedure for ratification			Constitutional
Belgian CC. Lisbon II	Substantive provisions protected under only procedure for amendment			Constitutional
German FCC. Maastricht	Different substantive provisions, including some protected under eternity clause	***Eternity clause***	Yes: Ratification blocked	Constitutional
German FCC. Lisbon				Constitutional

Source: Primary sources and secondary literature (espec. Closa and Castillo, 2012; Closa, 2013a). Author's own elaboration.

and Castillo, 2012). It is also worth noting that out of the cases for which the consequence of a declaration of unconstitutionality was the parliamentary amendment of the constitution, the only one in which the treaty was declared constitutional was the second Maastricht case of the French Constitutional Council; this result could be explained either by the fact that a declaration of unconstitutionality of the treaty had already been issued or by the fact that on this occasion in particular, the claimant was not a pro-treaty executive.

For the group of cases for which the consequence of a declaration of unconstitutionality would have consisted in the need to hold a referendum, again, the findings of previous studies (Wendel, 2011; Closa 2013a; Closa and Castillo, 2012) were confirmed, so that except for the *Crotty* case courts avoided the participation of citizens in processes of treaty ratification. But once again, the surprise came with the qualitative analysis of the cases: as Table 6.7 shows, in the majority of the cases, citizens had a clear pro-ratification stance, and hence a referendum not only was not risky, but could have been used to legitimize the processes of ratification. In Spain, 72 per cent of surveyed citizens considered the Maastricht Treaty to have positive effects. In Germany, where no referendums were held, 70 per cent of respondents considered the Maastricht Treaty to have positive effects, and 54 per cent supported the Lisbon Treaty. Sixty-six per cent of Belgian citizens and 51 per cent of Slovenian ones supported membership of the EU at the time of the Lisbon Treaty ratification, whereas only 11 per cent rejected membership in both of the countries. In some of these cases, constitutional or other constraints might have rendered difficult the call for a referendum. But in other cases courts or political actors had the option to hold referendums, although they seemed to avoid them despite their appealing democratic connotations. The reasons for this might be that accepting a referendum in one country could have legitimized petitions for referendum in other neighbouring, more Euro-sceptical member states, that political elites did not feel comfortable with such an idea despite the positive information provided by polls or simply, following a legalistic logic, that courts actually considered that constitutions did not require or allow referendums to be called. Of course, all of these explanations could have converged and reinforced each other in the cases.

In the group of cases in which constitutional amendment would have required dissolution of the chambers (plus referendum), declarations of unconstitutionality never took place. The Spanish Constitutional Treaty illustrates the dynamics underlying these cases. The reasoning of the court in that case avoided a clash between the principle of supremacy of the constitution and the principle of primacy of EU law. To do so, the court constructed a complex and well-known doctrine according to which both were compatible (Mayer, 2005), with the principle of primacy not implying a hierarchical supremacy of EU law over the national legal system, but just a 'displacement' of the effectiveness of internal law (Alonso García,

2005: 1020). Thus, the Constitutional Treaty could be found constitutional (Castillo, 2013a). Furthermore, the qualitative analysis of political costs has showed how Belgium was at the time of the rulings suffering from high political instability and hence the need for a constitutional amendment was especially dangerous, to the point that some academics called for a new procedure of constitutional reform that allowed Belgium to ratify treaties incompatible with the constitution without the need to dissolve the parliament (Behend, 2012: 18).

Finally, in Germany, despite the aggressive doctrine of the constitutional court in its Maastricht and Lisbon cases, and despite the fact that it critically reflected on issues such as the democratic principle or German sovereignty (see Grimm, 2009; Bieber, 2009; Lock, 2009), it never made the crucial step of declaring unconstitutional the treaties on such grounds, which would have probably activated the mechanism of the 'eternity clause'. The court opted instead for declaring its own *Kompetenz-Kompetenz* (Closa, 2013a). But bad news for the European Court of Justice was not necessarily bad news for the political actors aiming at the ratification of the treaties, whose main and most immediate need had been satisfied.

In general, no court brought to a dead end a process of ratification of any of the treaties, despite the many chances for that to occur (Closa, 2013b). NHCs seemed to play a controlled role in their intervention in the processes of treaty ratification. Although they were free to decide on the constitutionality of the treaties and were formally constrained only by their legal systems, the empirical information points at them taking other factors into consideration, showing a conservative attitude in which they cared about the status quo and the interests of pro-treaty political elites, avoiding political crisis and facilitating smooth and unproblematic processes of ratification (see also Closa, 2013a; Closa and Castillo, 2012). Some commentators dared to suggest how costly a declaration of unconstitutionality could be: regarding the Czech Constitutional Court Bříza (2009: 155) said that 'one could hardly expect the Court to seriously question the whole system on which the EU is founded, when much more powerful courts in Europe did not make such an open challenge'. The assertion illustrates how difficult it was for courts to deviate from the plan of ratification.

Conclusions

NHCs' rulings on European Union treaties were the object of pressure by political elites, sometimes rather explicitly. Just to mention one example, during the German ratification of the Lisbon Treaty, Interior Minister Wolfgang Schäuble urged the court to exhibit 'self-restraint' since he had 'no doubt that the Lisbon treaty corresponds completely with the constitution'.[10] The more recent rulings of the German court about the measures to deal with the crisis in the eurozone have confirmed this impression, with Karlsruhe being the focus of attention of the international press, European political movements and institutional actors. Of course, this fact has important implications in normative terms, particularly regarding the separation between branches of government, the independence of the judiciary in a democratic society and the rule of law in constitutional systems. Since this research is mainly empirical, I will not enter into these important normative debates here, although it must be acknowledged that the normative questions raised by this chapter are as important as the empirical findings that have been provided.

This being said, it must be underlined that judicial behaviour should not be reduced to its political dimension. If political variables had an impact on judicial behaviour, they did so in subtle, indirect and sophisticated ways. It is important to avoid the simplistic depiction of courts as puppets of political actors with no agency or interests of their own. In addition, to say that political factors played a role in judicial decisions is not incompatible with the assertion that legal elements are also part of the explanation, as the previous chapter showed. Furthermore, it has already been shown that legal and political aspects converged in many instances. In addition, other institutional and judicial explanatory conditions played a role, as will be explained in the next chapter. All of these dimensions of the cases – legal, political, institutional – matter and are necessary in order to understand the rulings. It is precisely the interaction between all of these types of causal conditions that may explain judicial behaviour in all its complexity.

Notes

1 *Der Spiegel*, 1 January 2007 www.spiegel.de/international/europe/0,1518,633702,00.html (19.04.2012).
2 *Der Spiegel*, 1 July 2009 www.spiegel.de/international/europe/0,1518,633691,00.html (12.01.2011).
3 *Der Spiegel*, 3 November 2009 www.spiegel.de/international/europe/0,1518,659038,00.html (01.04.2012).
4 I include in this category the Polish ruling on the Lisbon Treaty. In such ruling, Art. 90.3 of the constitution is widely discussed by the court, although it is not clear whether claimants actually alleged that referendum according to such provision should be held. Facing this problem, I opted for the most conservative option and also included the case in the category.
5 In the table, percentages are calculated from the total of actors voting either in favour of or against the treaty. In the cases of the French ratifications of the Maastricht and Constitutional treaties, the parliament did not intervene since they were carried out in referendum; thus, no information about the positions of the French MPs existed for the Constitutional Treaty, whereas for the Maastricht Treaty I had to use the results of the vote on the constitutional amendment session, as a constitutional amendment was requested by the first ruling of the Constitutional Council. In Ireland, the problem was not the absence of a parliamentary vote on the ratification of the treaty, but

the fact that the results of this vote were not representative of the preferences of political actors. The *Crotty* case in Ireland was surrounded by a volatile political scenario: changes in the political context made the different parties reconsider and modulate their stances. The Single European Act had been negotiated under a coalition government of *Fine Gael* and the Labour Party; at the time when the treaty had to be discussed in the chamber, *Fianna Fáil* expressed a relatively sceptical position towards it. However, in 1987 new elections were held and *Fianna Fáil* took power; in the new parliament, *Fianna Fáil* obtained 44.1 per cent of the deputies, *Fine Gael* obtained 27.1 per cent and its former ally the Labour Party obtained 6.4 per cent; the rest of the chamber was distributed among the Progressive Democrats, with 11.8 per cent of the seats, DL with 3.7 per cent and others with 6.9 percent of deputies (Holmes, 1996: 192) After winning the elections, *Fianna Fáil* changed its position and showed clearer support for the treaty. The stances of the parties were made clear with the occasion of the referendum subsequent to the ruling of the Supreme Court. In it, the only party officially against the ratification was the Workers Party (Holmes, 1996: 194). The Labour Party was in a difficult situation: although they had participated in the negotiation of the treaty, a majority of its militants were against it; to find a solution, the party avoided taking an official position and gave freedom to its members to campaign however they wished. The constitutional amendment necessary in order to ratify the treaty was passed in referendum. Subsequently, all the parties supported ratification in the parliament as a sign of respect for the will of the people (Luthardt, 1993: 59). Given the merely symbolic nature of this vote, it cannot be taken into account in order to measure political actors' preferences.

6 Official results of referendums were selected as a first option if they existed. If referendums did not take place, as a second option, I selected questions of the Eurobarometer regarding the treaty. The Eurobarometer presented such questions for the Maastricht and Constitutional treaties; however, for the Amsterdam and Lisbon treaties, such questions were not made. Thus, as a third option, I chose available national surveys on positions towards the treaty. Finally, in a number of cases, official referendums did not take place and Eurobarometers and national surveys were not made regarding the position of the citizenry towards the treaty. In these cases, the only available option was to use as a proxy general questions of the Eurobarometer regarding positions towards the EU, in which I opted for the question 'Do you think that your country has benefited from membership to the European Union?' When Eurobarometer had to be selected as the source of information, I always chose the edition closest in time to the rulings of the courts. Given the heterogeneity in the sources of information in this regard, I adopted a conservative strategy, so even if I will review in the next lines the stances of the citizens in a qualitative manner, this information will not be the basis of any condition in the qualitative comparative analysis (QCA) analysis in Chapter 8.

7 The second point of the claim seemed to be an already-made answer for the court, since the government specifically asked whether Article 93 of the constitution was sufficient to consider the aforesaid aspect of the treaty as constitutional, and, otherwise, if the same constitutionality could be declared through the interplay of Articles 13.2 and 11 of the constitution. Finally, the government asked which procedure of constitutional reform would have to be followed in case of a negative answer.

8 *El País*, 13 December 2004 http://elpais.com/diario/2004/12/13/espana/1102892417_850215.html (19.04.2012).

9 German Federal Constitutional Court, Cases 2 BvE 2/08 et al. (*Lisbon*), paragraphs 240–1.
10 *Der Spiegel*, 10 February 2009 www.spiegel.de/international/germany/0,1518, 606693,00.html (19.04.2012).

References

Alonso García, R. (2005) 'The Spanish Constitution and the European Constitution: The script for a virtual collision and other observations on the principle of primacy', *German Law Journal* 6(6): 1002–24.

Aragon, M. (1993) 'La Constitución Española y el Tratado de la Unión Europea: La reforma de la constitución', *Revista Española de Derecho Constitucional* 14(42): 9–26.

Barnes, J. (2007) 'Bringing the courts back in: Interbranch perspectives on the courts in American politics and policy making', *Annual Review of Political Science* 10: 25–43.

Barret, G. (2009), 'Taking the direct route – The Irish Supreme Court decision in Crotty, Coughlan and McKenna (No. 2)', UCD Working Papers in Law, Criminology & Socio-Legal Studies Research Paper 8/2009, at http://papers.ssrn.com/sol3/papers.cfm?abstract_id=1400029 (20.06.2012).

Baum, L. (1994) 'What judges want: Judges' goals and judicial behavior', *Political Research Quarterly* 47(3):749–68.

Behendt, C. (2012) 'The process of constitutional amendment in Belgium', at http://orbi.ulg.ac.be/bitstream/2268/107111/1/Belgium%20-%20Constitutional%20amendment%20-%20final%20version%20%28Behrendt%29.pdf (05.11.2012).

Bieber, R., (2009) ' "An association of sovereign states": Comments on the German Constitutional Court's decision on the Lisbon treaty', *European Constitutional Law Review* 5(3): 391–406.

Bříza, P. (2009) 'The Czech Republic. The Constitutional Court on the Lisbon treaty. Decision of 26 November 2008', *European Constitutional Law Review* 5(1): 143–64.

Carcassonne, G. (1999) 'Amendments to the French Constitution: One surprise after another', *West European Politics* 22(4): 76–91.

Castillo, P. (2013a) 'La Política Judicial del Tribunal Constitucional en los procesos de ratificación de tratados de la Unión Europea: Aproximación desde un nuevo realismo jurídico', *Revista de Estudios Políticos* 159:107–38.

Castillo, P. (2013b) 'Playing the judicial card. Litigation strategies during the process of ratification of the Lisbon Treaty', *European Law Journal* 20(5): 630–48.

Castillo de la Torre, F., (2005), 'Tribunal Constitucional (Spanish Constitutional Court), opinion 1/2004 of 13 December 2004, on the treaty establishing a constitution for Europe', *Common Market Law Review* 42(4):1169–1202.

Clayton, C. (2002) 'The supply and demand sides of judicial policy-making', *Law and Contemporary Problems* 65(3): 69–85.

Closa, C. (2009) 'Much ado about little: Continuity and change in the European union policy of the Spanish socialist government (2004–8)', *South European Society and Politics* 14(4): 503–18.

Closa, C. (2013a) 'National higher courts and the ratification of European Union treaties', *West European Politics* 36(1): 97–121.

Closa, C. (2013b) *The Politics of Ratification of European Union Treaties*, London: Routledge.

Closa, C. and Castillo, P. (2012), 'National Courts and Ratification of European Union treaties', in Evas, T., Lord, C., and Liebert, U. *Multilayered Representation in the European Union. Parliaments, Courts and the Public Sphere*, Berlin: Nomos, pp.129–57.

Dahl, R. (1957) 'Decision-making in a democracy: The Supreme Court as a national policy-maker', *Journal of Public Law* 6: 279–95.

De Witte, B. (2004) 'The process of ratification of the Constitutional Treaty and the crisis options: A legal perspective', *EUI Working Paper LAW No. 2004/16* at http://cadmus.eui.eu/bitstream/handle/1814/2831/law04–16.pdf;jsessionid=05EE3A663DA3DCCBDF286C9341335439?sequence=1 (23.04.2012).

Delpérée, F. (1991) 'The process for amending the Belgian Constitution', *Canadian Parliamentary Review* 14(3): 1–6.

Dyevre, A. (2010) 'Unifying the field of comparative judicial politics: Towards a general theory of judicial behaviour', *European Political Science Review* 2(2): 297–327.

Epstein, L. and Knight, J. (2000) 'Toward a strategic revolution in judicial politics: A look back, a look ahead' *Political Research Quarterly* 53(3): 625–61.

Eriksen, E. O. and Fossum, J. E., (2011) 'Bringing European democracy back in – Or how to read the German Constitutional Court's Lisbon Treaty ruling', *European Law Journal* 17(2): 153–71.

Eskridge, W. (1991) 'Reneging on history? Playing the court/congress/president civil rights game', *California Law Review* 79(3): 613–74.

Galanter, M. (1974) 'Why the "haves" come out ahead: Speculations on the limits of legal change', *Law and Society Review* 9(1): 95–160.

Gangas Peiró, P. (2000) 'El sistema político de Francia', en Alcántara Sáez, M., *Sistemas Políticos de la Unión Europea*, Valencia: Tirant Lo Blanch.

Gärditz, K. and Hillgruber, C. (2011) 'Should Karlsruhe be the guardian of the Basic Law?' in Guérot, U. and Hénard, J., *What Does Germany Think About Europe?*, European Council on Foreign Relations, www.ecfr.eu/page/-/ECFR36_GERMANY.pdf (08.03.2012).

Garoupa, N., Grembi V. and Amaral Garcia, S. (2008) 'Judicial independence and party politics in the Kelsenian constitutional courts: The case of Portugal', *University of Illinois College of Law, Law and Economics Working Papers*, Paper 95.

Grimm, D. (2009) 'Defending sovereign statehood against transforming the European Union. Comments on the German Constitutional Court's decision on the Lisbon Treaty', *European Constitutional Law Review* 5(3): 353–73.

Häberle, P. (2009) 'La regresiva "sentencia Lisboa" como "Maastricht-II" anquilosada', *Revista de Derecho Constitucional Europeo* 12: 397–429.

Handler, J. (1978) *Social Movements and the Legal System: A Theory of Law Reform and Social Change*, San Diego: Academic Press.

Heining, H. M. (2011) 'The political and the Basic Law's Sozialstaat principle – Perspectives from constitutional law and theory', *German Law Journal* 12(11): 1887–1900.

Holmes, M., (1996) 'Irish Political Parties and the European Union', in Caffney, J. (ed.) *Political Parties and the European Union*, London: Routledge.

Holmes, O.W. (1997 [1897]) 'The path of the law', *Harvard Law Review* 110(5): 991–1009.

Hönnige, C. (2011) 'Beyond judicialization: Why we need more comparative research about constitutional courts', *European Political Science* 10(3): 346–58.

Hug, S. (2002) *Voices of Europe. Citizens, Referendums, and European Integration*, Lanham: Rowman & Littlefield.

Joerges, C. (2010) 'The Lisbon Judgement, Germany's Sozialstaat, the ECJ's Labour-Law Jurisprudence, and the Reconceptualisation of European Law as a New Type of Conflicts Law', in Fischer-Lescano, A., Georges C., and Wonka A. (eds.) *The German Constitutional Court's Lisbon Ruling: Legal and Political Science Perspectives*, ZERP DIskussionpapier 1/2010, at www.mpifg.de/people/mh/paper/ZERP%20Discussion%20Paper%201.2010.pdf.

Kumm, M. (2005) 'The jurisprudence of constitutional conflict: Constitutional supremacy in Europe before and after the Constitutional Treaty', *European Law Journal* 11(3): 262–307.

Lock, T. (2009) Why the European Union is not a state. Some critical remarks. Comments on the German Constitutional Court's decision on the Lisbon Treaty, *European Constitutional Law Review* 5(3): 407–20.

Loewestein, K. (1955) 'The Bonn Constitution and the European community treaties. A study on judicial frustration', *The Yale Law Journal* 64: 805–39.

López Aguilar, J. F., (1992) 'Maastricht y la problemática de la reforma de la Constitución (Unión Europea, derechos de los extranjeros y reforma constitucional: teoría y *case study*)', *Revista de Estudios Políticos* 77: 57–93.

Mayer, F.C. (2005) 'Supremacy – Lost? – Comment on Roman Kwiecién', *German Law Journal* 6(11): 1497–1506.

Mayer, F.C. (2010) 'Rashomon in Karlsruhe – A reflection on Democracy and Identity in the European Union', NYU Jean Monnet Working Paper 05/10, at http://centers.law.nyu.edu/jeanmonnet/papers/10/100501.pdf (08.03.2012).

Meessen, K.M. (1993) 'Hedging European integration: The Maastricht judgment of the Federal Constitutional Court of Germany', *Fordham International Law Journal* 17(3): 515–30.

Möller, K. (2010) 'After the Lisbon Ruling: Where Is Social Democracy?', in Fischer-Lescano, A., Georges C., and Wonka A. (eds.) *The German Constitutional Court's Lisbon Ruling: Legal and Political Science Perspectives*, ZERP Diskussionpapier 1/2010, at www.mpifg.de/people/mh/paper/ZERP%20Discussion%20Paper%201.2010.pdf.

Neuman, G. (2012) 'The brakes that failed: Constitutional restriction of international agreements in France', *Cornell International Law Journal* 45(2): 257–365.

Pérez-Bustamente, R. (2008) *Historia Política y Jurídica de la Unión Europea*, Edisofer: Madrid.

Pritchett, H. (1948) *The Roosevelt Court*, New York: Macmillan.

Schnapper, D. (2010) *Une sociologue au Conseil constitutionnel*, Paris: Gallimard.

Schutte, C. (2005) 'Case note: Spain. Tribunal Constitucional on the European constitution. Declaration of 13 December 2004', *European Constitutional Law Review* 1(2): 281–92.

Shapiro, M. and Stone Sweet, A. (2002) *On Law Politics and Judicialization*, Oxford: Oxford University Press.

Slaughter, A.-M. and Mattli, W. (1997) 'The Role of National Courts in the Process of European Integration: Accounting for Judicial Preferences and Constraints', in Slaughter A.-M., Stone Sweet A. and Weiler, J. H. H., *The European Court and National Courts: Doctrine and Jurisprudence. Legal Change in Its Social Context*, Oxford: Hart Publishing, pp.253–77.

Stone Sweet, A. (2002) 'Constitutional courts and parliamentary democracy', *West European Politics* 25(1): 77–100.

Stone Sweet, A. (2010) 'The European Court of Justice and the judicialization of EU governance', *Living Reviews in European Governance* 5(2): 1–50.

Torreblanca, J.I. and Sorroza, A. (2005) 'Principales datos sobre el proceso de ratificación de la Constitución Europea en España', *Real Instituto Elcano – Documento de Trabajo* (DT) 8/2005.

Tsebelis, G. (2002) *Veto Players: How Political Institutions Work*, Los Angeles: Sage.

Vallinder, T. (1994) 'The judicialization of politics – A world-wide phenomenon: Introduction', *International Political Science Review* 15(2): 91–99.

Volcansek, M. (2007) 'Appointing judges the European way (rethinking judicial selection: A critical appraisal of appointive selection for state court judges)', *Fordham Urban Law Journal* 9(42), at http://law2.fordham.edu/publications/articles/400flspub8524.pdf (10.10.2012).

Wendel, M. (2011) 'Lisbon before the courts: Comparative perspectives', *European Constitutional Law Review* 7(1): 96–137.

Whittington, K. (2000) 'Once more unto the breach: Post-behavioralist approaches to judicial politics', *Law and Social Inquiry* 25(2): 601–34.

Ziller, J. (2008) 'The Law and Politics of the Ratification of the Lisbon Treaty', in Griller, S. and Ziller, J., *The Lisbon Treaty. EU Constitutionalism Without a Constitutional Treaty?*, Vienna: Springer, pp. 309–34.

7 The Judicial Dimension

Institutional Design and Decisional Dynamics

Introduction: The Judicial Dimension

The judicial arena has its own rules. Courts are strategic actors (Boucher and Segal, 1995; Epstein et al, 2001) whose behaviour is constrained by the *sui generis* nature of the judicial field and the rules that govern their setting up and actions. These constraints are multifaceted. They relate to the fact that courts are institutions, and hence their institutional design conditions the range of actions of which they are capable (see Hall and Taylor, 1996). They also relate to the fact that courts are not isolated, but operate within a network of European judiciaries (Gelter and Siems, 2012; Claes and de Visser, 2012). Courts may react to their own previous decisions, as suggested by some literature (Lax and Rader, 2010; Richards and Kritzer, 2002), or to the case law of other courts. All of these aspects point at the explanatory capacity of variables which vary in their nature, but which have something in common: they go beyond purely legalistic or political accounts of judicial conduct and underline the need to take into account the idiosyncrasy of the judicial field and of judicial institutions in order to understand courts' behaviour.

This chapter is divided into two main sections. After this brief introduction, I will explore aspects related to courts' institutional design, in the belief that it may constrain judicial behaviour. I will begin by considering national higher courts' (NHCs') formal guarantees of independence in order to test the assumption that more independent courts are more capable of seeking their own goals; subsequently, I will explore NHCs' powers of review, in the belief that it may be a powerful explanation for courts' variation in the reception of the doctrine of *Kompetenz-Kompetenz*. After having explored institutional aspects, in the next section I will focus on the interaction among courts' decisions. I will explore sequences of decisions by the same court on the same treaty, the link between statements of *Kompetenz-Kompetenz* and decisions on the merits and the impact of some courts' decisions on the rulings of their counterparts in the context of processes of cross-fertilization. I will finish by offering some brief conclusions.

Institutional Constraints and Judicial Behaviour

Neoinstitutionalism has become the dominant approach in the subfield of judicial politics (Redher, 2007). One of the core assumptions of neoinstitutionalism is that the design of the institutions constrains the behaviour of actors (Hall and Taylor, 1996). Courts' institutional design may become relevant when trying to understand judicial decisions, since a wide variation exists both with regard to courts' formal guarantees of independence and to courts' powers to review. In this section, these two aspects will be separately analyzed.

The Design of the Institution and Courts' Guarantees of Independence

The institutional design of NHCs is closely related to the functions that they are to perform. If they are to act as a counterbalancing power against the political branches of government, if they are to annul legislation passed by legislative majorities, if they are to defend citizens' constitutional rights against their violations committed by the public powers, NHCs have to be designed in a manner that ensures that pressures from the rest of the political actors cannot constrain their behaviour. Bühlmann and Kunz (2011: 318) define judicial independence as follows: 'Distinctive for judicial independence is that the decisions of the judges are exclusively based on the law and are not influenced by specific political interests or the other constitutional powers'. However, this definition is probably too optimistic in that it assumes that in the absence of external pressures courts would restrain themselves to neutrally apply the law to the cases, instead of pursuing their own preferred policy options. Closer to the theoretical assumptions of this research, an alternative definition of judicial independence would suggest that courts are independent as long as they are capable of making decisions free from the influence of other actors and as long as they are capable of seeking their own goals without having to worry about the consequences for other institutions (Ferejohn, Rosenbluth and Shipan, 2004: 3).

In order to maximize judicial independence, constitutional systems bestow on NHCs certain guarantees of independence. Such formal guarantees of independence are usually listed in the constitution in order to prevent majorities in power from curtailing them to their advantage. Among the most important ones, the following can be found: duration of term of office, prohibition of successive appointments, guarantees against removal, requirement of certain professional backgrounds and consensual nomination mechanisms. Elsewhere I have reviewed in detail all of these dimensions of judicial independence (see Castillo 2012), and Table 7.1 summarizes that information for the period covered by this book. By aggregating all of those dimensions, a general index of judicial independence is displayed.[1]

Table 7.1 Institutional design and degree of independence

Institution	*Term of office*	*Re-appointment*	*Removal*	*Appointment*	*Background*	*Total Score*
German Federal Constitutional Court	Twelve years (more than two legislative mandates)	No	Only in limited situations foreseen in the law	Half of magistrates elected by each legislative chamber, super-majorities required	Legal	4.46
Spanish Constitutional Court	Nine years (more than two legislative mandates)	No	Only in limited situations foreseen in the law	Two magistrates elected by the government, two magistrates elected by the Council of the Judiciary and four by each of the parliamentary chambers by super-majorities	Legal	4.46
Belgian Constitutional Court	Lifetime	No	Only in limited situations foreseen in the law	Appointed by the king from a list presented by each chamber, passed by two-thirds majorities	Half legal, half former ministers of parliament (MPs)	4.3
Latvian Constitutional Court	Ten years (more than two legislative mandates)	No	Only in limited situations foreseen in the law	Seven magistrates elected by the parliament with absolute majority; three of them at proposal of at least ten MPs, two proposed by the Council of Ministers and two by the Plenary of the Supreme Court	Legal	4.26
Irish Supreme Court	Lifetime	No	Only in limited situations foreseen in the law	Formally nominated by the president, actually elected by the government	Legal	4.2

Polish Constitutional Court	Ninc years (more than two legislative mandates)	No	Only in limited situations foreseen in the law	Proposed by fifty deputies or the president of the Seijm; appointed by absolute majority	Legal	4.04
Czech Constitutional Court	Ten years (more than two legislative mandates)	Yes	Only in limited situations foreseen in the law	Elected by the president of the republic, confirmed by the senate	Legal	3.06
Slovakian Constitutional Court	Twelve years (more than two legislative mandates)	Yes	Only in limited situations foreseen in the law	Ten magistrates elected by the president of the republic, over a list of twenty justices proposed by the parliament	Legal	3.06
French Constitutional Council	Nine years (fewer than two presidential terms)	No	Only in limited situations foreseen in the law	Three thirds elected in a discretionary way by the president of the republic, the National Assembly and the senate; former presidents of the republicare members ex officio	None	2.53

Source: Castillo (2012), constitutional and legal regulation. Author's own elaboration.

As can be seen in the table, two big groups can be distinguished according to formal guarantees of independence. The group of NHCs with high guarantees of independence consists of institutions with consensual procedures for the appointment of magistrates. This is indeed an extremely relevant institutional feature. The former justice of the Polish Constitutional Court Marek Safjan (2008) identified the appointment of justices as one of the reasons why politics are present in constitutional courts. In general, when more institutions and actors are involved in the nomination of justices, judicial independence increases (Herron and Randazzo, 2003: 426). At the top of the list, the Spanish Constitutional Court and the German Federal Constitutional Court can be found, with consensual procedures of appointment, prohibition of reappointment and long mandates. The institutional design is similar in Latvia, even though here only an absolute majority of the parliament is necessary to appoint justices. In addition, justices in the Belgian Constitutional Court and the Irish Supreme Court enjoy lifetime mandates.

In the group of NHCs with lower guarantees of independence the Czech, Slovak and French ones can be found. The Czech and Slovak courts permit re-appointment of magistrates, which is usually considered an incentive to judicial docility (Garoupa et al, 2008: 3; Herron and Randazzo, 2003: 425), and the president of the republic has a large degree of discretion over appointments. In the case of the French Constitutional Council, members are not required to possess a legal background, the procedure for appointment is scarcely consensual and the length of the mandate of justices is shorter than two presidential terms.

It has to be taken into account that, despite these formal guarantees of independence, political actors enjoy de facto mechanisms of court curbing (Clark, 2009; Kelemen, 2012) which allow them to enjoy a certain degree of control over judicial outcomes (Favoreu, 1994; Hönnige, 2009). The procedure for nomination of justices, capable of creating 'loyalty to the appointer' (Garoupa et al, 2008: 3), is particularly important in this regard. As was recently suggested (Castillo, 2012), a number of scholars have found a certain politicization of courts despite formal guarantees of independence, in particular due to the mechanisms for the appointment of magistrates, for institutions such as the Spanish Constitutional Court (Favoreu, 1994: 115), the German Federal Constitutional Court (Favoreu, 1994: 65; Hönnige, 2009: 972) and the Irish Supreme Court Casey (1987: 239), just to mention a few examples.

In general, this scenario seems to create tension between formal judicial guarantees of independence and links between courts and political actors. More independent courts are expected to be more capable of seeking their own goals, but even in the case of the most independent courts, political actors possessed mechanisms to exercise a certain control over magistrates. Empirical evidence (see Table 7.2) seems to point at a rather complex interaction between these elements, in which more independent

Table 7.2 Correlations between judicial independence and courts' decisions

			Independence
Spearman's rho	Unconstitutionality	Correlation Coefficient	–0.424
		Sig. (two-tailed)	0.090
		N	17
Spearman's rho	*Kompetenz*	Correlation Coefficient	0.552*
		Sig. (two-tailed)	0.022
		N	17

* Correlation is significant at the 0.05 level (two-tailed).

courts did seem to be more prone to pursue their own agenda, but only with regard to those issues which did not contradict the political actors' main preferences.

As can be seen in Table 7.2,[2] the association between judicial independence and declarations of *Kompetenz-Kompetenz* is significant (at the 0.05 level) and is positive; it can be interpreted that more independent courts were more capable of pursuing their own agenda, and thus were more prone to make empowering statements of *Kompetenz-Kompetenz*. The German case may well illustrate how judicial independence is important both in itself and as a proxy of judicial strength in order to explain statements of *Kompetenz-Kompetenz*. Karlsruhe, the most independent court of those studied in this research, is a powerful institution, responsible for the harshest statements of *Kompetenz-Kompetenz* and, to a large extent, for the very creation of the doctrine; indeed, as this chapter will show, other less powerful institutions tried to legitimize their statements of *Kompetenz-Kompetenz* quoting the precedent of this influential court. In turn, the association between judicial independence and courts' declarations of unconstitutionality is non-significant and negative; more independent courts were not more prone to declaring the unconstitutionality of the treaties. The French case may be responsible to a large extent for these results: four out of six declarations of unconstitutionality were made by the least independent court, the French Constitutional Council. It has to be taken into account, however, that this reading of the cases may be conditioned by the epistemological bias derived from the use of bivariate correlations. By turning to qualitative comparative analysis (QCA) in Chapter 8, a complementary approach will be offered. This will be based, not on general trends and associations between 'independent' and 'dependent' variables, but on interactions between explanatory conditions in concrete cases. From the perspective of QCA, when judicial independence interacts with other explanatory conditions, it might be crucial to understand the outcomes of judicial decision making in specific cases.

Courts' Powers to Review EU Secondary Law and the Question of Kompetenz-Kompetenz

Institutional constraints may affect NHCs' decisions in a second way. The absence of mechanisms through which they can review the constitutionality of European Union secondary law may prevent them from declaring their *Kompetenz-Kompetenz*. Dyevre (2013) recently suggested that the French Constitutional Council's limitations in its powers of review may explain why, unlike the German Federal Constitutional Court, the Council has not made statements of *Kompetenz-Kompetenz*. The assumption in this book is that the threat to declare European Union secondary law contrary to the constitution —the doctrine of *Kompetenz-Kompetenz*—is unrealistic and will not be done in the absence of real mechanisms to carry out such review. In this regard, for NHCs to declare the doctrine of the 'ultimate word', two circumstances must occur: the existence of procedures which courts may eventually use to review EU secondary law, and the lack of existence of a generally accepted interpretation of those procedures as excluding the review of European secondary law.

In general, NHCs have at their disposal many ways to carry out assessments of the constitutionality of legislation (for a review in European countries, see Ferreres, 2004). One good example is that of the German Federal Constitutional Court (see *inter alia*, Rupp, 1960; Kommers, 1998). In this institution, three main procedures are available in order to initiate a review before the court (see Stone Sweet, 2002: 86 ff.). The first of them is 'abstract regulation control' – Article 76 ff. of the constitution – according to which the constitutionality of statutes may be assessed 'in abstracto' by the court if one of the actors entitled to initiate the review – political actors such as executives, a number of members of the legislative chambers, Länder, etc. – decides to do so. The second way is 'specific regulation control' – Article 80 ff. of the constitution; in this case, the assessment by the constitutional court is the result of the remission by an ordinary judge of a question on the constitutionality of one of the norms that are to be applied in a case under his or her jurisdiction. The third way is 'constitutional complaint' – Article 90 ff. of the constitution; in this case, it is not political actors or other courts who question the constitutionality of a norm, but citizens who allege the violation of their constitutional rights. Constitutional review of European Union secondary law may be carried out through these procedures, particularly through the two latter ones; constitutional complaint may be particularly useful when citizens claim a violation of any of their constitutional rights by European law, and specific regulation control may allow judges to ask the constitutional court whether European law is contrary to the constitution in concrete cases.

These are the three most common procedures – but not the only ones – to carry out the constitutional review of legislation in the institutions analyzed in this book. One exceptional case is that of the Irish Supreme Court. This institution obviously does not follow the Kelsenian model and thus it displays certain differences vis-à-vis the rest of NHCs. However, in the Irish Supreme Court, equivalents for most of the procedures of constitutional review can be found. An equivalent for abstract regulation control exists for the institution: the president of the republic, before signing a bill, can refer it to the Supreme Court for the assessment of its constitutionality; if the court finds it contrary to the constitution, the bill cannot be signed. In addition, an equivalent for constitutional complaint exists, in that citizens claiming violation of their fundamental rights by a law can bring it before the Supreme Court for the assessment of its constitutionality. No equivalent for specific regulation control exists, though – only the parties can refer bills to the Supreme Court for its review. However, in principle, the powers of review of the Supreme Court are wide enough to permit review of European Union secondary law. Despite this, Article 29.4 of the Irish Constitution, which establishes the pre-eminence of European Union secondary law, is a strong constraint on the court. Still, this provision has not impeded the Irish court from challenging the primacy of EU law in certain cases (see on the *Grogan* case the piece by Colvin, 1991).

Thus, overall, one can observe institutions with wide powers of review, making them capable in principle of reviewing pieces of EU secondary legislation. There are some exceptions, though. The French Constitutional Council was clearly the institution with the most limited powers of review. It is true that the Council had undergone a dramatic empowering evolution in the previous decades. Schnapper (2010) cites the *Liberté d'association* ruling[3] of 1971 and calls it a '*révolution juridique*'. In it, the Council declared the unconstitutionality of a law for the first time. She also mentions the constitutional amendment of 1974, after which sixty deputies or senators are entitled to ask the court to initiate the review of legislation (see also Stone Sweet, 1992). However, despite this, the powers of review of the Council have been clearly limited, at least during the period analyzed by this research, when compared with other NHCs. As Garlicki (2007: 45) put it, 'France is [at that time] the only European country in which constitutional adjudication takes the form, almost exclusively, of a preventive review'. The French Council only enjoyed at the time of the decisions powers equivalent to 'abstract regulation control', and this procedure is scarcely adequate for the assessment of European secondary law given its *ex ante* nature. The powers of the Council have been far from those of the rest of the European courts, particularly those based on a Kelsenian model, for two main reasons: the Council has lacked capacity to initiate the review of legal norms *ex post* – once they have been enacted – and has also lacked capacity to review constitutional complaints. Taking into account that the assessment of European directives or regulations could only take place once they are enacted and generally after a party claims a violation of its constitutional rights by them, the actual possibilities for the Council to review EU secondary law would be clearly limited.

In Belgium the restriction is not a consequence of the regulation of the procedures for constitutional review, but of how these have been interpreted. In this country the most important judicial institutions exclude the possibility to review European Union secondary law. The *Cour de Cassation* has considered that EU secondary law ranks even higher than the constitution,[4] whereas the Council of State grounded in Article 34 of the Belgian Constitution the capacity of European institutions to exercise transferred competences without being bound by the very constitution.[5] Although the Constitutional Court apparently had never explicitly debated the question, some of its rulings could point at a tacit acceptance of the primacy of European Union secondary law even over constitutional provisions.[6] With regard to the interpretations of legal scholars, although some controversy exists around the question, some authors suggest that the Belgian Constitutional Court only has jurisdiction to review the constitutionality of acts adopted by federal or regional parliaments of Belgium (Lejeune, 2010: 124–25). In the opinion of the former president of the *Cour d'arbitrage* – the current constitutional court – Michel Melchior, a direct challenge to the constitutionality of European law would be inadmissible, although the acts assenting to the treaties can be brought before the court. Melchior minimized the possibilities of reviewing the constitutionality of European Union secondary law on European-friendly grounds, particularly taking into account that such solution would involve the violation by Belgium of its international obligations (Claes, 2006: 641).

The Belgian situation is similar to that of Austria, in which a positive attitude of courts towards European integration also can be found (Hiebler, 1999). In Austria, a doctrinal consensus exists around the idea that the review of EU law is outside the powers of review of the constitutional court (Fuch and Lachmayer, 2008: 233), and supremacy of European law would be accepted even over constitutional law (Posh, 2008: 276). However, unlike in the Belgian case, the Austrian Constitutional Court always rejected the claims against EU treaties on formal grounds, so the court never had the chance to approach the question of its *Kompetenz-Kompetenz*.

For those institutions whose powers of review were restricted, *Kompetenz-Kompetenz* was never declared. In other words, having wide powers of review seemed to be a quasi-necessary condition for statements of *Kompetenz-Kompetenz*. However, changes in the constraints faced by the French and Belgian courts may alter this situation. In France, after a constitutional amendment '*de modernisation des institutions de la Vème République*' passed on 23 July 2008 (after the Lisbon decision), the control *ex post* of constitutionality and the possibility for citizens to initiate constitutional complaints have been introduced to the French Constitutional Council (Fabbrini, 2008). After this new empowerment of the Council, will a more demanding attitude by the institution be observed? Will this be the beginning of its membership in the group of courts claiming their 'ultimate word' in European matters?

Interactions between Judicial Decisions

Judicial decisions interact with one another, and previous decisions may condition subsequent ones. This topic has been approached by a number of authors, who have focused on the impact of precedents on judicial behaviour (Lax and Rader, 2010; Richards et al, 2006). But the interaction between judicial decisions may take place in more complex and intricate manners. In this section some of them will be described.

Sequences: Decisions by the Same Court on the Same Treaty

In some occasions, NHCs were asked more than once to review the constitutionality of the same treaty: the French Constitutional Council for the Maastricht Treaty, and the Belgian and Czech constitutional courts for the Lisbon Treaty. In addition, two claims were presented before the Austrian Constitutional Court for the Lisbon Treaty, but both were rejected on formal grounds. In these sequences of rulings, earlier decisions seemed to have an impact on later ones. But instead of creating dynamics of 'path dependency' (Pierson, 2000; Levi, 1997; Stone Sweet, 2004) in which courts persevered in their stances in subsequent rulings, these sequences seemed to incite NHCs to change their behaviour, so that their decisions in later rulings were different from those made in earlier ones. The very fact that an earlier dispute had already been solved seemed to incentive NHCs to decide differently on latter ones.

This variation may be explained by a mix of variables of a legal and political nature. On the one hand, in some cases issues could be already considered *res judicata*: a legal solution to the petition had been already given, and thus another response on the same issue would be neither legally advisable nor necessary. However, against this line of argumentation, the parties could always allege a conflict with the constitution for different reasons or with regard to different constitutional provisions than those put forward on previous cases. On the other hand, political factors could also be part of the explanation for variation in these sequences of cases; as said earlier, courts behave strategically (Boucher and Segal, 1995; Epstein et al, 2001), so once a court has already made what it considers the necessary strategic move on one ruling, it may be pointless to repeat such moves on subsequent ones.

Sometimes variations in NHCs' decisions may be explained through a purely legal and commonsensical approach. This is the case of the French

Constitutional Council. As stated earlier, for the Maastricht Treaty three claims were presented before the Council. In the first of them, the Council declared the unconstitutionality of the treaty; in the second, it declared the treaty's constitutionality; and finally, the third case ended without a substantive decision on the merits. The precedent of the first case played a role in the second one, when the French Constitutional Council noted that the treaty had already been assessed and that a new assessment was only adequate in two situations: in the case that the constitution, once amended, was still contrary to one or more stipulations of the treaty, or in case a new rule had been incorporated into the constitution with the effect of creating an incompatibility with the content of the treaty[7] (Stefanini, 2003). This is the reason why the Council dismissed parts of the petition of the second case on the grounds that they were *res judicata*, such as the infringement by the new Article 8b(1) of the European Community Treaty – the right for EU nationals to vote and stand as a candidate in local elections – of paragraph 3 of the Declaration of Rights of 1789, or the contradiction between the treaty and Articles 3 and 24 of the constitution regarding people's sovereignty and the basic regulation of the legislature. In addition, taking into account the comprehensive review carried out in the first ruling, it is not surprising that the second one found no incompatibilities between the treaty and the constitution.

When the third case was brought before the Council, it declared its lack of competence to assess the constitutionality of a rule passed in referendum: 'direct expression of the national sovereignty'.[8] However, even if the procedure to pass the treaty had been a different one, it would have been difficult for the Council to review its constitutionality for the third time. Something similar happened in the Belgian case, although the Belgian Constitutional Court, unlike the French Constitutional Council, did not underline the fact that the question had already been an object of review in previous cases and limited itself to assess the legitimacy of the questions raised by the claimants. In the second case, the points put forward by the claim were different from those raised in the first complaint, and this permitted the court to make a new assessment of the treaty, whereas in the third ruling, timing impeded a new review on the merits of the case (the appeal had been lodged sixty days after the publication of the law).[9]

In the Czech Lisbon saga, variation in the court's decisions took place with regard to the *Kompetenz-Kompetenz* doctrine. With regard to its decisions on the merits, the question whether a second ruling on the same treaty could be issued was analyzed by the court. The Czech Constitutional Court acknowledged that in its first ruling it had already stated that a new petition for review of the same treaty 'would evidently be barred as regards the now-contested provisions'.[10] But then it moved on to describe the conditions in which the impediment of *res judicata* should apply by saying that in a restrictive understanding it had to involve both an identical provision of the international treaty contested by a petition and simultaneously identical grounds claimed for its conflict with the constitutional order.[11] This restrictive understanding allowed the court to briefly assess the content of the new claim and determine which of its parts could be reviewed, concluding that despite the 'finality, non-changeability, and binding nature of an enforceable decision by the Constitutional Court'[12] there was room for one more ruling on certain questions. In this sense, the fact that unlike in the first case a review of the treaty as a whole – and not just of some provisions – was asked for in the second case seemed to be particularly important for the court to accept a new assessment. This is not to say that the court agreed to review the whole content of the claim: many points, including the five questions by President Klaus, who stated that the court 'did not get a complete and convincing answer to them in the proceeding or later',[13] were finally dismissed.

As was said earlier, it was regarding the question of *Kompetenz-Kompetenz* in which a certain variation between the two rulings existed. In its first ruling on the Lisbon Treaty, the Czech court reflected on the compatibility of Article 10a of its constitution with the treaty; Article 10a par. 1 of the Czech Constitution permits the delegation of only 'certain powers of the bodies of the Czech Republic' to supranational institutions, and therefore an unlimited transfer of sovereignty is prohibited: certain limits exist on the transfer that are to be specified mainly by the legislature[14] (see Bříza, 2009). With this background, the court stated that

> The Constitutional Court of the Czech Republic will (may) also – although in view of the foregoing principles – function as an ultima ratio and may review whether any act of Union bodies exceeded the powers that the Czech Republic transferred to the European Union under Art. 10a of the Constitution. However, the Constitutional Court assumes that such a situation can occur only in quite exceptional cases; these could be, in particular, abandoning the identity of values and, as already cited, exceeding the scope of conferred competences.[15]

Curiously enough, in the second claim, the petitioners placed a greater emphasis on the question of the powers of the Czech Constitutional Court vis-à-vis the Court of Justice of the European Union, giving the Czech court the excuse for a more far-reaching reflection on the question. However, in this occasion, the court decided to water down its approach (Castillo, 2013). In his brief, President Klaus asked the court 'to define in a final list the elements of the "essential core" of the constitutional order, or more precisely of a sovereign democratic state governed by the rule of law',[16] an idea that was rejected by the court which considered it to be a political question (Komarek and editors, 2009: 346). In addition, during the hearings the petitioners argued that Article 19(1) of the treaty made the European Court of Justice 'superior in interpretation of the

"Treaties"' to the Constitutional Court of the Czech Republic'. According to the petitioners (Castillo, 2013), who had quoted the German Lisbon ruling (Slosacik, 2009: 3):

> [I]nterpretation of any supplements or amendments to the Treaty of Lisbon by the European Union Court of Justice will have priority over interpretation of them by the constitutional court of an EU Member State. This applies in the event of the court's decision-making on consistency of an international treaty with the constitution or the constitutional order.[17]

Thus, the claimants were offering the court a golden chance to go further in its doctrine of *Kompetenz-Kompetenz*. But the chance was rejected by the court. Although it incidentally acknowledged the stance taken in Lisbon I,[18] the Czech court limited itself to declare the petition unfounded and to remind that the possibility existed 'of removing any potential inconsistency not only through priority application of norms of Community law, but also through constitutional amendments'[19] (Castillo, 2013).

What is the explanation for this evolution in the court's attitude? Two points have to be stressed. The first of them relates to the sequence of rulings; given that in its first ruling the court had already dealt with the question of its *Kompetenz-Kompetenz* and declared its capacity in an emergency situation to protect its constitution against European Union law, there was no need to repeat such an uncomfortable doctrine again and for the same treaty. This is not to say that since the court had established the doctrine once, it will never state it again; possibly the question will appear again in the future in the rulings of the Czech magistrates. But once for the Lisbon Treaty was probably enough. A second explanation relates precisely to the claim and the claimants; the very fact that the petitioners tried to force the court to insist on the doctrine could have provoked the contrary effect. In this sense, it is worth recalling what Sadurski (2008) called 'reassurance strategy': by using its legal argumentation, a court 'can minimize the costs of creating "winners" and "losers", and establish a high degree of legitimacy for himself'. For instance, according to this approach the Czech court in its first ruling declared the constitutionality of the treaty, but simultaneously partially declared its own *Kompetenz-Kompetenz* in order to placate the most Euro-sceptic sectors. In the second ruling, though, the court seemed to prefer distancing itself from such Euro-sceptic actors; in refusing their rather explicit invitation to mark 'red lines' around European Union secondary law and the ECJ, the court rejected the supporters of Klaus as allies and made clear that despite the doctrinal stance taken on the first ruling, it was not on the side of Euro-scepticism.

The Relation between Decisions on the Merits and Decisions of Kompetenz-Kompetenz

Rulings may be understood as sets of messages addressed to different interlocutors (Tzanakopoulos, 2012). With their decisions on the merits, courts send a message to political actors regarding the possibilities to ratify the treaty. But in addition to decisions on the merits, rulings on European Union treaties included a second kind of message mainly addressed to the Court of Justice: statements of *Kompetenz-Kompetenz*. The doctrine of *Kompetenz-Kompetenz* may be seen as an interpretative strategy by the courts. This kind of strategy has been long used by judiciaries. In his work, French scholar Edouard Lambert (2010 [1921]) explained how from 1883 onwards, the American Supreme Court had been using 'the principle of interpretation' so it had de facto removed from the constitution Section V of the Fourteenth Amendment, thus curtailing the powers of the legislative branch. One century later, NHCs seemed to repeat this smooth move in order to expand their powers in the process of European legal integration, using the 'principle of interpretation' in order to construct the doctrine of *Kompetenz-Kompetenz*.

Decisions on the merits and statements of *Kompetenz-Kompetenz* were not simply two parallel and detached parts of the rulings. On the contrary, NHCs seemed to articulate them together in a more general strategy (Closa, 2013). Paradoxically, they seemed to be replicating the strategy historically used by the Court of Justice against that institution. Alter (1998) has shown how the Court of Luxembourg mobilized in a strategic way both decisions on the merits and interpretative decisions. The aim of the ECJ was to expand the EU legal system 'far from the desire of the member states and beyond their control', and it did so by playing with the different time horizons of politicians 'which translates into different preferences for judges and for politicians regarding the outcome of individual cases'. In its case law, the ECJ developed the principles of direct effect and primacy through its interpretation in rulings whose final decisions on the merits did not challenge political actors' preferences. The best example is probably that of the case *Costa v. ENEL*.[20] It is not only one of the most important landmarks in the evolution of EU law (Stiernstrom, 2005; Joerges, 2006), but also shows the interplay between a national government, an NHC and the European Court of Justice. In the case, an Italian citizen – Mr. Costa – opposed the nationalization of the Italian electricity sector with the argument that it violated the Treaty of Rome, with the Italian justice – *Giudice Conciliatore of Milan* – referring the case to the Italian Constitutional Court and to the European Court of Justice. The Italian Constitutional Court concluded that in the case there was a collision between the Treaty of Rome, incorporated in the Italian legal system in 1958, and the electricity nationalization law enacted in 1962, but that following a chronologic criterion, the second one was to be applied. In response, the European Court of Justice avoided a conflict with the Italian Constitutional Court *with regards to the merits of the case*, by avoiding a declaration that the Italian law violated EC law. But the ECJ used the chance to state that a particular citizen had the ability to raise a point of European Community law against a national government before the courts of that state and insisted on the 'special and original nature' of the European legal system (Kwiecień, 2005: 1481), creating the starting point for the primacy principle (Stein, 1964).

In NHCs' rulings the logic seems to be similar. In only one ruling, NHCs could make simultaneously two moves: their decision on the merits and their 'interpretative decision' of *Kompetenz-Kompetenz*. The hypothesis in this book is that a relation between the two of them exists. Closa (2013) defined this relation in terms of 'strategy': statements of *Kompetenz-Kompetenz* would be one of the strategies followed by NHCs to declare treaties constitutional, whatsoever their reasons to make such a final decision might be. However, from the viewpoint of this book, such a relation goes beyond that: statements of *Kompetenz-Kompetenz* are not simply a *strategy*, but one of the very reasons explaining why courts declared treaties constitutional. Furthermore, the absence of statements of *Kompetenz-Kompetenz* is one of the explanatory conditions for courts' decisions of unconstitutionality. The empirical information supports this idea: every time an NHC declared its *Kompetenz-Kompetenz*, it declared the treaty constitutional (for the Lisbon Treaty, see Castillo, 2013).

If one focuses on the paradigmatic *Maastricht-Urteil* ruling of the German Federal Constitutional Court, a strategy similar to that followed by the European Court of Justice can be found. The German court gave a green light to the ratification of the treaty by declaring its constitutionality, but at the same time it declared its own *Kompetenz-Kompetenz* in the interpretative part of the ruling. In so doing, it satisfied the short-term preferences of political actors – unproblematic ratification of the treaty – but it also satisfied its own long-term preferences – empowerment. The argumentation in the *Maastricht-Urteil* ruling has to be interpreted as a form of conditionality – nonetheless, it was called '*Solange* III' (Makowski, 1995) – and understood as a transaction. The doctrine of *Kompetenz-Kompetenz* seems to counter-balance the temptation of European institutions to act beyond the conferred powers. According to the ruling, the German court would declare contrary to the constitution European Union secondary law adopted *ultra-vires* or violating constitutional rights of German citizens, so the German state could be deemed to remain sovereign despite the transfer of power (MacCormick, 1995; Baquero, 2008). In this sense, the subtle message by the German court is not that the treaty is declared constitutional *despite* the critical argumentation that culminated in the statement of *Kompetenz-Kompetenz*, but precisely *because* of that critical argumentation. As Schorkopf (2009: 1119) put it, the Lisbon Treaty was found 'compatible with the Basic Law (. . .) so long as it is applied within the framework outlined by the Federal Constitutional Court'. In other words, the treaty was declared constitutional as long as it was interpreted as respecting the *Kompetenz-Kompetenz* of the German state, and as long as the German Federal Constitutional Court could ensure it in the future. Declarations of constitutionality of the treaty and statements of *Kompetenz-Kompetenz* were two sides of the same coin; they came together in the same judicial pack.

What is more striking is that this combination of statements of *Kompetenz-Kompetenz* and declarations of constitutionality is found in the rest of the rulings. Not only the Maastricht and Lisbon rulings of the German Federal Constitutional Court, but also the Spanish Constitutional Treaty ruling and the Czech Lisbon I ruling, and even the Polish and Latvian Lisbon rulings, combine harsh or soft approaches to the doctrine *Kompetenz-Kompetenz* with declarations of constitutionality. Schönberger (2009: 1201) has underlined the legal paradox underlying combinations of statements of *Kompetenz-Kompetenz* and declarations of constitutionality on the merits in rulings such as *Lissabon-Urteil*: 'There is probably no other judgment in the history of the Karlsruhe Court in which the argument is so much at odds with the actual result.' However, empirical information seems to insist that such an association is particularly frequent. It could be said that the doctrine of *Kompetenz-Kompetenz* allowed NHCs to declare European treaties constitutional by giving them a role 'as masters and controllers of the process' (Closa, 2013: 112) capable of ensuring the prevalence of their national constitution even once the treaty was entered into force. In addition, only when the doctrine of *Kompetenz-Kompetenz* was absent from the rulings did courts dare to declare treaties unconstitutional. Finally, it is important to note that statements of *Kompetenz-Kompetenz* should not only be seen as an auxiliary justification for decisions on the merits, a mere judicial 'strategy' (Closa, 2013) that courts could decide whether to use or not. Instead, statements of *Kompetenz-Kompetenz* have their own causation and are not the result of an unconstrained judicial decision, but the result of the interplay of different explanatory conditions, and at the same time such statements have explanatory capacity when accounting for courts' decisions on the merits.

Cross-fertilization: The Leading Role of Karlsruhe

The history of European legal integration is partly a history of conflict, a history which began with the doctrines of supremacy and direct effect of the Court of Justice, and in which NHCs had more to lose than to win. As Stone Sweet (2004: 22) said,

> It is also clear that positive incentives "to play the Eurolaw game" do not apply to all judges (. . .) National constitutional courts have good reasons to resist the development of a European "constitutional" order that might subsume the national order.

As suggested by Stone Sweet, not all NHCs have been enthusiastic about the evolution of European Union law, and some of them have tried to resist the principles developed by the ECJ. In this subsection, I will try to show that the position of NHCs in this regard has been the result of processes of informal coordination between courts in such a way that decisions by some courts were observed and imitated by other ones, thus creating dynamics of European constitutional cross-fertilization.

The history of European legal integration could be divided into three phases, which partially, but not exactly, correspond with those put forward by Weiler (1991). In the first phase, the European Court of Justice began to develop the principles that today structure European Union law, such as primacy and direct effect. In the second phase, NHCs slowly began to accept those principles. In the third phase, though, some NHCs started to show signs of resistance, which materialized in the *Kompetenz-Kompetenz* doctrine. European judicial politics have slowly evolved from the first to the second and then to the third phase. Hjalte Rasmussen (2000: 378–79) already had an intuition about this evolution and summarized the situation by asserting that

> during the first 25 years or so of the EC Treaty, a recurrent theme of numerous meetings of specialists in Community law was this: how long will it take before the Member States acknowledge that they have to accept unconditionally the supremacy of Community law over their own constitutions? (. . .) By the end of the 20th Century, the diametrically opposed question has come into currency. At this point in Community history it is regularly asked when Community law and its Court will acknowledge that most state constitutional provisions remain, as a matter of principle, forbidden land for Community law's claim to an exception-free supremacy for the Treaty and all the laws deriving thereof.

The first phase of European judicial dialogue begins with the creation of the core principles of European legal order by the Court of Luxembourg (see Weiler, 1991; Mayer, 2005). In 1963, in *Van Gend and Loos*, the European Court of Justice declared that European Union law that creates rights for individuals is directly enforceable before national courts if it is sufficiently precise, clear and unconditional:[21] it was the birth of the doctrine of direct effect (Craig, 1992; Eleftheriadis, 1996; von Bogdandy, 2008: 397). Soon after that, in *Costa v. ENEL*, the Court of Justice established the principle of primacy (Reestman, 2005) by stating that European Union law enjoys precedence over national law when enacted within the scope of powers of the European Union.[22] Considering this background, from the 1970s onwards, the European Court of Justice detailed and extended its doctrine in cases like *Van Duyn*,[23] *Simmenthal*,[24] *Marshall*,[25] *Foto-Frost*,[26] etc.

On the other side of the equation, however, one finds NHCs. If the European Court of Justice had been able to develop its doctrine thanks to the collaboration of national lower courts and the procedure of preliminary reference (Maher, 1994; Weiler, 1999), it found it more difficult to convince NHCs to accept the newly created principles of European Union law. The principles of direct effect and supremacy, in addition to the powers of review of the European Court of Justice, marked the end of the interpretative monopoly of constitutional courts across Europe. The paradigmatic example of this resistance against the doctrine of the European Court of Justice is the national 'side' of the *Costa/Enel* decision (see Del Duca and Mortillaro, 1999). The Italian Constitutional Court refused the primacy of European Union law on the grounds that the European Community treaties had been passed through Italian statutory law and, therefore, could not have priority over other rules of the same hierarchical level.[27] This attitude, however, soon began to be abandoned by NHCs. Slowly, one by one, many NHCs began to accept the doctrines of supremacy and direct effect (Kumm and Ferreres, 2005: 473), along with the rest of their implications, even if they based their approach on their internal constitutional law. In *Le Ski* in 1971, the Belgian *Cour de Cassation* accepted the principles of direct effect and supremacy[28] (Dehousse, 2000). In Italy, the decision in *Frontini Franco* partially reversed the previous case law of the Italian Constitutional Court. The Italian court asserted the separation between the European and Italian legal systems and accepted the doctrines of primacy and direct effect on the basis of Article 11 of the Italian Constitution, although in case of conflict (Rossi, 2008: 66), lower courts were expected to send the question to the Italian Constitutional Court for a decision on the matter[29] (La Pergola and Del Duca, 1985). In France, the principles of direct effect and primacy were accepted in the *Jacques Vabre* decision[30] (Dutheil de la Rochère, 1998). The principles created by the ECJ would soon become part of the legal common sense of the European NHCs. As for those countries that joined the Communities when the principles of primacy and direct effect had already been asserted by the European Court, de Witte (2011: 349–50) considers that they implicitly accepted the doctrine of the ECJ along with the *acquis communautaire* at the time of their accession.

Wondering how it was possible that the doctrinal construction of the European Court of Justice was accepted by national courts, Weiler (1999: 32–33) pointed, among other reasons, to a snowball effect:

> Once some of the highest courts of a few of the Member States endorsed the new constitutional construct, their counterparts in other Member States heard more arguments that those courts should do the same, and it became more difficult for national courts to resist the trend with any modicum of credibility.

This reading points to two important elements. First, a European network of NHCs, mutually observing and learning from one another, had been created. Second, these NHCs now needed coordination. When some of them began to accept the doctrine of the European Court of Justice, the judicial 'common sense' started to change in favour of the Court of Luxembourg. The principles of primacy and direct effect were no longer an exotic construction, unacceptable from the viewpoint of internal constitutional law; after they had gained the respect of some NHCs, they gained also legitimacy in the eyes of the rest of them.

In the third stage, however, things began to change, and NHCs began to show new signs of resistance. It is true that there was always a certain tension between the European Court of Justice and NHCs, since the latter did not generally accept the 'intrinsic primacy' of European law (Giorgi and Triart, 2008) and grounded it in their internal constitutional law. But the *Solange* decisions (Rossi, 2008: 67; Rosenfeld, 2008: 419; Sadurski, 2008: 1) clearly constitute a landmark in the evolution of the European judicial dialogue, which were later on complemented with the *Kompetenz-Kompetenz* doctrine. Although the trend had been until that moment one of expansion of the powers of the European Court of Justice and of acceptance of its doctrine, the doctrinal stance of the German court created a limit on these widening powers (Weiler, 2002). With it, Karlsruhe apparently wanted to recover some of its lost powers and set a limit on the primacy of European Union law. The stance of the German court was a brake on the expansionist approach of the European Court of Justice and would soon find an echo in the rulings of other NHCs, in a process of so-called 'Solange contagion' (Davies, 2012: 428). In my view, the same characteristics that featured the process of acceptance by NHCs of the doctrine of the Court of Luxembourg – mutual observation, slow mutation of the judicial common sense, cross-fertilization, etc. – also played a role when these courts decided to resist the doctrine of the European Court of Justice. Although the authorship of the *Kompetenz-Kompetenz* doctrine is commonly attributed to the German Federal Constitutional Court, the fact is that it should be considered a collaborative project, in which more courts – and particularly, the Italian Constitutional Court – had a role (see Kumm and Ferreres, 2005: 474, Kumm, 2005:2 64; Sadurski, 2008: 5). This challenge to the European Court of Justice was thus the result of slow, incremental and somehow informally coordinated case law by national courts.

The origins of the resistance by NHCs can be traced back to the *Frontini Franco* ruling of the Italian Constitutional Court, which developed the doctrine of *controlimiti*. Although the court accepted in this decision the precedence of community law, it did so on the basis of Article 11 of its national constitution. Accordingly, the core of the Italian Constitution and the fundamental rights of citizens constituted a red line to be respected by EU law, and thus the very treaties themselves could be, in an exceptional situation, an object of review, with occasion of an act of secondary law (Claes, 2006: 502–03). This approach was confirmed, even radicalized, in the *Fragd* ruling[31] in which the court 'went so far as to state that it could control the consistency of individual rules of EC law with the fundamental principles of the Italian Constitution, particularly (but not only) in the field of human rights' (De Witte, 2011: 353). Meanwhile, the German Federal Constitutional Court started its *Solange* saga (see Reich, 1996; Rosenfeld, 2008), with its steps forward (*Solange I*)[32] and backward (*Solange II*).[33] The fact is that this background seemed to pave the way for the *Maastricht-Urteil* ruling: *Kompetenz-Kompetenz* was not a sudden and unexpected doctrine, but a new episode of a sequence taking place not only in Germany but also, at least, in Italy (see Mayer, 2003; Krämer, 2010: 18). Furthermore, *Maastricht-Urteil* was not even the last episode. In its Maastricht decision the Danish *Højesteret*[34] backed the *Kompetenz-Kompetenz* doctrine by importing it into Denmark (Lachmann, 1998; Harck and Olsen, 1999; Follesdal, 2010). It considered that European law violating the fundamental rights of Danish citizens would be unconstitutional and that the powers transferred to the European Union only allowed for legislation passed within the scope of those powers, with Danish courts having the capacity to review whether community secondary legislation respected the limits of the competences surrendered (Claes, 2006: 625). This reception of the *Kompetenz-Kompetenz* doctrine meant that the German decision was much more than an extraordinary episode soon to be forgotten; far from being a marginal and recalcitrant doctrine, the legal discourse of Karlsruhe found its echo in the Danish Supreme Court. *Kompetenz-Kompetenz* had found its confirmation in the legal argumentation of another court. From that moment onwards, it would no longer be unthinkable for another court in Europe to pose a similar challenge to the European Court of Justice.

The core idea under this narrative is that some courts' statements of *Kompetenz-Kompetenz* played a role as a precedent for subsequent ones. The more courts that had already claimed their right to a 'last word', the more legitimacy other courts would feel they had to repeat the move. Precedent could be used by NHCs in other countries as a basis for their own decisions in a process of cross-fertilization (see Jacobs, 2003). For instance, when the German Federal Constitutional Court issued its Lisbon ruling, Baquero (2010: 19) warned that 'the judgment could have a domino effect on other constitutional courts, especially those of those countries most affected by the prestige of German public law organs'. Once again, Baquero's intuition was confirmed by the facts. In their rulings, NHCs not only referred to their own previous case law, but also to the case law of other European counterparts – with a special emphasis on that of Karlsruhe – which they acknowledge as a source of inspiration. As Gelter and Siems (2012) said, '[C]ross-citations can show to what extent courts use foreign law as a justification for a judicial decision'.

In its first ruling on Lisbon, for instance, the Czech Constitutional Court drew explicitly on the doctrine of the German Federal Constitutional Court (Bříza, 2009: 159; Castillo, 2013). The Czech court stated that '[i]n the case law of other constitutional courts – which we can take as inspiration – we can consider fundamental especially the decision of the German Federal Constitutional Court (GCC), Solange II and the Maastricht decision'[35] and then moved on to explain the German doctrine in two long and comprehensive paragraphs, including the question of *Kompetenz-Kompetenz*. However, this was just an introduction before further comments on other NHCs' approaches. Curiously enough, the Czech court not only summarized the stances of its counterparts, but also reflected on them, showing its agreement with the critical attitude of other courts but also sometimes watering down the tone (see Wendel, 2011: 137). It is worth mentioning that, in turn, the German court also referred to the Czech doctrine in its ruling,[36] albeit in a more discrete manner, thus completing a scenario of mutual observation (Niedobitek, 2009: 1273). The Czech court also referred to the Polish doctrine in terms of the possibility of ruling out the jurisdiction of the European Court of Justice to evaluate the conferral of competences on the European Union, although the Czech court considered that '[a]lthough, in terms of the dogmatics of domestic constitutional law, we can agree with that conclusion to a certain extent, it is questionable whether it is necessary to formulate it as sharply as the Tribunal did'.[37] Still, it must be made clear that the main focus of attention of the Czech court is the German doctrine of *Kompetenz-Kompetenz*, of which the Czech Constitutional Court offers a soft interpretation:

> The Maastricht decision meant a qualitative shift; however, we can obviously agree with the opinion that the Federal Constitutional Court's Maastricht doctrine (*Kompetenz-Kompetenz*) is more in the nature of a potential warning, but need not ever be used in practice.[38]

The practice of referring to the rulings of other NHCs was taken even more seriously by the Polish Constitutional Court (see Wendel, 2011: 137), which in its Lisbon decision devoted one part of the ruling to summarizing the rest of decisions on the treaty by its Czech, German, Hungarian, French, Latvian and Austrian counterparts.[39] The thorough systematization carried out by the Polish court merits attention as a comprehensive approach to the topic, closer to academic doctrinal studies than to usual court rulings. Similarly, a reference to the German case law can be found in the Latvian ruling; even if only incidental and intended to distance itself from its German counterpart,[40] the quotation showed the salience of the German doctrine in other countries and the fact that the Latvian court was taking note of what was happening in Karlsruhe. Finally, a general reference to similar rulings by other NHCs is made by the Spanish Constitutional Court in its Constitutional Treaty declaration, in which the court refers to 'well-known decisions by constitutional courts in some states, in the so-called doctrine of the dialogue between constitutional courts and the European Court of Justice'[41] (see Castillo de la Torre, 2005).

This series of cross-references highlights two issues. First, NHCs were aware of the decisions of their counterparts on the same treaties, and they saw their own ruling as just one more in a longer series of rulings about European primary law. Second, the influence of rulings by other NHCs, and particularly that of the often-quoted rulings of the German Federal Constitutional Court, is manifest. This influence is sometimes made explicit and used as a basis for courts' own legal argumentation. In general, precedents of *Kompetenz-Kompetenz* by other courts, and particularly that of the *Maastricht-Urteil* decision, seemed to play a role in subsequent repetitions of the doctrine by other NHCs. Courts knew that their counterparts were adopting an empowering interpretation of their capacity to enforce their own constitution even against European Union secondary law and, led by Karlsruhe, they probably felt tempted or obliged to join in. In his influential theory of counterpunctual law Maduro (2003: 42) stated that for the European legal system to be a coherent plural legal system horizontal – and not only vertical – coherence was also necessary, so that NHCs should be aware of the decisions of one another and accommodate their rulings accordingly. The paradox is that the best example of this European cross-national process of observation between national courts has been constructed precisely around the conflict with the European Court of Justice, with the *Kompetenz-Kompetenz* doctrine at its core.

Conclusions

The judicial field has its own dynamics. NHCs did not only seem to interact with political or legal variables, but their behaviour seemed to a large extent influenced also by phenomena occurring in the judicial field. On the one hand, the design of the institution with regard both to judicial independence and courts' powers of review imposed constraints on courts' behaviour and was particularly useful in explaining statements of *Kompetenz-Kompetenz*. On the other hand, the interaction between decisions played an important role in judicial behaviour: courts' former decisions explained variation in subsequent ones, statements of *Kompetenz-Kompetenz* seemed to condition courts' decisions on the merits and some NHCs' decisions were imitated by other institutions in processes of cross-fertilization. This discovery demonstrates that accounts of courts' behaviour must go beyond two oversimplified explanations: the legalist one, according to which courts simply apply the law to the cases, and the political one, according to which only political variables matter.

Although each of these two explanations partially account for judicial behaviour, both of them have to be combined with variables that relate to the very internal dynamics of the judicial field, which constrains actors by imposing many of the rules of the game.

The review of separate 'independent variables' ends here. So far this book has tried to make a thorough description of the cases in their different dimensions and to provide for a better understanding of many patterns explaining judicial behaviour. But one more thing needs to be done: trying to understand the interaction between all these different explanations of courts' decisions. In the next chapter, with the help of QCA, this will be done.

Notes

1 See the final appendix for specification of operationalization.
2 Spearman's rho coefficient was used, as the variables did not follow a normal distribution. Operationalization of the variables is described in the methodological appendix.
3 French Constitutional Council, decision DC 71–44.
4 Belgian *Cour de Cassation*, case S.02.0039.N. of 2 June 2003.
5 Council of State, legislative division, legal opinion n° 37.954/AV, 15 February 2005 (*European Constitution*), *Doc. Parl.*, Senate, 2004–2005, n° 3–1091/1, pp. 526–546; Council of State, legislative division, legal opinion n° 44.028/AV (*Lisbon Treaty*), *Doc. Parl.* Senate, 2007–2008, n° 4–568/1, p. 343.
6 Belgian Constitutional Court, judgment n° 130/2010 of 9 December 2010.
7 French Constitutional Council, Decision No.92–312 (*Maastricht II*), paragraph 5.
8 French Constitutional Council, Decision No. 93–313 (*Maastricht III*), paragraph 5.
9 Belgian Constitutional Court, Decision 156/2009 (*Lisbon III*), paragraph B.2.
10 Czech Constitutional Court, decision PL. ÚS 29/09 (*Lisbon II*), paragraph 96.
11 Czech Constitutional Court, decision PL. ÚS 29/09 (*Lisbon II*), paragraph 97.
12 Czech Constitutional Court, decision PL. ÚS 29/09 (*Lisbon II*), paragraph 99.
13 Czech Constitutional Court, decision PL. ÚS 29/09 (*Lisbon II*), paragraph 103.
14 Czech Constitutional Court, decision PL. ÚS 29/09 (*Lisbon II*), paragraph 109.
15 Czech Constitutional Court, decision PL. ÚS 29/09 (*Lisbon II*), paragraph 120.
16 Czech Constitutional Court, decision PL. ÚS 29/09 (*Lisbon II*), paragraph 69.
17 Czech Constitutional Court, decision PL. ÚS 29/09 (*Lisbon II*), paragraph 88.
18 Czech Constitutional Court, decision PL. ÚS 29/09 (*Lisbon II*), paragraph 150.
19 Czech Constitutional Court, decision PL. ÚS 29/09 (*Lisbon II*), paragraph 172.
20 *Costa v. Ente Nazionale per L'Energia Elettrica (ENEL)*, ECJ Case 6/64 (1964).
21 *NV Algemene transport: en expeditie onderneming Van Gend & Loos v. Nederlandse administratie der belastingen*, ECJ case 26/62.
22 *Costa v. Ente Nazionale per L'Energia Elettrica (ENEL)*, ECJ Case 6/64.
23 *Yvone van Duyn v. Home Office*, ECJ Case 41/74.
24 *Administrazione delle finanze dello stato v. Spa Simmenthal*, ECJ Case 106/77.
25 *M. H. Marshall v. Southampton and South-West Hapshire Area Health Authority*, ECJ Case 152/84.

26 *Foto-Frost v. Hauptzollamt Lübeck-Ost*, ECJ Case 214/85.
27 Italian Constitutional Court, decision 15/64 of 24 February 1964, *Costa v. ENEL*.
28 Belgian *Cour de Cassation*, decision of 27 May 1971, *SA Fromagerie franco-suisse Le Ski*.
29 Italian Constitutional Court, decision 183/73 of 27 December 1973, *Frontini*.
30 French *Cour de Cassation*, decision of 25 May 1975, *Société des cafés Jacques Vabre*.
31 Italian Constitutional Court, decision of 23 April 1989, *S.p.a. Fragd v. Amministrazione delle Finanze*.
32 German Constitutional Court, decision of 29 May 1974, *Internationale Handelsgesellschaft* (Solange I).
33 German Constitutional Court, decision of 22 October 1986, *Wünsche Handelsgesellschaft* (Solange II).
34 Danish Supreme Court, decision of 6 April 1998, Treaty of Maastricht, UfR 1998, 800. The ruling of the Danish Supreme Court assesses the constitutionality of the Maastricht Treaty. However, the proceedings before the court began when the treaty was already ratified, so it is not included in the object of study of this research in a strict sense. However, although this ruling is excluded from the core of the analysis, it, of course, has to be included as part of the more general explanation.
35 Czech Constitutional Court, decision PL. Ús 19/08 (*Lisbon I*), paragraph 116.
36 German Federal Constitutional Court, decision 2 be 2/08 et al. (*Lisbon*), paragraph 338.
37 Czech Constitutional Court, decision PL. ÚS, 19/09 (*Lisbon I*), paragraph 139.
38 Czech Constitutional Court, decision PL. ÚS, 19/09 (*Lisbon I*), paragraph 139.
39 Polish Constitutional Court, decision K32/09 of 24 November 2010 (*Lisbon*), part 3.
40 'The summoned person, dr.iur. Aivars Endziņš, a professor at the Department of Public Law at the School of Business Administration, "Turība," noted that sovereignty cannot be restricted or limited otherwise, i.e., "sovereignty either exists or not". Unlike, for example, the Federal Republic of Germany, the Republic of Latvia has provided that sovereignty exists and it is associated with the right to "final say" that is provided in Article 68 (2) of the Satversme'. Latvian Constitutional Court, decision 2008–35–01 (Lisbon), part 6.
41 Spanish Constitutional Court, declaration 1/2004 (Constitutional Treaty), part II.3.

References

Alter, K. (1998) 'Who are the "masters of the treaty"?: European governments and the European Court of Justice', *International Organization* 52(1):121–47.

Baquero, J. (2008), 'The legacy of the Maastricht-Urteil and the pluralist movement', *European Law Journal* 14(4): 389–422.

Baquero, J. (2010) 'A judicial Götterdämmerung. The Lisbon decision of the German Constitutional Court', in Auel, K. and Baquero, J., *Karlruhe's Europe*, Notre Europe Studies and Research 78, at: www.notreeurope.eu/uploads/tx_publication/Etud78-Karlsruhe_sEurope-en_01.pdf (15.02.2015).

Boucher, R. and Segal, J. (1995) 'Supreme Court justices as strategic decision makers: Aggressive grants and defensive denials on the Vinson court', *The Journal of Politics* 57(3): 824–37.

Bříza, P. (2009) 'The Czech Republic. The constitutional court on the Lisbon Treaty. Decision of 26 November 2008', *European Constitutional Law Review* 5(1): 143–64.

Bühlmann, M. and Kunz, R. (2011) 'Confidence in the judiciary: Comparing the independence and legitimacy of judicial systems', *West European Politics* 34(2): 317–45.

Casey, J. (1987), *Constitutional Law in Ireland*, London: Sweet & Maxwell.

Castillo, P. (2012), '"Guardar al defensor de la Constitución" Sobre la indepedencia de la jurisdicción constitutional : Evaluación de alternativas institucionales', *Estudio de Progreso 69/2012*, Madrid: Fundación Alternativas.

Castillo, P. (2013) 'Playing the judicial card. Litigation strategies during the process of ratification of the Lisbon Treaty', *European Law Journal* 20(5): 630–48.

Castillo de la Torre, F., (2005) 'Tribunal Constitucional (Spanish Constitutional Court), opinion 1/2004 of 13 December 2004, on the treaty establishing a constitution for Europe', *Common Market Law Review* 42(4): 1169–1202.

Claes, M. (2006) *The National Courts Mandate in the European Constitution*, Oxford: Oxford University Press.

Claes, M. and de Visser, M. (2012) 'Are you networked yet ? On dialogues in European judicial networks', *Utrech Law Review* 8(1): 100–14.

Clark, T. (2009) 'The separation of powers, court curbing, and judicial legitimacy', *American Journal of Political Science* 53(4): 971–989.

Closa, C. (2013) 'National higher courts and the ratification of European Union treaties', *West European Politics* 36(1): 97–121.

Colvin, C. (1991) '*Society for the Protection of Unborn Children (Ireland) Ltd. v. Grogan*: Irish abortion law and the free movement of services in the European Community', *Fordham International Law Journal* 15(2): 476–526.

Craig, P. (1992) 'Once upon a time in the West: Direct effect and the federalization of EEC Law', *Oxford Journal of Legal Studies* 12(4): 453–79.

Davies, B. (2012) 'Pushing back: What happens when member states resist the European Court of Justice? A multi-modal approach to the history of European law', *Contemporary European History* 21(3): 417–35.

De Witte, B. (2011) 'Direct Effect, Primacy and the Nature of the Legal Order' in Craig, P. and De Búrca, G. *The Evolution of EU Law*, Oxford: Oxford University Press, pp. 323–62.

Del Duca, P. and Mortillaro D. (1999) 'The maturation of Italy's response to European Community law: Electric and telecommunication sector institutional innovations', *Fordham International Law Journal* 23(3): 536–605.

Dehousse, R. (2000) 'L'Europe par le droit: plaidoyer pour une approche contextuelle', *Politique européenne* 2000/1(1): 63–83.

Dutheil de la Rochère, J. (1998) 'Les implications constitutionnelles pour un État de la participation à un processus d'intégration régional', *Revue International de droit comparé* 50(2): 577–93.

Dyevre, A. (2013) 'European integration and national courts: defending sovereignty under institutional constraints?', *European Constitutional Law Review* 9(1): 139–68.

Eleftheriadis, P. (1996) 'The direct effect of community law: Conceptual issues', *Yearbook of European Law* 16(1): 205–21.

Epstein, L., Knight, J. and Martin, A. D. (2001) 'The Supreme Court as a strategic national policymaker', *Emory Law Journal* 50: 583–611.

Fabbrini, F. (2008) 'Kelsen in Paris: France's constitutional reform and the introduction of a posteriori constitutional review of legislation', *German Law Journal* 9(10): 1297–1312.

Favoreu, L. (1994) *Los Tribunales Constitucionales*, Barcelona: Ariel.

Ferejohn, J., Rosenbluth, F., and Shipan, C., (2004), 'Comparative judicial politics', at www.yale.edu/polisci/rosenbluth/Papers/comparative%20judicial%20 politics.pdf (16.10.2011).

Ferreres, V. (2004) 'The European model of constitutional review of legislation: Toward decentralization?', *International Journal of Constitutional Law* 2(3):461–91.

Follesdal, A. (2010) 'Normative political theory and the European Union', at http://papers.ssrn.com/sol3/papers.cfm?abstract_id=1704462 (11.07.2012).

Fuch C. and Lachmayer, K. (2008) 'European Community law in Austria', *International Constitutional Law Journal* 2(4): 233–34.

Garlicki, L. (2007) 'Constitutional courts versus supreme courts', *International Journal of Constitutional Law* 5(1): 44–68.

Garoupa, N., Grembi V. and Amaral Garcia, S. (2008) 'Judicial independence and party politics in the Kelsenian constitutional courts: The case of Portugal', *University of Illinois College of Law, Law and Economics Working Papers*, Paper 95.

Gelter, M. and Siems, M. (2012), 'Networks, dialogue or one-way traffic? An empirical analysis of cross-citations between ten of Europe's highest Courts', *Utrecht Law Review* 8(2): 88–99.

Giorgi, F. and Triart, N. (2008) 'National judges, community judges: Invitation to a journey through the looking glass: On the need for jurisdictions to rethink the inter-systemic relations beyond the hierarchical principle', *European Law Journal* 14(6): 693–717.

Hall, P. and Taylor R. C. R. (1996) 'Political science and the three new institutionalisms', *MPIfG Discussion Paper 99/6* Cologne: Max Planck Institute for the Study of Societies.

Harck, S. and Parlmer Olsen, H. (1999) 'Decision concerning the Maastricht Treaty. 1998 Ugeskrift for Retsvaesen, H 800', *The American Journal of International Law* 93(1): 209–14.

Herron, E. S. and Randazzo, K. A. (2003) 'The relationship between independence and judicial review in post-communist courts', *Journal of Politics* 65(2): 422–38.

Hiebler, U. (1999) 'Austria's accession to the European Union: Impacts on the national legal order', *Journal of International Relations and Development* 2(2): 187–215.

Hönnige, C. (2009) 'The electoral connection: How the pivotal judge affects oppositional success at European constitutional courts', *West European Politics* 32(5): 963–48.

Jacobs, F. (2003) 'Judicial dialogue and the cross-fertilization of legal systems: The European Court of Justice', *Texas International Law Journal* 38(3): 547–57.

Joerges, C. (2006) '"Deliberative political processes" revisited: What have we learnt about the legitimacy of supranational decision-making', *Journal of Common Market Studies* 44(4): 779–802.

Kelemen, D. (2012) 'The political foundations of judicial independence in the European Union', *Journal of European Public Policy* 19(1): 43–58.

Komarek, J. and editors (2009) 'The Czech Constitutional Court's second decision on the Lisbon Treaty of 3 November 2009', *European Constitutional Law Review* 5(3): 345–52.

Kommers, D. P., (1998) 'The Federal Constitutional Court in the German political system', *Journal of Theoretical Politics* 26(4): 470–91.

Krämer, R. (2010) 'Looking through Different Glasses at the Lisbon Treaty: The German Constitutional Court and the Czech Constitutional Court', in Fischer-Lescano, A., Joerges, C. and Wonka, A. *The German Constitutional Court's Lisbon Ruling: Legal and Political Science Perspectives*, ZERP Diskussionapapier 1/2010, at www.mpifg.de/people/mh/paper/ZERP%20Discussion%20Paper%201.2010.pdf (12.06.2012).

Kumm, M. (2005) 'The jurisprudence of constitutional conflict: Constitutional supremacy in Europe before and after the Constitutional Treaty', *European Law Journal* 11(3): 262–307.

Kumm, M. and Ferreres, V. (2005) 'The primacy clause of the Constitutional Treaty and the future of constitutional conflict in the European Union', *International Journal of Constitutional Law* 3(2–3): 473–92.

Kwiecień, R., (2005) 'The primacy of European Union Law over national law under the Constitutional Treaty', *German Law Journal* 6(11): 1479–69.

La Pergola, A. and Del Duca, P. (1985) 'Community law, international law and the Italian Constitution', *American Journal of International Law*, 79(3): 598–621.

Lachmann, P. (1998) 'The Treaty of Maastricht vs. the Danish Constitution', *Nordic Journal of International Law* 68: 365–68.

Lambert, E. (2010 [1921]) *El Gobierno de los Jueces*, Madrid: Tecnos.

Lax, J., and Rader, K. T. (2010) 'Legal constraints in Supreme Court decision making: Do jurisprudencial regimes exist?', *The Journal of Politics* 72(2): 273–84.

Lejeune, Y. (2010) *Droit Constitutionnel Belge. Fondements et institutions*, Brussels: Larcier.

Levi, M. (1997) 'A Model, a Method, and a Map: Rational Choice in Comparative and Historical Analysis', in Lichbach M. and Zuckerman, A., *Comparative Politics: Rationality, Culture and Structure*, Cambridge: Cambridge University Press, pp. 19–41.

MacCormick, N. (1995) 'The Maastricht-Urteil: Sovereignty now', *European Law Journal* 1(3): 259–66.

Maduro, M. (2003) 'Las formas del poder constitucional de la Unión Europea', *Revista de Estudios Políticos* 119: 11–55.

Maher, I. (1994) 'National courts as European Community courts', *Legal Studies* 14(2): 226–43.

Makowski, K. (1995) 'Solange III: The German Federal Constitutional Court's decision on accession to the Maastricht Treaty on European Union', *University of Pennsylvania Journal of International Business Law* 16(1): 155–79.

Mayer, F. C. (2003) 'The European Constitution and the courts. Adjudicating European constitutional law in a multilevel system', Walter Hallstein Institut Paper 15/03, at www.whi-berlin.de/documents/whi-paper1503.pdf (20.05.2012).

Mayer, F. C. (2005) 'Supremacy – Lost? – Comment on Roman Kwiecién', *German Law Journal* 6(11): 1497–1506.

Niedobitek, M. (2009) 'The Lisbon case of 30 June 2009 – A comment from the European law perspective', *German Law Journal* 10(8): 1267–76.

Pierson, P. (2000) 'Increasing returns, path dependency, and the study of politics', *The American Political Science Review* 94(2): 251–67.

Posch, A. (2008) 'Community law and Austrian constitutional law', *International Constitutional Law Journal* 2(4): 272–283.

Rasmussen, H. (2000) 'Confrontation or Peaceful Co-existence? On the Danish Supreme Court's Maastricht Ratification Judgment', in O'Keeffe, D. *Judicial Review in European Union Law*, The Hague: Kluwer Law International, pp. 377–90.

Redher, B. (2007) 'What is political about jurisprudence? Courts, politics, and political science in Europe and the United States', MPIfG Discussion Paper, Max Planck Institute for the Study of Society, Cologne (Germany).

Reestman, J.-H. (2005) 'Primacy of union law', *European Constitutional Law Review* 1(1): 104–07.

Reich, N. (1996) 'Judge-made Europe á la carte: Some remarks on recent conflicts between European and German constitutional law provoked by the banana litigation', *European Journal of International Law* 7(1):103–07.

Richards, M.J. and Kritzer, H.M. (2002) 'Jurisprudencial regimes in the Supreme Court decision making', *American Political Science Review* 96(2): 305–20.

Richards, M.J., Smith, J.L. and Kritzer, H.M. (2006) 'Does Chevon matter?', *Law and Policy* 28(4): 444–69.

Rosenfeld, M. (2008) 'Rethinking constitutional ordering in an era of legal and ideological pluralism', *International Journal of Constitutional Law* 6(3–4): 415–54.

Rossi, L.S. (2008) 'How fundamental are fundamental principles? Primacy and fundamental rights after Lisbon', *Yearbook of European Law* 27(1): 65–87.

Rupp, H. (1960) 'Judicial review in the Federal Republic of Germany', *The American Journal of Comparative Law* 9(1): 29–57.

Sadurski, W. (2008) "Solange, chapter 3": Constitutional courts in Central Europe – Democracy – European Union', *European Law Journal* 14(1): 1–35.

Safjan, M. (2008) 'Politics and constitutional courts. A judge's personal perspective', EUI Working Papers Law 2008/10, at http://cadmus.eui.eu/bitstream/handle/1814/8101/LAW-2008–10.pdf?sequence=1 (07.05.2012).

Schnapper, D. (2010) *Une Sociologue au Conseil Constitutionnel*, Paris: Gallimard.

Schönberger, C. (2009) 'Lisbon in Karlsruhe : Maastricht's epigones At sea', *German Law Journal* 10(8): 1201–18.

Schorkopf, F. (2009) 'The European Union as an association of sovereign states: Karlsruhe's ruling on the Treaty of Lisbon', *German Law Journal* 10(8): 1219–40.

Slosarcik, I. (2009) 'The Treaty of Lisbon & the Czech Constitutional Court: Act II', CEPS Policy Brief 197/27.

Stefanini, M. (2003) 'Jurisprudence du Conseil Constitutionnel', *Revue Française de Droit Constitutionnel 54*: 363–89.

Stein, E. (1964) 'Toward supremacy of the treaty. Constitution by judicial fiat: On the margin of the Costa case', *Michigan Law Review* 63(3): 491–523.

Stiernstrom, M. (2005) 'The relationship between community law and national law', Jean Monnet/Robert Schuman Paper Series 5(33) at http://aei.pitt.edu/8162/ (20.03.2012).

Stone Sweet, A. (1992) *The Birth of Judicial Politics in France. The Constitutional Council in Comparative Perspective*, Oxford: Oxford University Press.

Stone Sweet, A. (2002) 'Constitutional courts and parliamentary democracy', *West European Politics* 25(1): 77–100.

Stone Sweet, A. (2004) *The Judicial Construction of Europe*, Oxford: Oxford University Press.

Tzanakopoulos, A. (2012) 'Judicial Dialogue in Multi-Level Governance: The Impact of the Solange Argument', in Fauchald O. K., and Nollkaemper, A. (eds) *The Practice of International and National Courts and the (De-)Fragmentation of International Law*, Oxford: Hart, pp. 185–215.

Von Bogdandy, A. (2008) 'Pluralism, direct effect, and the ultimate say: On the relationship between international and domestic constitutional law', *International Journal of Constitutional Law* 6(3–4): 397–14.

Weiler, J. H. H. (1991), 'The transformation of Europe', *The Yale Law Journal* 100(8): 2403–83.

Weiler, J. H. H. (1999) *The Constitution of Europe. "Do the New Clothes Have an Emperor?" and Other Essays on European Integration*, Cambridge: Cambridge University Press.

Weiler, J. H. H. (2002) 'A constitution for Europe? Some hard choices', *Journal of Common Market Studies* 40(4): 563–90.

Wendel, M. (2011) 'Lisbon before the courts: Comparative perspectives', *European Constitutional Law Review* 7(1): 96–137.

8 Judicial Behaviour as a Result of Complex Causation

A QCA Approach to the Juridical Dynamics of Treaty Ratification

Presentation: Judicial Behaviour as the Result of Conjunctural Causation

The previous chapters have assessed how certain variables individually impacted judicial behaviour. It was shown that judicial decisions were highly dependent on inputs of various types. Far from being a purely legalistic exercise, national higher courts' (NHCs') decision making was a result of the action of contextual, institutional, juridical and extra-juridical explanatory variables. A legalistic approach to NHCs' rulings on European Union treaties would have simply highlighted courts' decisions and hid the actual processes of judicial decision making. However, this research has analyzed such processes from a realist perspective, showing that various socio-political factors impacted the behaviour of judges. More precisely, this book has showed that there is more than application of law to the cases in the episodes reviewed, even when the law is also an important factor to understanding the decisions of the courts.

However, up to now the analysis has not fully taken into account causal complexity, as it has tried to understand how certain variables *individually* contributed to explain the behaviour of NHCs. Now it is time to put all of the explanations together to complete the puzzle of the role of NHCs in the processes of the ratification of European Union treaties. Utilizing qualitative comparative analysis (QCA) will help accomplish this task. QCA is a methodology based on set theory and Boolean algebra. Unlike stochastic statistics, in which the impact of each variable upon a phenomenon is usually analyzed individually, QCA focuses on the interaction between explanatory conditions in the production of an outcome (Ragin and Sonnett, 2004).[1] Additionally, QCA allows the analysis of medium-N objects of study in which the number of cases is too small for techniques such as regressions. Using QCA, in the following pages the impact of all explanatory conditions on courts' decisions will be jointly analyzed. Courts' decisions will finally be understood as the result of complex combinations of explanatory conditions.

This chapter is organized as follows. After this short introduction, the two 'dependent variables' of the research will be analyzed separately. First, the following question will be answered: Under which circumstances did national courts dare to make statements of *Kompetenz-Kompetenz* that challenged the doctrine and role of the European Court of Justice? In addition, the paths that led to the absence of declarations of *Kompetenz-Kompetenz* in the rulings will be also explained. Subsequently, the following question will be explored: Under which circumstances did national courts dare to declare the unconstitutionality of European Union treaties, thus endangering their process of ratification? In addition to answering this question, the chapter will try to explain the circumstances that led to the absence of the outcome – the declaration of constitutionality of the treaty. Finally, some brief conclusions will be offered.

The Question of *Kompetenz-Kompetenz*: Courts' Quest for Self-empowerment

As it is widely known, Hart's (1997) rule of recognition is a specific type of secondary rule whose content would be 'what the constitution says is law'. As the source of validity of the whole legal system, the validity of the rule of recognition cannot be assessed. In this regard, the only analysis about the rule of recognition that can be made is the verification of its de facto existence. The rule of recognition only exists as a practice, complex but usually concordant, of courts, public servants and citizens when they identify the law with reference to certain criteria, and thus its existence is a matter of fact (Hart, 1997). Observe that Hart's definition included the expectation that all the actors share the same criteria of identification of the source of validity of the legal system. This is precisely what has been missing in the area of European judicial politics, where the Court of Justice of the European Union identified such a source of validity in the founding treaties of the European Union (MacCormick, 1995: 261), whereas NHCs did so in their national constitutions (Weiler, 2002; Posch, 2008: 274). What has been called judicial dialogue is the civilized expression of a struggle for the establishment of a rule of recognition.

This struggle drives us to Bourdieu because, in this case, it is the rule of recognition that establishes who has the power to 'say the law' (2001: 169). Pierre Bourdieu considered the juridical field an arena in which different actors competed for the 'power to say the law', that is, the power to make binding interpretations about the general rules of the legal system. In this struggle courts are not the only actors, but they are the most important ones. In the case of this research, the struggle for the establishment of a rule of recognition is simultaneously the struggle for the power to 'say the law'. NHCs defend a rule of recognition whose content would be 'what the constitution says is law,' which in their doctrinal construction gives them the last word even in matters of European Union law.

The ECJ defends a rule of recognition that would state that 'what the founding treaties say is the law', which allows it to control the interpretation of the EU legal system. The subject of this section can only be understood by taking into account the Hartian and the Bourdieuan perspectives together. The questions that could arise from a Hartian perspective alone would be of a normative and prescriptive nature, including 'which one should be the rule of recognition?' Complementing Hart with Bourdieu, the research moves towards a question of an empirical and positivist nature, namely 'what determines each court's option for one or another rule of recognition?' In other words, what explains NHCs' different positions towards the question of *Kompetenz-Kompetenz*?

The Path-breaking Maastricht-Urteil *and Its Followers: Paths to Declarations of* Kompetenz-Kompetenz

The question of *Kompetenz-Kompetenz* was addressed by NHCs in six different rulings. However, as explained in Chapter 4, wide variation in the approaches of the different courts existed. Earlier in this research it was hypothesized that two paths could lead to statements of *Kompetenz-Kompetenz*. The first consisted of the absence of a constitutional clause acknowledging the primacy of EU law (in Tables 8.1 and 8.2 referred to as 'PRIMACY'), combined with sufficient powers of review of the court ('REVIEW_POWERS') and a high judicial independence ('INDEPENDENCE'). In the second path, in addition to the absence of the primacy clause and the presence of wide powers of review of the court, it was expected that previous declarations of *Kompetenz-Kompetenz* by other NHC could cross-fertilize new courts, having as a result new statements of the doctrine ('CROSSFERTILIZATION'). Additionally, it was theorized that the existence of a constitutional clause imposing conditions on the exercise of powers by the EU ('CONDITIONS') would contribute to the outcome, as well as the fact that it was the first case before that court for that treaty ('FIRST_CASE').

QCA analysis helps us understand causation of statements of *Kompetenz-Kompetenz* in a configurational manner: explanatory conditions were deemed to interact with one another in producing the outcome. In Table 8.1, as in the rest of the tables in this chapter, uppercase indicates the presence of an explanatory condition, and lowercase indicates its absence, and the multiplication symbol ('*') means the logical 'AND'. The 'solution coverage' indicator shows to what extent the overall solution covers all the cases in which the outcome of interest was observed. The 'solution consistency' indicator shows the extent to which all the cases included in the solution had the outcome of interest. Individual paths also have specific indicators of consistency, raw coverage (the coverage of that path) and unique coverage (the coverage of that path which does not overlap the coverage of other paths of the solution).

Table 8.1 Intermediate solution for the presence of *Kompetenz-Kompetenz*

Configuration	*Raw Coverage*	*Unique Coverage*	*Consistency*	*Cases*
FIRST_CASE* REVIEW_POWERS* primacy* INDEPENDENCE* CONDITIONS	0.529100	0.211322	0.879454	Ge_Maas (0.940476,1) Ge_Lisb (0.940476,1) Lv_Lisb (0.826353, 0.5)
FIRST_CASE* REVIEW_POWERS* primacy* CROSSFERTILIZATION	0.697778	0.380000	0.792929	Pl_Lisb (0.95,0.5) Ge_Lisb (0.88,1) Lv_Lisb (0.82, 0.5) Cz_Lisb1 (0.69,0.75) Sp_Const (0.52,0.75)
Solution coverage: 0.909100				
Solution consistency: 0.831950				

Table 8.1 lists two configurations, or 'paths'. These two paths account for every case in which a statement of *Kompetenz-Kompetenz* was made (solution coverage is 0.91). In addition, solution consistency is 0.83, meaning that over 80 per cent of cases covered by these solutions presented the outcome of interest.

The solutions are very interesting. 'Enabling' and 'unleashing' conditions were identified. Enabling factors were shared by the two paths; in both paths, the primacy of European Union law was not declared by the constitution, the court had wide powers of review and the case was the first for that treaty before that court. Thus, these explanatory conditions provided the structural part of the explanation: the interplay between these conditions constitutes the background over which declarations of *Kompetenz-Kompetenz* are possible. In Boolean terms, they are 'quasi-necessary' conditions.

However, beyond these quasi-necessary conditions, unleashing factors that are different for each path were identified. One path represents the German cases, especially the *Maastricht-Urteil* ruling. In this path, the additional combination with a constitutional clause imposing substantive conditions on the exercise of powers by the European Union and with a high judicial independence can be observed. The only case specific to this path is the *Maastricht-Urteil* ruling, because the other two cases covered by this first path are also covered by the second path (they are 'overdetermined'). It is widely acknowledged that *Maastricht-Urteil* was a special case: this is the path-breaking ruling in which *Kompetenz-Kompetenz* was declared for the first time in decisions on European Union treaties. The first path confirms and accounts for this specificity. For a court to dare challenge the European Court of Justice when nobody had done it before in such a clear and explicit manner, it had to be a strong and independent institution, which was the case with the German court. It also was necessary for the court to have a solid legal ground, such as Article 23 of the German Constitution, which embodied a large list of principles to which the European Union was expected to be 'committed': democratic, social and federal principles; the rule of law; the principle of subsidiarity and basic rights equivalent to those protected under the German Basic Law. Some research indeed confirms the relevance of these explanatory conditions, particularly the salience of Article 23 of the German Basic Law, in driving the court towards declaring its *Kompetenz-Kompetenz*. In one analysis, Grimm (1996: 230) argues that from 1992 onwards, Article 23 of the German Constitution explicitly defines limitations to the powers of the European Union in which an exception to its primacy could be grounded.

In the second path, the unleashing factors are simpler: previous statements of *Kompetenz-Kompetenz* by other courts, and particularly the precedent of *Maastricht-Urteil*, in the presence of the quasi-necessary conditions, seemed to encourage courts to issue new statements of *Kompetenz-Kompetenz*. The fears regarding the imitation effect of the German doctrine (Baquero, 2010: 19) seemed to be well founded. The cases covered only by this path were the Polish Lisbon ruling, the Czech Lisbon ruling, the Latvian Lisbon ruling and the Spanish Constitutional Treaty ruling. These courts were not all highly independent, as shown by the Czech instance (see Sadurski, 2005). Unlike in the German constitution, in these cases demanding constitutional provisions regarding the European Union cannot be observed. In such a scenario, declaring *Kompetenz-Kompetenz* and thus challenging the doctrine of the European Court of Justice would have been difficult for these institutions. However, because at least one precedent of that doctrine existed, these courts could find external support for their claims, grounding them in the case law of one of the most prestigious courts in Europe. The fact that some of these rulings explicitly quote *Maastricht-Urteil* (see Bříza, 2009: 159; Wendel, 2011: 137; Castillo de la Torre, 2005) confirms this impression. It is not surprising that a ruling by the German Federal Constitutional Court had this impact on other courts. In fact, this is a particular case of a more general pattern observed by Gelter and Siems (2012), that is, the importance of the German court among its counterparts as one of the most cited courts in the case law of other NHCs.

Finally, two cases were included simultaneously in both paths: the Latvian and German Lisbon rulings. Thus, these cases may be explained by either one solution or the other. In the case of the German Lisbon ruling, its inclusion in the first path seems quite realistic. For the Latvian ruling, however, the court is less independent than the German court, and if its European clause is explored in a qualitative manner (see Chapter 5), it can be found that it is not as detailed and demanding as the German clause. In addition, in this ruling *Kompetenz-Kompetenz* was not fully stated. Therefore, this case will most likely be explained by the second path, in particular, by the precedent of *Maastricht-Urteil*.

ECJ-friendly Rulings: Explaining the Absence of the Kompetenz-Kompetenz Doctrine

It is good practice in QCA to conduct an analysis for the negation of the outcome, 'since it can either help to understand the causal logic driving to positive cases and/or can generate substantively interesting insights in their own rights' (Wagemann and Schneider, 2007: 26). Indeed, in the cases covered by this book, such analysis was of theoretical interest. In the vast majority of the rulings, *Kompetenz-Kompetenz* was not declared by courts. This is surprising given that declarations of *Kompetenz-Kompetenz* are empowering and, in principle, all NHCs should thus have the same interest in stating such a doctrine.

Table 8.2 identifies four different causal paths to the absence of *Kompetenz-Kompetenz* statements, which cover almost completely the cases with the outcome of interest (solution coverage: 0.88). At the same time, these paths nearly exclusively explained cases in which declarations of *Kompetenz-Kompetenz* were absent (solution consistency: 0.97). At first sight, the four paths seemed to be the reverse of the analysis conducted for the presence of the outcome. A closer look, however, reveals their specificities, and thus causal asymmetry.

The table shows that the absence of constitutional clauses imposing conditions on the exercise of powers by the European Union is quasi-necessary for the absence of declarations of *Kompetenz-Kompetenz*. This has to be understood in the context of the deterministic logic of QCA, since *empirically* this explanatory condition was always absent in rulings not declaring *Kompetenz-Kompetenz*. Using a less deterministic formulation, this finding suggests that the absence of such a constitutional provision clearly provides a disincentive to courts to declare their right to a last say in matters relating to EU law.

Combining the absence of this legalistic explanatory condition with other essentially institutional explanatory conditions, four different paths emerge. In the first path, the defining feature seems to be the restriction on NHCs' powers to review EU law, thus creating a structure of scarce incentives to declare *Kompetenz-Kompetenz*. This path accounts for every ruling of two different institutions: the French Constitutional Council and the Belgian Constitutional Court. To understand this path, it is essential to consider the reversible nature of this condition. In Belgium, it was primarily a doctrinal construction that excluded European

Table 8.2 Intermediate solution for the absence of *Kompetenz-Kompetenz*

Configuration	*Raw Coverage*	*Unique Coverage*	*Consistency*	*Cases*
conditions* review_powers	0.560000	0.280652	1.000000	Fr_Maas1 (1,1) Fr_Maas2 (1,1) Fr_Amst (1,1) Fr_Const (1,1) Fr_Lisb (1,1) Bel_Lisb1 (1,1) Bel_Lisb2 (1,1)
conditions* crossfertilization	0.496800	0.177482	0.955385	Ir_ESA (0.95,1) Fr_Maas1 (0.95,1) Sp_Maas (0.95,1) Fr_Maas2 (0.95,1)
conditions* independence* first_case	0.147153	0.060301	1.000000	Fr_Maas2 (0.8938,1) Cz_Lisb2 (0.803766,1)
conditions* independence* PRIMACY	0.082819	0.039501	1.000000	Sk_Const (0.803766,1)
Solution coverage: 0.884603				
Solution consistency: 0.974444				

Union secondary law from the powers of review of the Belgian Constitutional Court. As such, the constraints implied by this condition are not as rigid as those derived from explicit legal or constitutional provisions are, even when the Europhile tradition of this court could prevent it from challenging the ECJ (see Vandamme, 2008; Bossuyt and Verrijdt, 2011). Moreover, in France, the institutional conditions that discouraged the Council from declaring its *Kompetenz-Kompetenz* recently experienced a dramatic shift, with the powers of review of the institution being substantially enlarged, particularly with the new possibility for the Council to hear claims brought by citizens in defence of their rights (Fabbrini, 2008). If the analyses are correct, then, the Council should be expected to position itself closer to its German counterpart in the future.

In the second path, it can be found that one of the unleashing elements that was observed in rulings declaring *Kompetenz-Kompetenz* was missing: the existence of a previous statement of *Kompetenz-Kompetenz* by other courts. Thus, in these cases cross-fertilisation was simply not possible. As it was shown, many European courts found support for their declarations of *Kompetenz-Kompetenz* in the doctrine of the German

Federal Constitutional Court, which they explicitly quoted. For obvious reasons, then, rulings issued before *Maastricht-Urteil* did not contain such statements, including the Irish *Crotty* case and the French and Spanish cases on the Maastricht Treaty. Statements of *Kompetenz-Kompetenz* were likely not even on the agendas of these courts at that time.

Finally, the third and fourth paths share a condition: the scarce independence of the courts. This condition is combined in the third path with the fact that the case was a second ruling on the same treaty, which accounted for both the second French ruling on Maastricht and the second Czech ruling on Lisbon. For the fourth path, the absence of a constitutional clause imposing conditions on the exercise of powers by the European Union and the scarce independence of the court are combined with the presence of a constitutional clause declaring the primacy of European Union law. This path is the most law oriented in the analysis, and constitutional provisions play a preeminent role. It also confirms one of the theoretical assumptions of this study: that positivist explanations of judicial behaviour in social sciences must integrate law into the analyses. This path accounts for the Slovak Constitutional Treaty case in which a constitutional frame clearly constrains a weak court and makes issuing statements of *Kompetenz-Kompetenz* unthinkable.

Decisions on the Merits: National Courts Playing in a Supranational Arena

What was suggested in the previous chapters in relation to courts' decisions on the merits could be considered a clear attack against exclusively legalistic explanations. As Burley and Mattli (2006: 229) noted, legalism could be seen as an approach 'that denies the existence of ideological and sociopolitical influences on the Court's jurisdiction'. However, earlier in this book it has been demonstrated that certain variables of a political nature can sometimes provide better explanations for judicial outcomes than legal ones, even when the legal background remains a core explanatory dimension of judicial behaviour. The approach in this research, thus, has been a realist one.

A Not-So-Dangerous Outcome: Paths to Declarations of Unconstitutionality

Declarations of unconstitutionality seem the most surprising outcomes of judicial decision making given the existing pressures in favour of treaty ratification and the capacity of political elites to control courts. This outcome has been previously studied in some pieces (Closa and Castillo, 2012; Closa, 2013a, 2013b; Castillo, 2013), which were taken as the starting point for the analysis in this research. The findings of these pieces may be summarized by the following statement by Closa (2013a: 115), who points at three variables as relevant to understanding declarations of unconstitutionality:

> [A]ll cases in which constitutional reform was an immediate and direct consequence of court rulings [except for the Crotty case] contain the following institutional features: procedures of constitutional reform not requiring the intervention of veto points (via either referendums or intervening elections); appeals activated by the executive (. . .); and adjudication taking place in specialized jurisdictions.

Although this book agrees with most of the implications of this statement, there are some differences with earlier research of which the reader must be aware. First, this book considers the absence of veto points not only in cases of a declaration of unconstitutionality of the content of the treaty, but also in cases of a declaration of unconstitutionality of its procedure of ratification (see Chapter 6). Second, it is believed that a larger number of explanatory conditions, such as statements of *Kompetenz-Kompetenz* and judicial independence, are necessary to explain the outcome. Third, by using QCA, this book aims to achieve a different perspective of the causal paths producing declarations of unconstitutionality. In particular, QCA will allow the understanding of interactions between explanatory conditions in the production of the outcome.

In Chapter 2 it was hypothesized that two paths could lead to declarations of unconstitutionality. In the first path, the absence of a statement of *Kompetenz-Kompetenz* (in Tables 8.3 and 8.4 referred to as 'KOMPETENZ'), combined with parliamentary amendment of the constitution as a possible route to circumvent the judicial veto to ratification ('PARLIAMENTARY_AMENDMENT'), was expected to lead to the outcome. In the second path, the absence of statements of *Kompetenz*-Kompetenz was combined with a high judicial independence ('INDEPENDENCE') which allowed the court to challenge the preferences of political actors. Additionally, the type of court (in Tables 8.3 and 8.4 'SUPREME_COURT' refers to an NHC which is part of the judicial branch, as opposed to Kelsenian specialized courts) and the fact that the claimant was member of the executive ('CLAIMANT_EXECUTIVE') were deemed to have an impact on judicial decision making.

After the analysis, two different paths to declarations of unconstitutionality were identified, although the first accounted for the majority of cases.

The indicators for coverage and consistency of the overall solution are perfect: every declaration of unconstitutionality was covered by the solution (solution coverage: 1.0), and every case covered by the solution was a declaration of unconstitutionality (solution consistency: 1).

First, a quasi-necessary condition was observed: the absence of a declaration of *Kompetenz-Kompetenz* in the ruling. This supports the idea that

Table 8.3 Intermediate solution for declarations of unconstitutionality

Configuration	*Raw Coverage*	*Unique Coverage*	*Consistency*	*Cases*
kompetenz* PARLIAMENTARY_ AMENDMENT* CLAIMANT_ EXECUTIVE	0.8333333	0.833333	1.000000	Fr_Maas1 (1,1) Sp_Maas (1,1) Fr_Amst (1,1) Fr_Const (1,1) Fr_Lisb (1,1)
kompetenz* SUPREME_COURT* INDEPENDENCE	0.166667	0.166667	1.000000	Ir_SEA (1,1)
Solution coverage: 1.000000				
Solution consistency: 1.000000				

statements of *Kompetenz-Kompetenz* are important to explanations of decisions on the merits. Statements of *Kompetenz-Kompetenz* were more than a strategy that courts used to justify declarations of constitutionality (as had been suggested by Closa, 2013a): the absence of such statements causally explains courts' declarations of unconstitutionality. Indeed, statements of *Kompetenz-Kompetenz* had an autonomous causation, as it was suggested in the previous subsection. Once this quasi-necessary condition was in place, combinations of conditions produced the outcome differently in each case.

The first path could be called one of 'controlled declarations of unconstitutionality', and it confirms and supports the findings of previous qualitative studies (Closa and Castillo, 2012; Closa, 2013a; Castillo, 2013a). It accounted for more than 80 per cent of the declarations of unconstitutionality: the four declarations of unconstitutionality by the French Constitutional Council and the Maastricht Treaty declaration of the Spanish Constitutional Court. What this path suggests is that these cases, rather than being challenging rulings endangering the process of ratification of the treaties, were 'controlled proceedings' (Closa and Castillo, 2012) initiated by pro-treaty executives in which a declaration of unconstitutionality was costless because of the existence of simple procedures of constitutional amendment. Moreover, control of the overall process was given back to political elites, and it was always possible to proceed with treaty ratification (Closa and Castillo, 2012; Closa, 2013a). However, although it confirms the main findings of previous research, this path also complements them by suggesting the importance of the quasi-necessary condition 'absence of statement of *Kompetenz-Kompetenz*'. This condition is essential to understanding these cases. The declarations of the Spanish Constitutional Court are a good example. One difference between the Maastricht Treaty and Constitutional Treaty cases in Spain – in addition to the different rigidities of the provisions affected – is that, in the first case, the doctrine of *Kompetenz-Kompetenz* was still off NHCs' agenda, whereas the second case occurred long after the *Maastricht-Urteil* ruling put it in a prominent position in the European judicial dialogue. In the Maastricht case the court declared the treaty unconstitutional, but *Kompetenz-Kompetenz* had not been stated, and thus the ruling as a whole did not seem extremely challenging. In the Constitutional Treaty declaration, the combination was the opposite: a moderate statement of *Kompetenz-Kompetenz* was made, but now the court declared the treaty constitutional precisely by doctrinally circumventing a possible clash between the primacy of EU law and the supremacy of the constitution. In that case, a logical connection could be doctrinally reconstructed between the soft statement of *Kompetenz-Kompetenz* of the Spanish court and the avoidance of a declaration of unconstitutionality of the primacy of EU law. In addition, the French cases follow a similar logic. Because the French Constitutional Council had limited powers of review, it never declared its *Kompetenz-Kompetenz*; in this context declarations of unconstitutionality were more reasonable options. Thus, in this path we find rulings that make compatible two of the NHCs' institutional goals: political stability and self-empowerment.

The second path only accounts for the ruling on the Single European Act in Ireland and demonstrates that, beyond the exceptional character of that case (as argued by Closa, 2013a), a small number of interacting explanatory conditions played an essential role in this episode. The causal path points to institutional elements as explanatory conditions for the declaration of unconstitutionality, including being a supreme court rather than a Kelsenian court and being a highly independent institution, in addition to the absence of a statement of *Kompetenz-Kompetenz*. Unlike the other declarations of unconstitutionality, which demonstrated collaboration between courts and politicians, this ruling posed a challenge to political elites, which was explained by the specific institutional design of the court: the idiosyncrasy and high independence of the Irish Supreme Court explain why the judges dared to declare the treaty unconstitutional.

Closa (2013a) explained that other elements also could have acted as causal mechanisms for the challenging Irish declaration of unconstitutionality. It is worth summarizing and complementing that explanation. *Crotty* is the only case initiated by a citizen – and by an opponent of ratification – that produced a declaration of unconstitutionality. This is surprising given the fact that, as the previous analysis showed, the general pattern was that treaties were only declared unconstitutional at the request of pro-treaty executives when these maintained control over the overall process. Indeed, the ruling was said to have embarrassed the Irish government, which was committed to ratification (O'Connor, 1987: 762). The surprising outcome of the *Crotty* case can be understood as the result of many exceptional circumstances. First, the result of the vote within the court was adjusted: two of five judges of the Supreme Court actually rejected the declaration of unconstitutionality (Barret, 2009: 11). One more vote in favour of the Single European Act could have produced a declaration of constitutionality. Second, in challenging the preferences of political actors, the Irish Supreme Court was not more institutionally independent than other courts, such as the German or Belgian courts, which never dared to take such a crucial step. However, the *Crotty* case is the only ruling issued by a supreme court that is part of the ordinary judiciary. The other institutions were specialized constitutional courts. Although commentators have emphasized political control over the nomination of the judges of the court (Casey, 1987: 239), in the Irish Supreme Court, all nominees had judicial careers and were appointed for life. Therefore, the combination of being a supreme court and a highly independent institution could have produced an outcome that would not have been caused by either of these conditions individually. Third, *Crotty* was the first of the cases covered by this book in which a court entered into the merits of the case. The pattern that later emerged, with declarations of constitutionality being the most frequent outcome of proceedings, had not yet materialized. The Irish Supreme Court could not rely on the experience of other courts in understanding the costs of an uncontrolled declaration of unconstitutionality, and presumably political elites did not exercise pressure over courts during the 1980s as strongly as they did during later waves of treaty ratification. Lastly, although *Crotty* was a challenge to political elites, the political cost of the case was not enormous; after the declaration of unconstitutionality, the Irish people passed a constitutional amendment by a large majority, which could be foreseen by the polls (García Díez and Mateos Díaz, 2000: 352). According to one commentator, at the time of the ruling, a referendum seemed a safe option for ratification (Barret, 2009: 14). Finally, Closa (2013a: 116) refers to the *ex ante* nature of the case that *Crotty* shared with the other declarations of unconstitutionality; however, the fact that other *ex ante* cases were declared constitutional, such as the Spanish Constitutional Treaty case, may question this idea and point towards the stronger explanatory capacity of the institutional path suggested by the previous QCA analysis.

Thanks to the sophistication of QCA, it has been shown that two completely different paths may produce a declaration of unconstitutionality of a treaty. For one path, declarations of unconstitutionality were under the control of political elites, whereas for the second path the declaration of unconstitutionality partially challenged their preferences. This fact points to two different models of relations between courts and political actors. Two final reflections are in order. First, it cannot be known how far courts would have gone in challenging the preferences of political actors in other scenarios. The Irish Supreme Court seems to be an exception among cooperative courts, and even in that case a constitutional amendment in referendum seemed unproblematic. It is hard to say what the outcome of the proceedings would have been if the Irish society had

had a more Euro-sceptic stance. Second, as has been previously explained, declarations of unconstitutionality have become less frequent over time. Subtle learning by courts and political actors, as well as increases in pressure over courts, may underlie this trend and could play a role in future waves of judicialized treaty ratifications. Even in the presence of an exceptional institutional setting such as that of the Irish Supreme Court, new challenges to the process of ratification could be avoided.

'Green Light': Explaining Declarations of Constitutionality

As was said earlier, it is a good practice in QCA research to test the model for the absence of the outcome (Wagemann and Schneider, 2007: 26). The absence of the outcome of a declaration of unconstitutionality is substantively the declaration of constitutionality of the treaty. Although declarations of unconstitutionality are more surprising outcomes, declarations of constitutionality are also interesting and deserve individual explanation. Indeed, although previous research (Closa and Castillo, 2012, Closa, 2013a, 2013b) had provided relevant information to understand declarations of unconstitutionality, the *causes* of declarations of constitutionality remain largely unexplored (even if certain strategies followed by courts in these cases have been described). The analysis (Table 8.4) produced three different paths to declarations of constitutionality.

Table 8.4 Intermediate solution for declarations of constitutionality

Configuration	*Raw Coverage*	*Unique Coverage*	*Consistency*	*Cases*
supreme_court* claimant_ executive* parliamentary_ amendment	0.818182	0.181818	1.000000	Ge_Maas (1,1) Sk_Cons (1,1) Cz_Lisb1 (1,1) Bel_Lisb1 (1,1) Lv_Lisb (1,1) Ger_Lisb (1,1) Bel_Lisb2 (1,1) Cz_Lisb2 (1,1) Pl_Lisb (1,1)
supreme_ court*claimant_ executive* independence	0.363636	0.090909	1.000000	Fr_Maas2 (1,1) Sk_Cons (1,1) Cz_Lisb1 (1,1) Cz_Lisb2 (1,1)
supreme_court* parliamentary_ amendment* KOMPETENZ	0.545455	0.090909	1.000000	Ge_Maas (1,1) Sp_Const (1,1) Cz_Lisb (1,1) Lv_Lisb (1,1) Ge_Lisb (1,1) Pl_Lisb (1,1)
Solution coverage: 1.000000				
Solution consistency: 1.000000				

The overall solution had a perfect coverage (1.0) and a perfect consistency (1.0). This means that all declarations of constitutionality were covered by the solution and that all the cases covered by the solution were declarations of constitutionality.

In this solution, being a specialized constitutional court – a Kelsenain court or similar – is a quasi-necessary condition for the outcome. This finding must be considered cautiously. The role of this condition in the solution can be explained by the fact that a supreme court had never declared a treaty constitutional; however, supreme courts had only one opportunity to do so: the *Crotty* case. In addition to that, it must be noted that being a Kelsenian court was not a sufficient condition for declarations of constitutionality to occur: it had to be combined with other conditions in order to have a causal impact.

The first path is the most relevant because it can account for the largest share of declarations of constitutionality: over 80 per cent. Unsurprisingly, this path is precisely the opposite of the most encompassing path for declarations of unconstitutionality. If declarations of unconstitutionality were mostly explained as 'controlled proceedings', the first path for declarations of constitutionality is one of completely uncontrolled proceedings. It demonstrates how courts systematically avoided satisfying the interests of opponents of ratification. In this path, cases were not initiated by Europhile executives, but by opponents of ratification, including ministers of parliament (MPs) and citizens. Indeed, in these cases, claimants asked for declarations of unconstitutionality whose consequences would have gone far beyond parliamentary amendment of the constitution. In most cases, a referendum for ratification was requested. Under these circumstances, courts never declared treaties unconstitutional, which explains why even if some ratifications had failed throughout the process of European integration – the European Defense Community (EDC) Treaty or Constitutional Treaty – this was never the consequence of a decision made by an NHC.

The second path includes four rulings, and it may be seen as a deviation from the *Crotty* case. As in *Crotty*, claimants in these cases were not pro-treaty executives, but opponents of ratification; however, in these cases, the elements that allowed the Irish Supreme Court to challenge pro-treaty political elites are missing. These courts are neither part of the judicial branch nor highly independent institutions, but scarcely independent, specialized constitutional courts. Indeed, the only case uniquely covered by this path, the second ruling of the French Constitutional Council on the Maastricht Treaty, illustrates the logic underlying these cases. The French Constitutional Council in its first Maastricht ruling declared the treaty unconstitutional at the request of the president of the republic. However, in the second case, for which most other conditions remained the same but the claimant was now a true opponent of ratification, the Council declared the treaty constitutional. Alternatively, however, this change in the decisions of the Council could be explained by the fact that the institution could have considered unnecessary a second declaration of unconstitutionality of the same treaty.

Finally, the third path is important because it shows the link between decisions on the merits and interpretative decisions and thus demonstrates that one of the main theoretical assumptions of this study holds true: that judicial behaviour is a complex set of decisions in which not only decisions on the merits matter, and that interpretative decisions might causally explain decisions on the merits. In summary, declarations of *Kompetenz-Kompetenz* demonstrate their relevance to explaining declarations of constitutionality through this path. This path accounts for six cases: the German Maastricht and Lisbon rulings, the Spanish Constitutional Treaty ruling, the Czech Lisbon I ruling and the Polish and Latvian Lisbon decisions. In addition to the general quasi-necessary condition of not being a supreme court, two other conditions are relevant: consequences of a declaration of unconstitutionality going beyond parliamentary amendment of the constitution, and the presence of a declaration of *Kompetenz-Kompetenz* in the ruling. Importantly, this path challenges one of the most repeated mantras by studies in European law and European judicial politics: that the German Federal Constitutional Court is a recalcitrant actor whose rulings are 'brakes to integration' (Baquero, 2010). Instead, it can be said that declarations of *Kompetenz-Kompetenz* and the rulings of the German court in general constitute an intelligent strategy by Karlsruhe to satisfy three institutional goals simultaneously: loyalty to the status quo of the European project and a cooperative attitude towards the preferences of other political actors, empowerment vis-à-vis the European Court of Justice and respect for its function as guardian of the German constitution in the face of the development of European Union law. In other words, with its rulings the German court facilitates ratification of the treaties while seeking a form of self-empowerment capable of facilitating a better protection of its national constitution in the medium run. In summary, this path demonstrates that far from being a threat to the European project, statements of *Kompetenz-Kompetenz* were one reason why courts declared the constitutionality of the treaties and facilitated their ratification.

Conclusions

In this chapter, the complex causation of judicial behaviour was accounted for. The QCA techniques helped to understand the interactions among explanatory conditions. The analysis demonstrated that diverse dimensions of judicial behaviour combine to produce the outcomes: judicial decisions were the result of interactions among legal, political and institutional conditions.

In the analysis of declarations of *Kompetenz-Kompetenz*, the most salient aspects were the inner dynamics of the judicial field and the process of imitation between courts. The solution confirmed the intuition by Dyevre (2013) regarding the importance of courts' powers of review, but also showed that other factors were relevant. It also underlined the importance of following 'integrative approaches' (Tamanaha, 1997) where legal and political explanatory conditions are combined. The specificity of the *Maastricht-Urteil* ruling and of the German Federal Constitutional Court was underlined by the solutions: only a court as institutionally strong as the German court could challenge the European Court of Justice in a context in which the latter was reigning supreme in the landscape of European legal integration. The *Maastricht-Urteil* ruling has to be understood in the context of the exceptional institutional and constitutional circumstances of the German court, in particular Article 23 of the Basic Law. However, once Karlsruhe made the first step it opened a Pandora's box. An increasing number of European NHCs would soon follow its path. The doctrine of *Kompetenz-Kompetenz*, which could have been only the heterodox and marginal offspring of the exceptional *Maastricht-Urteil* ruling, became a core element of the European judicial dialogue and a widely accepted approach to EU law among European constitutional courts.

The analyses of decisions on the merits highlighted two important elements. First, political explanations beyond legalistic narratives improve understanding of judicial behaviour. Second, statements of *Kompetenz-Kompetenz* are important to explain the outcomes of rulings. Two paths for declarations of unconstitutionality were found. They show opposite relationships between courts and political actors: a cooperative one (France and Spain) and a challenging one (Ireland). Both paths were based on the necessary precondition that self-empowerment was, for different reasons, not on NHCs' agendas at that time. Declarations of constitutionality fit the same underlying logic. They were sometimes a judicial action aimed at avoiding a political crisis. Other times they were the result of institutional constraints, which made courts incapable of challenging the preferences of political actors. Finally, they often were the consequence of NHCs empowering themselves through their interpretative decisions.

Overall, conjunctural analysis proved to be extremely useful to understand paths driving to the outcomes beyond the individual impact of the explanatory variables. Each path is a narrative that highlights the interaction between explanatory conditions. At the same time, conjunctural analysis shows that the same outcome can be produced by different combinations of events. I hope that this chapter has provided for an improved understanding of judicial behaviour in processes of ratification of EU treaties.

Note

1 In the following, only intermediate solutions will be displayed. QCA allows for three kinds of solutions: complex, parsimonious and intermediate solutions. In intermediate solutions, counterfactuals – combinations of explanatory conditions that did not actually occur – are utilized in the analysis only when there are theoretical grounds to do so. This is surely the only manner of capturing explanatory conditions that are truly relevant to the cases without oversimplifying causal paths by considering impossible counterfactuals (see Ragin and Sonnett, 2004). Indeed, in all these cases, after testing every possible solution, the intermediate ones provided the soundest responses to the research questions, without oversimplifications or excess complexity. Additional information about QCA analysis can be found in the "Methodological Appendix" at the end of this book.

References

Baquero, J. (2010) 'A Judicial Götterdämmerung. The Lisbon Decision of the German Constitutional Court', in Auel, K. and Baquero, J., *Karlruhe's Europe*, Notre Europe Studies and Research 78, at: www.notre-europe.eu/media/karlsruheeuropeauel-baquerocruznejuly10.pdf?pdf=ok (16.02.2015).

Barret, G. (2009), 'Taking the direct route – The Irish Supreme Court decision in Crotty, Coughlan and McKenna (No. 2)', UCD Working Papers in Law, Criminology & Socio-Legal Studies Research Paper 8/2009, at http://papers.ssrn.com/sol3/papers.cfm?abstract_id=1400029 (20.06.2012).

Bossuyt, M., and Verrijdt, W. (2011) 'The full effect of EU law and constitutional review in Belgium and France after the Melki judgement', *European Constitutional Law Review* 7(3): 355–91.

Bourdieu, P. (2001), *Poder, Derecho y Clases Sociales*, Bilbao: Desclee.

Bříza, P. (2009) 'The Czech Republic. The constitutional court on the Lisbon Treaty. Decision of 26 November 2008', *European Constitutional Law Review* 5(1): 143–64.

Burley, A.-M. and Mattli, W. (2006) 'Europe before the Court : A Political Theory of Legal Integration' in Eilstrup-Sangiovanni, M. (ed.) *Debates on European Integration*, Wales : Palgrave, pp. 226–49.

Casey, J. (1987), *Constitutional Law in Ireland*, London: Sweet & Maxwell.

Castillo, P. (2013) 'La Política Judicial del Tribunal Constitucional en los procesos de ratificación de tratados de la Unión Europea: Aproximación desde un nuevo realismo jurídico', *Revista de Estudios Políticos* 159:107–38.

Castillo, P. (2012), ' "Guardar al defensor de la Constitución" Sobre la independencia de la jurisdicción constitucional: Evaluación de alternativas institucionales', *Estudio de Progreso 69/2012*, Madrid: Fundación Alternativas.

Castillo de la Torre, F. (2005) 'Tribunal Constitucional (Spanish Constitutional Court), opinion 1/2004 of 13 December 2004, on the treaty establishing a constitution for Europe', *Common Market Law Review* 42(4): 1169–1202.

Closa, C. (2013a) 'National higher courts and the ratification of European Union treaties', *West European Politics* 36(1): 97–121.

Closa, C. (2013b) *The Politics of Ratification of European Union Treaties*, London: Routledge.

Closa, C. and Castillo, P. (2012) 'National Courts and Ratification of European Union Treaties', in Evas, T., Lord, C., and Liebert, U. *Multilayered Representation in the European Union. Parliaments, Courts and the Public Sphere*, Berlin: Nomos, pp. 129–57.

Dyevre, A. (2013) 'European integration and national courts: Defending sovereignty under institutional constraints?', *European Constitutional Law Review* 9(1): 139–68.

Fabbrini, F. (2008) 'Kelsen in Paris: France's constitutional reform and the introduction of a posteriori constitutional review of legislation', *German Law Journal* 9(10): 1297–1312.

García Díez F., and Mateos Díaz, A. (2000) 'El Sistema Político de Irlanda', en Alcántara Sáez, M. *Sistemas Políticos de la Unión Europea*, Valencia: Tirant Lo Blanch.

Gelter, M. and Siems, M. (2012) 'Networks, dialogue or one-way traffic? An empirical analysis of cross-citations between ten of Europe's highest courts', *Utrecht Law Review* 8(2): 88–99.

Grimm, D. (1996) 'The European Court of Justice and national courts: The German constitutional perspective after the Maastricht DECISION', *Columbia Journal of European Law* 3: 229–42.

Hart, H. L. A. (1997 [1961]) *The Concept of Law*, New York: Oxford University Press.

MacCormick, N. (1995) 'The Maastricht-Urteil: Sovereignty NOW', *European Law Journal* 1(3): 259–66.

O'Connor, J. (1987) 'L'Acte unique Européen devant la cour supreme d'Irlande (Affaire Crotty)', *Annuaire Français de Droit International* 33: 762–73.

Posch, A. (2008) 'Community law and Austrian constitutional law', *International Constitutional Law Journal* 2(4): 272–328.

Ragin, C. and Sonnett, J. (2004) 'Between complexity and parsimony: Limited diversity, counterfactual cases, and comparative analysis', Compass Working Paper Series, at www.compasss.org/wpseries/RaginSonnett2004.pdf (10.10.2012).

Sadurski, W. (2005) *Rights before Courts. A Study of Constitutional Courts in Post-communist States of Central and Eastern Europe*, The Netherlands: Springer.

Tamanaha, B. (1997) *Realistic Socio-Legal Theory*, New York: Oxford University Press.

Vandamme, T. (2008) 'Prochain Arrêt: La Belgique! Explaining recent preliminary references of the Belgian Constitutional Court', *European Constitutional Law Review* 4(1): 127–48.

Wagemann, C. and Schneider, C. (2007) 'Standards of good practice in qualitative comparative analysis (QCA) and fuzzy-sets', Compass Working Paper Series, at www.compasss.org/wpseries/WagemannSchneider2007.pdf (18.10.2012).

Weiler, J. H. H. (2002) 'A constitution for Europe? Some hard choices', *Journal of Common Market Studies* 40(4): 563–90.

Wendel, M. (2011) 'Lisbon before the courts: Comparative perspectives', *European Constitutional Law Review* 7(1): 96–137.

9 Conclusions and Some Final Reflections

Research on National Higher Courts in the Process of European Integration

More than half a century has passed since the writings of Karl Loewestein (1955) on the role of the German Federal Constitutional Court in the process of ratification of the European Defense Community Treaty. From the time in which Loewestein published his fascinating description of the case, the number of new European Union treaties has dramatically grown, and so has the number of rulings by national higher courts (NHCs). This research made a comprehensive review of all these rulings by describing and analyzing the behaviour of the courts with regard not only to decisions on the merits, but also to interpretative decisions. The book has tried to solve what were considered the most relevant puzzles posed by the rulings, scrutinizing courts from both a legal and political perspective and trying to provide for an 'integrative approach' (Tamanaha, 1997). I hope that the book has at least shed some light on its object of study and provided for a better understanding of the behaviour of judicial actors in the process of European integration.

This has been a multidisciplinary research. It has combined legal and political analysis of the rulings of NHCs on European Union treaties issued during their processes of ratification. The book has developed a reflection on the cases that combines comparative constitutional law, European law and judicial politics. From a legal perspective, this book could be considered a new form of legal realism; but unlike the traditional forms of legal realism, which only theorize socio-political explanations of judicial behaviour, this book has carried out an empirical analysis of the cases, using the methods of the social sciences and the theoretical knowledge of political science (see Shapiro, 1964). This multidisciplinary approach was necessary in order to understand the puzzles of the research and to answer the research questions, since rulings on European Union treaties, by their very nature, pose problems which go beyond the boundaries of one single discipline.

In this final chapter, after this introduction, I will make a summary of the findings of the book. Subsequently I will analyze in more detail the interaction between the two outcomes of the research: decisions on the merits and statements of *Kompetenz-Kompetenz*. Next, I will provide for a short reflection on new cases of NHCs in the context of the process of European integration before summarizing the challenges that future research in the field will have to face.

Summary of Findings

One of the main goals of this book was to provide for models of judicial behaviour which could account for NHCs' decisions. Among the most important of these decisions were courts' statements of *Kompetenz-Kompetenz*, in which NHCs declared their right to a 'last say' regarding the compatibility between the national constitution and EU secondary law. One way to approach this phenomenon could have consisted of following the legalistic narrative provided by courts in their rulings. According to this narrative, the *Kompetenz-Kompetenz* doctrine would be no more than the necessary consequence of a rigorous analysis of the national constitution. At the end of the day, it is national constitutions which authorize member states to ratify European Union treaties and to transfer powers to the European Union. For that reason, European Union law in conflict with the constitutions of the member states would be unacceptable from the viewpoint of the internal legal system. To some extent, this legalistic approach seems to be internally coherent, and it provides for a reasonable explanation of courts' decisions. However, in underlining the legal reasons that NHCs had for making their statements of *Kompetenz-Kompetenz*, this reasoning hides the political dimension of the so-called judicial dialogue in the EU. Curiously enough, even law scholars such as Neil MacCormick (1999: 8–9) had intuitions about the political involvements of such judicial dialogue:

> Where a plurality of judgements each conclusive within a particular legal order can be passed, the question is: 'Which ought to prevail?' (. . .) Which is it least disadvantageous, all things considered, to ignore? In cases of conflict the answer to the latter question, the prudential answer, will be considerably affected by the weight and balance of conventional opinions and by power-relations (. . .). But in so far as power-relations enter the question, the issue is (. . .) one of politics.

As suggested by MacCormick, the political dimension of statements of *Kompetenz-Kompetenz* talks about power relations. This book assumed that one of the NHCs' institutional goals was self-empowerment and that a number of intervening factors could explain why some NHCs placed more emphasis on it than others. In this regard, the analyses carried out in the previous chapters pointed at the interaction between legal and political explanatory conditions. A good example of this interaction is the behaviour of the German Federal Constitutional Court. The German court is well known for having made the harshest rulings on European Union treaties. In those rulings, it openly challenged the European Court of Justice and its doctrine on the uniformity of EU law. The analyses found, on the one hand, that some clauses in the German Constitution had a protagonist role in grounding statements of *Kompetenz-Kompetenz*; in particular, the absence of a declaration of primacy of EU law and the presence of a strong conditionality in Art. 23 of the Basic Law – the commitment of the EU to democratic principles, fundamental rights, etc. – had a strong salience in explaining Karlsruhe's decisions. But together with this, political and institutional variables also played a role; in particular, the high institutional independence and strength of the German court, as well as the extent of its powers of review, allowed it to seek its own goals and to dare going further than any other NHC in the European Union.

Once Karlsruhe had done this, other NHCs saw the chance to make the same move and to seek their own empowerment. The analyses showed how the case law of the German court was often quoted by other NHCs. This phenomenon reinforces the idea that judicial institutions cross-fertilize and points at the creation of a network of European higher courts in constant indirect dialogue. The paradox is that, in defending their own constitutional systems from the potential excesses of the EU, European NHCs engaged in processes of flexible coordination and thus, to some extent, they could be said to have truly Europeanized. In order to avoid a top-down Europeanization imposed by the Court of Justice through the unconditional application of the primacy and direct effect doctrines, NHCs engaged in a process of horizontal Europeanization in which cross-national links were created between them. Of course, some NHCs did not participate in the process. Most notably, institutions such as the French Constitutional Council, the Belgian Constitutional Court, the Slovak Constitutional Court and the Irish Supreme Court avoided statements of *Kompetenz-Kompetenz*, at least in the rulings analyzed in this book. However, everything points at this being caused by contingent constraints, such as certain institutional designs. If the theory provided in Chapter 2 holds true and all NHCs share the same motivational background – the will to self-empower – these institutions should join the *Kompetenz-Kompetenz* doctrine at some point after these constraints are removed.

The analyses of decisions on the merits also revealed the importance of statements of *Kompetenz-Kompetenz* in a second way, as their absence turned out to be an important explanatory factor for declarations of unconstitutionality. Such analyses confirmed the findings of previous studies which had pointed at a cooperative relation between NHCs and pro-ratification political elites (Closa and Castillo, 2012; Closa, 2013). However, the analyses also revealed that in the case of some institutions, such as the Irish Supreme Court, a high judicial independence combined with a specific institutional setting could have driven towards a more challenging behaviour vis-à-vis the preferences of political actors. Regarding declarations of constitutionality, the analyses showed that NHCs often opted for these outcomes in proceedings initiated by opponents of ratification. NHCs thus preferred to set themselves apart from these actors and favoured a smooth ratification of the treaties. In some cases, this could have been facilitated by weak guarantees of independence of certain NHCs, whereas in other cases the explanation seems to be more closely related to the potentially grave consequences of a declaration of unconstitutionality. Finally, in some other cases, declarations of constitutionality seemed to be related to the fact that NHCs had adopted statements of *Kompetenz-Kompetenz* in the same ruling. This intriguing relation between decisions of *Kompetenz-Kompetenz* and decisions on the merits has been one of the most interesting findings of this book and will be commented on in more detail in the next section.

A Paradoxical Interplay between Judicial Decisions: The Four 'Types' of Rulings

As was suggested at the beginning of this book, rulings must be understood as a set of inter-related decisions on the merits and interpretative decisions through which courts express their preferences and interact with other actors. By linking decisions on the merits and interpretative decisions of *Kompetenz-Kompetenz*, a typology with four main 'types' of rulings can be constructed. Table 9.1 shows these 'ideal types', mentioning one ruling which could be consisted as an example of each them.

In the first ideal type, NHCs declare their *Kompetenz-Kompetenz* together with the constitutionality of the treaty. The paradigmatic example of this type is the *Maastricht-Urteil* ruling by the German Federal Constitutional Court – although the Lisbon decision could also play this same role. This type of ruling may be counterintuitive to some degree from a legalist perspective. In the German rulings in particular, statements of *Kompetenz-Kompetenz* were the culmination of a very critical

Table 9.1 The four 'types' of rulings

	Constitutional	*Unconstitutional*
Kompetenz-Kompetenz	German FCC. Maastricht	–
No *Kompetenz-Kompetenz*	Belgian CC. Lisbon I	French CC. Maastricht

legal argumentation. Given the tone of the rulings and the abundant criticisms against European Union law, one could have expected these rulings to end up in a declaration of unconstitutionality. However, this was not the case. That is why Schönberger (2009: 1201) stated that

> [t]here is probably no other judgment in the history of the Karlsruhe Court in which the argument is so much at odds with the actual result. To the point of perplexity and bewilderment, the reader of the opinion is hardly able to find any reasons supporting the outcome of the case.

The opposite type is represented by rulings of the French Constitutional Council such as Maastricht I, rulings in which *Kompetenz-Kompetenz* is not declared and in which, indeed, the legal argumentation is scarcely critical, but which end up in a declaration of unconstitutionality of the treaty. These kinds of rulings cannot be deemed 'anti-ratification' despite their decision on the merits: they simply declare treaties unconstitutional without making further assessments about the development of the European Union or European legal integration (see Baquero, 2008). In declaring treaties unconstitutional, these rulings are not making an implicit criticism of the European Union, but they simply seem to have found that their constitution has to be amended because it and the treaty need to be more compatible. As was the case for the previous type, this type is also paradoxical, although for opposite reasons: treaties are declared unconstitutional even if the legal argumentation of the ruling has been less critical than in rulings such as *Maastricht-Urteil*.

Unlike the first two, the third type is not characterized by a paradoxical structure. In this type, the legal argumentation is not critical; indeed, *Kompetenz-Kompetenz* is not declared and treaties are declared constitutional. Courts' final decisions seem to logically follow from the tone of their legal argumentation. Examples of this type of ruling are the first and second rulings of the Belgian Constitutional Court on the Lisbon Treaty.

The last type is the most interesting one precisely because it lacks empirical cases. The combination of a critical legal argumentation, including a statement of *Kompetenz-Kompetenz* and a declaration of unconstitutionality, never took place, even though in legal terms it makes perfect sense. The paradox is that, whereas the first and second types of rulings abounded despite the fact that their structure was somehow counterintuitive from a legalist perspective, the fourth type lacked empirical cases despite its coherent structure. The solution for this puzzle may lie in the fact that this kind of ruling would have been, in political terms, extremely challenging and costly. Apparently, no court in the European Union wanted to play a role as an opponent of integration with such a recalcitrant stance. The question, however, is how long can Karlsruhe avoid this type of ruling without losing credibility (see Closa and Castillo,

2012). The German Federal Constitutional Court has expressed reservations regarding the democratic quality of the European Union. It has expressed concerns about how constitutional rights are respected in the frame of the process of integration. It has forced the interpretation of the treaties to modify the distribution of powers between the ECJ and itself. If the German court dislikes the political structure to which the treaties give rise, if it considers such structure to be at odds with the constitution that it has to defend, then the logical move would be to declare the treaties unconstitutional. On the contrary, if the treaties are constitutional, political assessments and criticisms are probably beyond the functions that a constitutional court ought to perform. With its rulings, the German court is satisfying neither the supporters nor the opponents of the status quo of the European project. Indeed, such rulings have merited several academic criticisms (*inter alia* Baquero, 2009; Häberle, 2009; Krämer, 2010). Until now, Karlsruhe has achieved a strategic equilibrium with its rulings. But the pressures on such a delicate equilibrium are strong. Some may expect the court to abandon its critical discourse, and others may want it to carry such discourse to its logical conclusion. Bound by its own case law, by the expectations it has created and by the need to conserve its credibility, the German court may encounter increasing pressures in the future which could have an important impact on its behaviour and its decisions.

The New Decisions of NHCs

One important challenge for the findings of this research relates to their generalizability. In particular, it would be relevant to know the extent to which the models of judicial behaviour provided by the analyses of this book will help in explaining future decisions of NHCs on European Union treaties. In principle, qualitative comparative analysis (QCA) models like those displayed in Chapter 8 only aim at 'modest generalization', so that it should be acknowledged that new cases in relatively different contexts might be subject to different causal forces and thus are in need of new explanatory models. At the same time, however, new rulings on European Union treaties will share with the cases covered by this book a large number of features, and thus, part of the patterns found for treaties such as Maastricht or Lisbon could help in explaining the behaviour of NHCs in new waves of treaty ratification.

In fact, after the process of ratification of the Lisbon Treaty, NHCs engaged in the review of instruments such as the European Stability Mechanism (ESM). The European Stability Mechanism was not a European Union treaty *stricto sensu*. That was one of the reasons why it was excluded from the object of study of this book. However, it is obvious that the ESM had important implications for the process of European integration, and so had the rulings issued on such instruments by institutions like the German Federal Constitutional Court, the Irish Supreme Court and the Estonian Supreme Court. It is worth mentioning that in these three cases, the ESM was declared constitutional. Are these cases a new example of the cost-avoiding behaviour traditionally exhibited by NHCs in former processes of ratification of European Union treaties? It is hard to say without a more detailed analysis, but certain information seems to point in that direction. For instance, De Witte and Beukers (2013: 805) suggested that a declaration of unconstitutionality by the Irish Supreme Court could have had a high cost in the form of a relapse in the sovereign debt crisis, while recalling that ratification of the ESM Treaty in Germany was essential for its entry into force (2013: 815 ff.).

This being said, the rulings on the ESM were subject to different constraints and intervening variables than those covered by this book. To begin with, ratification in all European Union member states was not essential for this treaty to enter into force. This could disempower NHCs and, at the same time, render declarations of unconstitutionality less costly. At the same time, rulings on the ESM provoked one of the most relevant episodes of the European 'judicial dialogue' so far: the first preliminary reference of the German Federal Constitutional Court to the European Court of Justice. This book has analyzed the challenging statements of *Kompetenz-Kompetenz* by Karlsruhe, so the shift of the German court towards a more cooperative attitude must likely be explained from a different approach. However, the preliminary reference made by the German Federal Constitutional Court should not make anyone think that the *Kompetenz-Kompetenz* doctrine will be abandoned. It should be recalled once again that the history of the German rulings on European Union treaties has plenty of invitations to collaborate, which, however, did not prevent Karlsruhe from showing its deep disagreement with some of the core doctrines of the Court of Luxembourg.

Future Normative and Empirical Challenges

This book does not exhaust the topic of the participation of NHCs in the process of European integration. In empirical terms, I could think of at least three dimensions in which further research is still necessary. First, as said earlier, a number of new rulings have been issued on instruments such as the European Stability Mechanism (see *inter alia* Schmidt, 2013; Wendel, 2013; Schneider, 2013). This implies that, as has been suggested, NHCs have an increasing protagonism in the process of European integration. But it also points at the need to carry out further research in order to understand the law and politics of these and any other new rulings. Second, many statements of *Kompetenz-Kompetenz* have been issued outside the processes of ratification of European Union treaties. Although hopefully this book has made a contribution to the understanding of the variation in NHCs' approach to this doctrine, future studies will have to include rulings issued in contexts other than treaty ratifications in order to better understand this phenomenon. Third, much can still be said about judicialization in processes of treaty ratification; in particular, although this book has provided information regarding what happens once the processes of ratification are judicialized, it still has to be known why judicialization took place in some countries and not in other ones, which were the constraints faced by potential claimants and which were the synergies between judicialization and other political strategies intended at blocking ratification.

But beyond these empirical problems, this research has made some contributions with important normative and philosophical implications. Many of the findings in this book deserve a serious theoretical reflection, both with regard to the inter-branch and the intra-branch dimensions (see Friedman, 2005) of the analysis. With regard to the interaction between NHCs and other political actors, for instance, the suggestion that in many cases courts took into account political considerations when deciding on the constitutionality of treaties so that their decisions avoided political costs poses a serious problem in terms of the ideal of the rule of law and of the supremacy of the constitution, as courts are expected to neutrally and apolitically apply the law to the cases. Furthermore, the fact that these political considerations mirrored the preferences of the most powerful political actors is problematic in terms of the principle of separation of powers and of the independence of the constitutional courts. Of course, the behaviour of NHCs could be normatively defended by saying that, through self-restraint, they avoided interfering with the political debate on whether or not the treaties should ratified, as a decision in this regard should be taken by democratically legitimized actors. More challenging decisions by NHCs could have been described as irritating examples of 'judicial activism'. But this justification is at odds with the premises of neoconstitutionalism: constitutional courts are indeed expected to play a counter-majoritarian role in modern democratic systems and to challenge the preferences of the political branches of government when this is necessary in order to safeguard the constitution.

With regard to the intra-branch dimension of the analysis, this book also provides some information for which normative reflection is necessary. In particular, this research has approached the question of the 'judicial dialogue' between the European Court of Justice and NHCs. Some authors have tried to frame the relation between these actors in terms of 'constitutional pluralism', which has been defined as 'a pluralism of constitutional jurisdictions each of which may raise equally valid normative constitutional claims vis-à-vis the EU' (Evas and Liebert, 2011; see also Maduro, 2008). Theories of constitutional pluralism usually insist on processes of implicit or explicit dialogue between national courts and the European Court of Justice and point towards the existence of subtle mechanisms through which all actors avoid judicial clashes. However, in these theories, the outcomes of the proceedings seem to be the result of the good will of judges (see Closa, 2013: 98) and thus no structural and institutionalized guarantees exist for the avoidance of open conflicts. Indeed, this book has shown that the number of NHCs claiming to have an ultimate capacity to review European Union secondary legislation has increased over time. In this scenario the risks of a clash grow, and thus a threat exists for the process of European legal integration: the musical harmony between the European legal melodies which Maduro (2003) theorized could at some point be interrupted by the creaky noise produced by NHCs. Is the process of integration ready to manage a potentially increasing risk of judicial conflicts? What are the implications of this for legal certainty and the coherence of the legal system(s)?

In summary, although this book leaves open a number of empirical and normative puzzles, it has also provided for some contributions which could turn out to be relevant in order to solve them. NHCs will continue to have an important role in the process of European integration, as they are European courts as much as national ones. Future research will have to use imaginative and multidisciplinary approaches in order to explain their behaviour, their relations with other actors and the normative implications of their decisions.

References

Baquero, J. (2008), 'The legacy of the Maastricht-Urteil and the pluralist movement', *European Law Journal* 14(4): 389–422.

Baquero, J. (2009) 'A judicial Götterdämmerung. The Lisbon decision of the German Constitutional Court', in Aziel, K. and Baquero, J., *Karlruhe's Europe*, Notre Europe Studies and Research 78, at: www.notreeurope.eu/uploads/tx_publication/Etud78-Karlsruhe_sEurope-en_01.pdf (15.08.2010).

Closa, C. (2013) 'National higher courts and the ratification of European Union treaties', *West European Politics* 36(1): 97–121.

Closa, C. and Castillo, P. (2012) 'National Courts and Ratification of European Union Treaties', in Evas, T., Lord, C., and Liebert, U. *Multilayered Representation in the European Union. Parliaments, Courts and the Public Sphere*, Berlin: Nomos, pp. 129–57.

De Witte, B. and Beukers T. (2013) 'The Court of Justice approves the creation of the European Stability Mechanism outside the EU legal order: Pringle', *Common Market Law Review* 50: 805–48.

Evas, T. and Liebert, U. (2011) 'Domestic Courts, National Political Actors and European Judiciary: New Form of Political Participation Through Multilevel Judicial Governance', *RECON Workshop "Strengthening Democracy in the EU – Alternative Forms of Representation"* Bremen, 14–15 July 2011.

Friedman, B. (2005) 'The politics of judicial review', *Texas Law Review* 84(2): 287–337.

Häberle, P. (2009) 'La regresiva "sentencia Lisboa" como "Maastricht-II" anquilosada', *Revista de Derecho Constitucional Europeo* 12: 397–429.

Krämer, R. (2010) 'Looking through Different Glasses at the Lisbon Treaty: The German Constitutional Court and the Czech Constitutional Court', in Fischer-Lescano, A., Joerges, C. and Wonka, A. *The German Constitutional Court's Lisbon Ruling: Legal and Political Science Perspectives*, ZERP Diskussionapapier 1/2010, at www.mpifg.de/people/mh/paper/ZERP%20Discussion%20Paper%201.2010.pdf (12.06.2012).

Loewestein, K. (1955) 'The Bonn Constitution and the European Community treaties. A study on judicial frustration', *The Yale Law Journal* 64: 805–39.

MacCormick, N. (1999) *Questioning Sovereignty*, Oxford: Oxford University Press.

Maduro, M. (2003) 'Las formas del poder constitucional de la Unión Europea', *Revista de Estudios Políticos* 119: 11–55.

Maduro, M. (2008) 'Interpreting European law: Judicial adjudication in a context of constitutional pluralism', Working Paper IE Law School, WPLS08–08.

Schmidt, S. (2013) 'A sense of déjà vu? The FCC's preliminary European Stability Mechanism verdict', *German Law Journal* 14(1): 1–20.

Schneider, K. (2013) 'Yes, but. . . one more thing: Karlsruhe's ruling on the European Stability Mechanism', *German Law Journal* 14(1): 53–74.

Schönberger, C. (2009) 'Lisbon in Karlsruhe: Maastricht's epigones at sea', *German Law Journal* 10(8): 1201–18.

Shapiro, M. (1964) 'Political jurisprudence', *Kentucky Law Journal* 52: 294–345.

Tamanaha, B. (1997) *Realistic Socio-Legal Theory*, New York: Oxford University Press

Wendel, M. (2013) 'Judicial restraint and the return to openness: The decision of the German Federal Constitutional Court on the ESM and the Fiscal Treaty of 12 September 2012', *German Law Journal* 14(1): 21–52.

10 Methodological Appendix

To facilitate the reading of the book, methodological specifications have been omitted from the text as much as possible. However, such specifications are a guarantee of rigour and replicability, so this methodological appendix is provided to present them. In the following pages I first justify the operationalization used in the research; second, I present the truth tables on which the qualitative comparative analysis (QCA) models in Chapter 8 are based and finally, I display the data matrix used.

Operationalization

Chapters 3 through 7 of this book provided detailed qualitative information about the phenomena explored. This qualitative information was the basis of the QCA analyses in Chapter 8, as it helped in justifying the scores assigned to the explanatory conditions and the outcomes. However, in order to transform this qualitative information into a QCA data matrix, certain operationalization rules had to be followed. In this section, these operationalization rules will be explained and justified. It must be taken into account that the analyses for the outcome '*Kompetenz-Kompetenz*' (and its absence) were carried out using fuzzy-set QCA, in which the cases admit fuzzy (and not only dichotomous) inclusions in the sets. Analyses for the outcome 'unconstitutionality' (and its absence), however, could not be fuzzy, since that outcome was dichotomous in nature, and hence crisp-set QCA had to be used. In crisp-set QCA, all conditions must be dichotomous, and this implies the need to dichotomize some of the fuzzy sets. Finally, the book has also included a few bivariate correlations, so operationalization of the variables used in such analyses will also be provided.

- *Declaration of unconstitutionality*. This was operationalized as a crisp set, in which declarations of unconstitutionality scored 1 and declarations of constitutionality scored 0. In bivariate correlations, the same operationalization was followed to construct a dichotomous variable.

- *Statements of Kompetenz-Kompetenz*. To analyze this question as an outcome of the models, differences regarding the phrasing of the doctrine made by each NHC had to be taken into account, so instead of a crisp set, a fuzzy set was used. To assign scores, and given that a previous quantitative measurement of the phenomenon suitable for calibration was not available, I used the method of direct assignment, in which 'a judge provides a numeric or linguistic membership value "out of her head" after considering the objects and relevant evidence' (Verkuilen, 2005: 469). In the method of direct assignment, scores are 'directly arrived at through expert knowledge', that is, 'based on theoretical and/or empirical knowledge' (Thiem and Dusa, 2013: 54). However, in order to minimize arbitrariness in assigning scores, I used an objective criterion based on the existing theoretical and qualitative knowledge on the cases; my aim was to assign scores that mirrored real differences between the rulings. Full inclusion in the set (score 1) was assigned when, after a critical legal argumentation, the national higher court (NHC) clearly asserted its capacity to assess the constitutionality of EU secondary law. Relative inclusion (score 0.75) was assigned when the court stated its capacity to assess the constitutionality of EU secondary law, although just as a theoretical option or after an EU-friendly legal argumentation. The cross-over point (0.5) was assigned in cases in which the NHC deals with the doctrine of *Kompetenz-Kompetenz*, but leaves open the question of whether it would review the constitutionality of EU secondary law in concrete cases. Full exclusion was assigned (score 0) when the court does not make any statement regarding its *Kompetenz-Kompetenz*. The operationalization is not symmetric: the score '0.25' is missing. This was a deliberate decision, and the reason behind it is that although the doctrine of *Kompetenz-Kompetenz* may be more or less present in the rulings – according to the way in which courts phrase it – it cannot be 'more or less absent', but simply absent. In bivariate correlations, the same operationalization was followed to construct a continuous variable.

  It must be noted that in QCA models *Kompetenz-Kompetenz* was not only analyzed as an outcome, but also was used as an explanatory condition for the outcomes 'declaration of unconstitutionality' and 'declaration of constitutionality'. Given the nature of such outcomes, these analyses were carried out using crisp-set QCA, and hence the *Kompetenz-Kompetenz* condition had to be transformed into a crisp one. To do so, cases in which *Kompetenz-Kompetenz* was not declared at all scored 0 and the rest of the cases (scores 0.5 to 1 in the fuzzy outcome) scored 1.
- *European clauses*. Following Claes (2005, 2007) four questions were taken into account, so four dichotomous independent variables were

created and used in bivariate correlations: (1) whether or not the constitution mentioned the European Union; (2) whether or not the constitution imposed specific requisites for the transfer of powers to international organizations; (3) whether or not the national constitution imposed substantive principles or requirements – most notably, respect for the democratic principles – on the exercise of powers by the supranational institutions to which powers are transferred; and (4) whether or not the national constitution explicitly granted primacy to European Union law over national law. The sources of information for these variables were the national constitutions, in many cases clarified with the help of legal doctrine. After a qualitative and quantitative assessment, it was considered that two out of these four issues –points (3) and (4) – had a particularly clear impact on NHCs' decisions and thus had to be introduced in the QCA model as crisp sets.

- *Type of claimant.* The focus of attention in this regard was whether the claimant was a member of the executive or not. To determine this, a crisp set was constructed based on the knowledge of the cases provided by the text of the rulings and secondary literature (Closa and Castillo, 2012; Closa, 2013).
- *Consequences of the ruling: parliamentary amendment.* When the ruling ends up in a declaration of unconstitutionality, in order to proceed with ratification, it is necessary either to amend the constitution, if the substantive content of the treaty has been declared unconstitutional (Closa and Castillo, 2012; Closa, 2013), or turn to an alternative procedure for ratification –referendum – if the declaration of unconstitutionality refers to the formalities of ratification. This may give rise to four different political scenarios (Closa and Castillo, 2012; Closa, 2013): (1) *parliamentary amendment of the constitution*, if the declaration of unconstitutionality affects parts of the constitution protected under this type of procedure of amendment; (2) *celebration of referendum*, if the declaration of unconstitutionality affects parts of the constitution protected under this type of procedure of amendment, or if the declaration of unconstitutionality refers to the formalities followed for ratification; (3) *amendment of the constitution by two subsequent legislatures*, which would require dissolution of the chambers and the celebration of new elections, if the declaration of unconstitutionality affects parts of the constitution protected under this type of procedure of amendment; and (4) *direct blockage* of the ratification, if the declaration of unconstitutionality affects parts of the constitution protected under an 'eternity clause'. As was already said, for supporters of ratification, amendment of the constitution in the parliamentary arena is the least grave consequence, since it gives back to political elites control of the overall process and makes it possible to continue with ratification in a riskless fashion (Closa and Castillo, 2012). To account for this, a

crisp set was built in which cases in that latter scenario scored 1 and cases in the rest of the scenarios scored 0.

However, operationalizing this condition was not simple. I mostly followed Closa (2013), but I also took into account the possibility of a declaration of unconstitutionality on the procedure of ratification. In some cases, the type of scenario subsequent to a declaration of unconstitutionality was unclear; for instance, when the constitution included two different procedures for constitutional amendment, an ordinary one and a rigid one. In this case, the content of the petition of the claimants was used to determine if the final decision of the court would refer to substantive aspects protected under the ordinary procedure for amendment, to substantive aspects protected under the rigid one or to the formalities of ratification. In cases where the allegations of the parties affected simultaneously two or more of the former, I opted for a conservative approach and the score was assigned according to the gravest possible scenario to which a declaration of unconstitutionality could give rise. The only exception to this rule is the French Constitution, which foresaw two alternative procedures for constitutional amendment: in referendum or in the parliamentary arena. Because the president of the republic is the actor who chooses the procedure for amendment at his or her will, in this case the less grave scenario – parliamentary amendment – is taken into account.

- *Judicial independence*. Ishiyama and Ishiyama's (2002) index of judicial independence was used as a starting point. This index presented certain advantages. First, it has found an echo in the literature and has been reproduced in other studies (Herron and Randazzo, 2003). Second, the index referred to constitutional courts in post-communist countries, which partially overlapped with the cases of this book. Ishiyama and Ishiyama's index allowed me to build up a quantitative variable. However, it was modified in order to adapt it to the needs of this research. Ishiyama and Ishiyama use six different items, each of them ranging from 0 to 1, thus obtaining an index ranging from 0 to 6. Its items are (1) capacity of other bodies to overturn judicial decisions; (2) extent of powers of judicial review; (3) length of magistrates' terms; (4) number of actors involved in the nomination process; (5) control over courts' own procedures; and (6) degree of difficulty in removing judges from office.

Out of these six issues, three were removed for different reasons. Two of them – capacity of other bodies to overturn judicial decisions and extent of powers of judicial review – were removed because they were being used as separate explanatory conditions. Capacity of other actors to overturn judicial decisions is at the core of the variable of 'consequences of ratification', whereas extent of powers of judicial review is one of the variables that was used to understand decisions of *Kompetenz-Kompetenz*. I opted for a conservative approach to avoid being redundant in the utilization of these items, and since they were being used in other explanatory conditions, I removed them from the index of judicial independence. The third item that was removed was control over courts' own procedures. I believed this item was too blurry, since every court has control over its own procedures through the means of interpretation of its own regulation. In turn, two new issues were added to the index: professional background of the magistrates – whether or not they had legal professions prior to their nomination – and whether or not they were renewable.

Altogether, the index was composed of five different issues. The first is term of office – scoring 1 if lifelong, 0.66 if longer than two mandates of any of the other relevant constitutional actors (executives and legislative chambers), 0.33 if shorter than two of these mandates and 0 if shorter than one parliamentary mandate. The second issue is the dismissal of magistrates – scoring 1 if these can only be removed from office under limited circumstances foreseen in the law and 0 if dismissal is at the discretion of one actor. The third dimension of judicial behaviour is renewability of magistrates – scoring 1 if magistrates were not renewable and 0 if renewable. The fourth dimension is the nomination procedure – scoring 1 if not elected by political actors, 0.8 if at least three-fifths super-majority in the legislative chamber is necessary, 0.6 if a majority less than three-fifths in the legislative chamber is sufficient but at least two more actors participate in the nomination, 0.4 if a majority less than three-fifths in the legislative chamber is sufficient and fewer than two more actors participate in the nomination, 0.2 if elected by two or more actors not including the legislative chambers and 0 if elected by only one actor different from the legislative chambers. Finally, the last issue in the index is the professional background of magistrates – scoring 1 if a legal background is required for all magistrates, 0.5 if required for some them and 0 if not required at all. Adding the scores for all issues, a quantitative index of independence was obtained ranging from 0 to 5. Information regarding the issues which form the index had been already gathered in previous studies (Castillo, 2012).

This index was used in quantitative analysis. But for fuzzy-set QCA analyses, this quantitative variable had to be transformed into a fuzzy set. To do this, calibration anchors had to be selected. Qualitative knowledge about the cases indicated that even for NHCs vested with high guarantees of independence, political actors found means to control the institutions, so small losses of formal guarantees of independence may translate into important losses of actual independence. That is the reason why the calibration points were set at high scores. The first calibration point was 4.5, which is close to 5, the maximum score; NHCs scoring 4.5 or higher are deemed to fully belong to the set of courts with high guarantees of independence. The lowest calibration point was set at 3.5 in order to account for the fact that these courts had only half of the possible score in at least three out of the five issues; NHCs scoring 0.35 or below were deemed to be fully excluded from the set of courts with high guarantees of independence. The intermediate calibration point was set at 4, since having only half of the possible score in two out of five items or a score of 0 in one of them indicated a transition towards NHCs for which judicial independence could be undermined in some aspects. Setting the calibration points in such a small interval was indeed an advantage: although the index ranged from 0 to 5, actual scores of the cases ranged from 4.8 to 2.53, so this variation, even if small, could be captured by the fuzzy set.

Finally, judicial independence was also used in the analyses for 'declarations of unconstitutionality' and 'declarations of constitutionality'. Since these analyses were carried out using crisp-set QCA, fuzzy sets could not be used, and hence judicial independence had to be transformed into a crisp set. To do so, 4 was used again as the threshold (this time for dichotomization), so cases with more than 4 points in the index of independence scored 1 in the set, and the rest of the cases scored 0.

- *Courts' powers of review.* To measure this, I created a crisp set. In general, courts have many ways to review legislation: abstract regulation control, specific regulation control and constitutional complaint. For an NHC to have actual possibilities to review EU law, two conditions have to be satisfied: that the majority of these procedures are available for the court and that they are interpreted as allowing the court to review not only national legislation, but also European. Cases in which NHCs satisfied these two requirements were included in the set, and cases in which at least one of these two conditions was not satisfied were excluded from that set.
- *First case.* A crisp set was created to account for whether the case was the first on that treaty before that NHC.
- *Cross-fertilization: precedents of Kompetenz-Kompetenz in other NHCs.* To construct a fuzzy set, I followed two steps. In the first step, I built an index indicating how many previous statements of *Kompetenz-Kompetenz* – in the cases covered by the book – existed for each ruling. In this index, the score for each case was the result of adding up the scores in the outcome '*Kompetenz-Kompetenz*' of all precedent cases. For instance, if for one case at least one previous full declaration of *Kompetenz-Kompetenz* by some other court existed (score 1) and also a soft declaration of *Kompetenz-Kompetenz*

(score 0.75) had been made by another court, the score of that case in the index was 1.75. Through this operationalization, I obtained a quantitative index which ranged between 0 and 4.5, in which 0 indicated that no precedents of *Kompetenz-Kompetenz* existed in any ruling by any other court, and 4.5 indicated that the six of the rulings in which *Kompetenz-Kompetenz* was stated had been already issued. According to my theoretical framework, the larger the number of precedents of *Kompetenz-Kompetenz* by other NHCs (the higher the score), the easier it was for a new NHC to also declare its *Kompetenz-Kompetenz*.

In a second step, I transformed this index into a fuzzy set using Ragin's direct method of calibration. Calibration thresholds chosen for this variable mirrored the relative importance of the existence of at least one precedent of *Kompetenz-Kompetenz* for the series. Full exclusion was set at 0 (no precedent existed) and full inclusion at 4.5 (all precedents had been issued). The intermediate calibration point was set at 0.9. The reason is that the intermediate calibration point had to take into account the existence of at least one precedent of a full statement of *Kompetenz-Kompetenz*, as this clearly marks the transition from the absence to the presence of precedents of the doctrine. But setting the anchor at 1 would have meant that cases in which at least one precedent existed would have scored 0.5 in the fuzzy set, and thus would not be included or excluded in the set of rulings with at least one precedent, when it is obvious that for these cases such a precedent existed. In setting the intermediate calibration point at 0.9, this problem was solved.

Truth Tables

Analysis for Presence of Kompetenz-Kompetenz

Since the outcome was fuzzy, an fsQCA analysis was carried out. Six different explanatory conditions were used. Two of them were legal in nature: the existence of a declaration of primacy of European Union law in the national constitution ('PRIMACY') and the existence of substantive conditions to the exercise of powers by the European Union ('CONDIT'); two more were institutional: the scope of powers of review of the court ('REVIEWPOWERS') and the institutional power of the court, using as a proxy its formal independence ('INDEPEN'); finally, two more referred to dynamics which are generated among rulings: the existence of previous statements of *Kompetenz-Kompetenz* by other courts ('PREVIOUS') and being the first ruling by that court on that treaty ('FIRST_CASE'). In total, six explanatory conditions were used in an analysis with seventeen cases, which places such analysis in the 'grey zone' of Axel Marx (2010) in which the possibilities of finding a contradiction-free model based on

Table A.1 Truth table for presence of *Kompetenz-Kompetenz*

indep	*Review*	*first_c*	*condit*	*Primac*	*Previous*	*number*	*Kompet*	*Raw consistency*
1	1	1	1	0	0	1	1	1.000000
0	1	1	0	0	1	1	1	0.959671
1	1	1	0	0	1	2	1	0.917256
1	1	1	1	0	1	2	1	0.817143
1	1	1	0	0	0	1	0	0.435729
0	0	0	0	0	0	1	0	0.000000
0	0	1	0	0	0	1	0	0.000000
0	1	1	0	1	1	1	0	0.000000
1	0	0	0	0	1	1	0	0.000000
1	0	1	0	0	1	1	0	0.000000
0	1	0	0	0	1	1	0	0.000000
1	1	1	0	1	0	1	0	0.000000
0	0	1	0	0	1	3	0	0.000000

random data ranges between 1 and 10 per cent.[1] This is moderately satisfactory, given that it is still far from the high-risk zone[2], that Marx's benchmarks are designed for crisp analyses and this one is fuzzy and that the research had showed solid theoretical and empirical reasons to suggest that these explanatory conditions could have an impact on the outcome.

When obtaining the truth table (see Table A.1), it is observed that some combinations display high consistency scores, and the rest show quite lower ones. There is a combination with a raw consistency of 0.817143, and the next combination with empirical cases has a consistency of 0.435729. For this reason, the consistency cut-off is set at 0.81. The cut-off chosen allowed me to include all the empirical cases with statements of *Kompetenz-Kompetenz*, despite the fact that some of them had fuzzy scores of 0.5 – a fact which lowers the consistency scores. Still, the cut-off was slightly higher than the standard cut-off of 0.8. In order to obtain an intermediate analysis, the contribution of the conditions to the outcome had to be decided. For the reasons made explicit throughout this book, all of them were expected to contribute to the outcome when present, except 'PRIMACY' which was deemed to contribute to the outcome when absent.

Analysis for Absence of Kompetenz-Kompetenz

As noted earlier, since the outcome was fuzzy, an fsQCA analysis was carried out (see Table A.2).

For this analysis, I used the same conditions as those employed for the presence of the outcome. The consistency cut-off was set at 0.86, above the standard level of 0.80, where a gap between the configurations existed. When asked to select prime implicants, I took the most conservative approach and marked all.[3]

Table A.2 Truth table for absence of *Kompetenz-Kompetenz*

indep	*reviewp*	*first_c*	*condit*	*Primac*	*previous*	*number*	*~kompet*	*Raw consistency*
0	0	1	0	0	1	3	1	1.000000
1	0	0	0	0	1	1	1	1.000000
1	1	1	0	1	0	1	1	1.000000
0	0	0	0	0	0	1	1	1.000000
0	0	1	0	0	0	1	1	1.000000
0	1	0	0	0	1	1	1	1.000000
0	1	1	0	1	1	1	1	1.000000
1	0	1	0	0	1	1	1	1.000000
1	1	1	0	0	0	1	1	0.862004
1	1	1	0	0	1	2	0	0.751337
0	1	1	0	0	1	1	0	0.645107
1	1	1	1	0	1	2	0	0.285714
1	1	1	1	0	0	1	0	0.145106

Regarding the expectations about the behaviour of the explanatory conditions, these were the opposite of those in the former analysis, for the same theoretical reasons made explicit throughout this book. All of them were deemed to contribute to the absence of declarations of *Kompetenz-Kompetenz* when absent, except 'PRIMACY' which was deemed to do it when present.

Analysis for Presence of Declaration of Unconstitutionality

In this case, the outcome was crisp (dichotomous), so a csQCA was carried out. As indicated, for the analysis five explanatory conditions were used. For the reasons made explicit throughout this book, four of them were deemed to contribute to the outcome when present: the claimant is a member of the executive ('CLAIMANT_EXE'), parliamentary amendment of the constitution in cases of declaration of unconstitutionality ('PARL_AM'), not being a specialized jurisdiction but an ordinary one ('SUPREME_C') and being a highly independent institution ('INDEPENDENCE'); on the contrary, the existence of a statement of *Kompetenz-Kompetenz* in the ruling ('KOMPETENZ') is associated with declarations of constitutionality and thus deemed to contribute to declarations of unconstitutionality when absent. With only five conditions, the analysis is in Marx's (2010) safe area in which the probability of obtaining a contradiction-free model based on random data is 0 per cent.

From the very moment of building the truth table (see Table A.3), the adequacy of the conditions used could be observed: configurations had a raw consistency of either 1.000000 or 0.000000, which indicated that no contradictions existed. The consistency cut-off was set at 0.99. When asked to select prime implicants, I opted for the most conservative option and marked all.[4]

Table A.3 Truth table for *declaration of unconstitutionality*

Compete	*parl_ am*	*claimant_ ex*	*supreme_c*	*indepen*	*number*	*Unconst*	*raw consistency*
0	1	1	0	0	4	1	1.000000
0	0	0	1	1	1	1	1.000000
0	1	1	0	1	1	1	1.000000
0	0	0	0	1	2	0	0.000000
0	0	0	0	0	2	0	0.000000
0	1	0	0	0	1	0	0.000000
1	0	0	0	1	4	0	0.000000
1	0	0	0	0	1	0	0.000000
1	0	1	0	1	1	0	0.000000

Table A.4 Truth table for *declarations of constitutionality*

Compete	*parl_ am*	*claimant_ ex*	*supreme_c*	*indepen*	*number*	*Const*	*raw consistency*
1	0	1	0	1	1	1	1.000000
1	0	0	0	1	4	1	1.000000
0	0	0	0	0	2	1	1.000000
0	0	0	0	1	2	1	1.000000
1	0	0	0	0	1	1	1.000000
0	1	0	0	0	1	1	1.000000
0	1	1	0	1	1	0	0.000000
0	0	0	1	1	1	0	0.000000
0	1	1	0	0	4	0	0.000000

Analysis for Absence of Declarations of Unconstitutionality (Presence of Declarations of Constitutionality)

For the absence of the outcome, I also carried out a csQCA analysis in which the same conditions as used for the analysis of its presence were tested. Expectations regarding the behaviour of the explanatory conditions were the opposite of those for the previous analysis: all of them were deemed to contribute to the declaration of constitutionality when absent, except 'KOMPETENZ' which was deemed to contribute to the outcome when present.

Again, in the truth table (see Table A.4) it was observed that configurations had a raw consistency of either 1.000000 or 0.000000. Thus, no contradictions existed. The consistency cut-off was set at 0.99.

Table A.5 QCA data matrix

Caseid	*kompetenz*	*komp_ crisp*	*Uncons*	*Review powers*	*first_ case*	*conditi*	*primacy*	*claimant_ exec*	*previous*	*parl_ am*	*supreme_c*	*Indepen*	*Inde_ crisp*
Ir_ESA	0	0	1	1	1	0	1	0	0,05	0	1	0,7685246	1
Fr_Maas_I	0	0	1	0	1	0	0	1	0,05	1	0	0,1062	0
Sp_Maas	0	0	1	1	1	0	0	1	0,05	1	0	0,9404756	1
Fr_Maas_II	0	0	0	0	0	0	0	0	0,05	1	0	0,1062	0
Ge_Maas	1	1	0	1	1	1	0	0	0,05	0	0	0,9404756	1
Fr_Amst	0	0	1	0	1	0	0	1	0,52	1	0	0,1062	0
Fr_Const	0	0	1	0	1	0	0	1	0,52	1	0	0,1062	0
Sp_Const	0,75	1	0	1	1	0	0	1	0,52	0	0	0,9404756	1
Fr_Lisb	0	0	1	0	1	0	0	1	0,69	1	0	0,1062	0
Sk_Cons	0	0	0	1	1	0	1	0	0,69	0	0	0,196234	0
Cz_Lis_I	0,75	1	0	1	1	0	0	0	0,69	0	0	0,196234	0
Bel_Lis_I	0	0	0	0	1	0	0	0	0,82	0	0	0,8581491	1
Lv_Lis	0,5	1	0	1	1	1	0	0	0,82	0	0	0,8263535	1
Ge_Lis	1	1	0	1	1	1	0	0	0,88	0	0	0,9404756	1
Bel_Lis_II	0	0	0	0	0	0	0	0	0,95	0	0	0,8581491	1
Cz_Lis_II	0	0	0	1	0	0	0	0	0,95	0	0	0,196234	0
Pl_Lis	0,5	1	0	1	1	0	0	0	0,95	0	0	0,5597136	1

Notes

1 Marx suggests that in increasing the number of explanatory conditions in csQCA, the probability to find contradiction-free models increases. Thus, the absence of contradictions in a model could be due to the saturation of explanatory conditions and not to the theoretical or empirical relevance of such conditions: with a high number of explanatory conditions, such a 'model' could be found even with random data.
2 For eight conditions, the probability would be higher than 33 per cent, whereas for five conditions, it would be 0 per cent.
3 For the implicants 'indepen*reivewpowers*FIRST_CASE*conditi*primacy*PREVIOUS' I had to choose either 'indepen*reviewpowers*FIRST_CASE*condition*primacy' or 'reviewpowers*FIRST_CASE*conditi*primacy*PREVIOUS'.
4 For the implicants 'kompetenz*PARL_AM*CLAIMANT_EXE*supreme_c*independ' and 'kompetenz*PARL_AM*CLAIMANT_EXE*supreme_c*INDEPEN' I had to choose either 'kompetenz*CLAIMANT_EXE' or 'PARL_AM*CLAIMANT_EXE'.

References

Castillo, P. (2012) ' "Guardar al defensor de la Constitución" Sobre la indepedencia de la jurisdicción constitutional: Evaluación de alternativas institucionales', *Estudio de Progreso 69/2012*, Madrid: Fundación Alternativas.

Claes, M. (2005) 'Constitutionalizing Europe at its source: The "European" clauses in the national constitutions – Evolution and typology', *Yearbook of European Law* 24(1): 81–125.

Claes, M. (2007) 'The Europeanisation of national constitutions in the constitutionalisation of Europe: Some observations against the background of the constitutional experience of the EU-15' *Croatian Yearbook of European Law and Policy* 3: 1–38.

Closa, C. (2013) 'National higher courts and the ratification of European Union treaties', *West European Politics* 36(1): 97–121.

Closa, C. and Castillo, P. (2012) 'National Courts and Ratification of European Union Treaties', in Evas, T., Lord, C., and Liebert, U. *Multilayered Representation in the European Union. Parliaments, Courts and the Public Sphere*, Berlin: Nomos, pp. 129–57.

Herron, E. S. and Randazzo, K. A. (2003) 'The relationship between independence and judicial review in post-communist courts'. *Journal of Politics* 65(2): 422–38.

Ishiyama, S. and Ishiyama, J. (2002), 'Judicial activism in post-communist politics', *Law and Society Review* 36(4): 719–42.

Marx, A. (2010) 'Crisp-set qualitative comparative analysis (csQCA) and model specification: Benchmarks for future csQCA applications', *International Journal of Multiple Research Approaches* 4(2): 138–58.

Thiem, A. and Dusa, A. (2013) *Qualitative Comparative Analysis with R. A User's Guide*, New York: Springer.

Verkuilen, J. (2005) 'Assigning membership in fuzzy set analysis', *Sociological Methods and Research* 32(4): 462–96.

Index

Note: Page numbers with *f* indicate figures; those with *t* indicate tables.

abstract regulation control 164
accident de parcours 134
Act Extending and Strengthening the Rights of the Bundestag and the Bundesrat in European Union Matters 104
Adams, J. 52
Aguilar, L. 145
Alberton, G. 77
Alter, K. 11, 89
Amsterdam Treaty 9; decisions on the merits of 59*f*; declaration of unconstitutionality and 58–9, 105–6; *Kompetenz-Kompetenz* statements and 71*t*, 78*t*, 79; petitions filed by citizens 128, 129*t*, 131*t*; ratification processes 127*t*; topics addressed in ruling of 87*t*
application of law to case 25–6
'A Realistic Jurisprudence: The Next Step' (Llewellyn) 121
Austrian Constitutional Court 9, 52, 61; Constitutional Treaty ruling 79; decisions on the merits by 61*f*; Lisbon Treaty ruling 56, 107–8, 167

Baquero, G. 82, 90
Baquero, J. 58, 177
Barret, G. 132
Barroso, J.M. 57, 135
Baum, L. 25
Belgian Constitutional Court 9, 61, 120; cases rejected on formal grounds 107; decisions on the merits by 61*f*; institutional design and degree of independence 160*t*; *Kompetenz-Kompetenz* doctrine and, absence of 77; legislative chambers requirements and 113–14; Lisbon Treaty 57, 71; statements of *Kompetenz-Kompetenz* 71*t*; treaty ratification statement of 144
Beukers T. 211
Bickel, A. 50
Bourdieu, P. 24, 33, 188
Bříza, P. 151
Bruner, M. 1
Brunnel, T. 3
Brunner, M. 103
Bühlmann, M. 159
Burley, A.-M. 194

Carbonnier, J. 12
Chalmers, D. 10, 37
Chaves, M. 10, 37
Christlich-Soziale Union (CSU) 57, 73, 134
Claes, M. 27, 28, 54–5, 76, 77, 109, 121
claimants: decisions on the merits and 130–3, 131*t*; described 127; judicializing process and 127–34; statements of *Kompetenz-Kompetenz* and 133–4, 133*t*; status of 128–30, 129*t*
claimant type 35–6
Closa, C. 5, 38, 39, 107, 134, 172, 194–5, 197, 198
common structure in rulings 100–1
concrete contradiction 105
configurational analysis 20
configurational hypotheses: for decisions on the merits 41–2; *for*

Kompetenz-Kompetenz decisions 33–4
consent 53
constitutional complaint 164
constitutional core concept 81–3
constitutional identity 104
constitutionality, declarations of 99–104; common structure in rulings 100–1; exceptionality of German rulings 102–4; overview of 99–100; political involvement 101–2
constitutional pluralism 212–13
constitutional review of EU treaties 48–62; *see also Kompetenz-Kompetenz,* doctrine of; birth of 49–53; decisions on the merits and 58–61, 59*f*, 61*f*; introduction to 48–9; outcomes of 56–8; ratification processes and 53–6
constitutional rights 102
Constitutional Treaty 60, 150–1; decisions on the merits of 59*f*; *Kompetenz-Kompetenz* statements and 78*t*, 79; national parliaments and 101; petitions filed by citizens 128, 129*t*
controlled declarations of unconstitutionality 196
controlled proceedings 196, 200
Costa v. ENEL 171, 174
countermajoritarian difficulty 50
Cour d'arbitrage 166
Cour de Cassation 166
cross-fertilization processes 173–9; European Court of Justice and 174; *Kompetenz-Kompetenz* doctrine and 176–8; national higher courts and 175–6, 179
Crotty, R. 1
Crotty v. An Taoiseach 1, 9, 58, 78, 80, 102, 104, 111, 119, 132, 141–2, 150, 197–9, 200
Czech Constitutional Court: decisions on the merits by 61*f*; declaration of constitutionality and 57, 61; European clause and 112; holding a referendum and 115; institutional design and degree of independence 161*t*; *Kompetenz-Kompetenz* statements of 71, 71*t*, 73–4; Lisbon I decision 55, 79, 135, 178; transfer of powers to EU and 115
Danish Supreme Court, Maastricht decision 55, 79
Davies, B. 30
deadlines, as rejection on formal grounds 107
decisions of judicial-type organs 7
decisions on the merits 34–42; analyses findings 207–8; claimants and 130–3, 131*t*; claimant type and 35–6; configurational hypotheses for 41–2; constitutional review and 58–61, 59*f*, 61*f*; court type and 39–40; described 22, 34–5; judicial independence and 40–1; *Kompetenz-Kompetenz* declarations and 37–9, 39*f*; political actors preferences and 36–7
declarations of constitutionality 99–104; common structure in rulings 100–1; exceptionality of German rulings 102–4; overview of 99–100; political involvement 101–2
declarations of unconstitutionality 104–7; consequences following 136–47, 137–8*t*; constitutional amendment scenario 139–40*t*, 139–41; eternity clause of Germany and 145–7; as harmless decisions 147–51, 149*t*; new elections and 142–5; referendums as result of 141–2, 142*t*
democratic deficit, of EU 85–6
De Witte, B. 53, 175, 211
'dire le droit' (to say the law) 24, 25, 29, 33
Dupéré, O. 77
Dyèvre, A. 4, 25, 31, 164, 202

EDC Treaty *see* European Defense Community (EDC) Treaty
EEC Treaty 59
Ehrlich, E. 121
empowerment of court 24–5
epistemic community of law 25
Epstein, L. 23
ESA treaty *see* European Single Act (ESA)
eternity clause, Germany 145–7, 151
Euratom Treaty 59
European clauses 27–8, 108–20; by case and correlations 110*t*; described 27–8; EU law and

109–13; overview of 108–9; powers of EU and 116–18; primacy of EU law and 28, 118–20; ratification and, regulating 113–16; substantive principles in 28
European Coal and Steel Community (ECSC) Treaty 59
European Court of Justice (ECJ) 20, 23, 24; *Costa v. ENEL* 69; cross-fertilization processes and 174; *Internationale Hadelgesseslschaft* 69; *Kompetenz-Kompetenz* doctrine and 67, 69, 192–4, 193*t*; rule of recognition and 188–9; *Van Gend and Loos* 69
European Defense Community (EDC) Treaty 9, 59–60, 205; decisions on the merits of 59*f*; *Kompetenz-Kompetenz* statements and 78; petitions filed by citizens 128, 129*t*, 130
European judicial integration: methodology in analysis of 12–14; study of 10–12
European Single Act (ESA) 58; decisions on the merits of 59*f*; declarations of unconstitutionality and 149*t*; European clauses and 110*t*; *Kompetenz-Kompetenz* statements and 78, 78*t*
European Stability Mechanism (ESM) 62, 210–11
Europhile rulings 73–5, 77
EU secondary law 166
EU treaties, constitutional review of 48–62; *see also Kompetenz-Kompetenz*, doctrine of; birth of 49–53; decisions on the merits and 58–61, 59*f*, 61*f*; introduction to 48–9; outcomes of 56–8; ratification processes and 53–6; rulings on, during ratification process 8*t*
ex ante review 54, 56, 165
exceptionality of German rulings 102–4
explanatory conditions 26
ex post review 54, 56, 165

formal grounds, cases rejected on 107–8
formal-positivist model of thinking 25
Fossum, J. E. 89–90
Freedom Party (FPÖ) 9
French Constitutional Council 7, 10, 31, 40; decisions on the merits by 61*f*; declarations of unconstitutionality 104–6; institutional design and degree of independence 161*t*; *Kompetenz-Kompetenz* doctrine and, absence of 76–7; Maastricht Treaty decision 57, 58, 71*t*, 100; powers of EU and 117; presumption of unconstitutionality 105
French Constitutional Council (Schnapper) 134

Galanter, M. 35
Garlicki, L. 165
Garret, G. 3, 11
Gauweiler, P. 57, 134
Gelter, M. 29, 177, 191
German Federal Constitutional Court 1, 7, 9, 31, 38, 205; decisions on the merits by 61*f*; European Defense Community Treaty 56; harsh statements of *Kompetenz-Kompetenz* 71*t*, 72–3, 207; institutional design and degree of independence 160*t*; Lisbon Treaty ruling 57; *Maastricht-Urteil* ruling 24–5, 57, 67, 68–9, 79; powers of review and 31; *Solange* I case 70; transfer of powers to EU and 116
Grimm, D. 191

Häberle, P. 90
Handler, J. 35
Hänsch, K. 57
Hart, H. L. A. 188
Herron, E. S. 31, 35
Hesse, K. 24
Hungarian Constitutional Court 9

independence guarantees, institutional design and 159–67, 160–1*t*
institutional constraints, judicial behaviour and 159–67; independence guarantees and 159, 160–1*t*, 162–3, 163*t*; *Kompetenz-Kompetenz* statements and 164–7
institutional design, independence guarantees and 159–67, 160–1*t*
institutionalist-externalist model 36

institutional objectives of courts 23–6; application of law to case 25–6; empowerment and 24–5; stability of political framework and 23–4
institutional self-empowering field of study 11, 21
insufficient demonstration, as rejection on formal grounds 107–8
integration clauses 27
integrative approaches 21, 27
inter alia 109
inter-branch interaction 3, 5–6
inter-court competition theory 89
intergovernmentalism 2–3
interpretative decisions 21–2
intra-branch interaction 3, 4–5
involuntary defection 5
Irish Supreme Court 1, 7, 9, 61, 208; decisions on the merits by 61*f*; declarations of unconstitutionality 104; European clause and 109, 111; European Single Act decision 58; institutional design and degree of independence 160*t*; *Kompetenz-Kompetenz* doctrine and, absence of 77; presumption of unconstitutionality 105; statements of *Kompetenz-Kompetenz* 71*t*
Italian Constitutional Court 171–2, 175

judicial activism 212
judicial behaviour, model of 20–42; decisions on the merits and 34–42; institutional objectives of courts and 23–6; interpretative decisions and 21–2; *Kompetenz-Kompetenz* decisions and 26–34; theoretical approach to 20–1
judicial decisions, consequences of 134–51; *see also* declarations of unconstitutionality
judicial decisions, interactions between 167–79; cross-fertilization processes and 173–9; decisions on the merits/*Kompetenz-Kompetenz* decisions 171–3, 208–9; same court/same treaty decisions 167–70
judicial decisions on EU treaties: consequences of 134–51 (*see also* declarations of unconstitutionality); overview of 6–10; rulings on 8*t*; types of 208–10, 208*t*
judicial dimension 158–80; cross-fertilization processes and 173–9; decisions on the merits and 171–3; institutional constraints and 159–67; introduction to 158; judicial decisions and 167–79; *Kompetenz-Kompetenz* statements and 164–7, 171–3
judicial independence 30–1, 40–1; courts' decisions and 163*t*; defined 159
judicialization of politics 48, 62; *see also* claimants; defined 127; processes of treaty ratification 127*t*

Karlsruhe *see* German Federal Constitutional Court
Keck, T. 36
Kelsen, H. 25, 50–1, 52
Klaus, V. 82
Knight, J. 23
Kompetenz-Kompetenz, doctrine of 66–91; absence of 192–4, 193*t*; accompanying legislation assessment and 80–1; approaches to, in EU treaty rulings 70–7, 71*t*; constitutional core concept and 81–3; cross-fertilization processes and 176–8; definition of 67–70; democracy and 85–6; evolution of, by treaties 78–80, 78*t*; history of 68–9; inter-court competition perspective of 70; introduction to 66–7; as political conflict 90–1; sovereignty and 83–5; topics addressed in rulings of 86–90, 87*t*
Kompetenz-Kompetenz decisions 3, 26–34; claimants and 133–4, 133*t*; configurational hypotheses for 33–4; decisions on the merits and 37–9, 39*f*, 171–3; European clauses and 27–8; harsh statements of 72–3; interpretative decisions and 22, 26; judicial independence and 30–1; moderate statements of 73–5; overview of 26–7; powers of review and 31–2, 164–7; preceding rulings of, by other courts 28–30, 30*f*; primacy of EU law and 118–20; QCA analysis of 188–94, 190*t*; ratification and 4–5; research findings 206–7; subsequent rulings on same treaty and 32–3

Krämer, R. 82
Kunz, R. 159

Lambert, E. 22, 171
Latvian Constitutional Court: Charter of Rights of the European Union 75; decisions on the merits by 61*f*; European clause and 112–13; holding a referendum and 114; institutional design and degree of independence 160*t*; *Kompetenz-Kompetenz* doctrine and 80; powers of EU and 117; statements of *Kompetenz-Kompetenz* 71*t*
law: application of, to case 25–6; epistemic community of 25; making good 25, 42; open texture of 25
legalist field of study 11, 21
legalistic discourse of courts 99–108; declarations of constitutionality 99–104; declarations of unconstitutionality 104–7; rejections on formal grounds 107–8
legal norms, definiteness of 26
legal realism 98
legal rules, judicial behaviour and 98–121; courts' legalistic discourse 99–108; discovery and, context of 120–1; European clauses and 108–20; introduction to 98–9; justification and, context of 120–1
legislative chambers, European clauses and 113–14
Leterme, Y. 144
Liberté d'association ruling 165
Lida, K. 5
Lisbon Treaty 9, 60, 71, 71*t*; decisions on the merits of 59*f*; eternity clause and 146; European integration and 100–1; exceptionality of 103–4; *Kompetenz-Kompetenz* statements and 78*t*, 79–80; petitions filed by citizens 128, 129*t*
Llewellyn, K. 121
Lock, T. 81, 84
Loewestein, K. 205

Maastricht Treaty 1, 9, 60; cases rejected on formal grounds and 107, 108; constitutionality of 79; decisions on the merits of 59*f*; declaration of unconstitutionality and 104–6, 150; European clause and 111–12; *Kompetenz-Kompetenz* statements 78*t*; petitions filed by citizens 128, 129*t*, 130; same court/same treaty decisions and 167, 168
Maastricht Urteil ruling 67; democratic deficit and 85–6; European clause and 111; European integration and 100; exceptionality of 103; harsh statements of *Kompetenz-Kompetenz* 72; *Kompetenz-Kompetenz* doctrine and 68–9, 79–80; national parliaments and 101
MacCormick, N. 33, 68, 76, 206
Maduro, M. 69, 179, 213
making good law 25, 42
manifest function of institution 25
Marbury, W. 52
Marbury v. Madison 51–2
Marshall, J. 52
Martinico, G. 53
material core concept 82
Mattli, W. 11, 20, 135, 194
McCloskey, R. 36
Melchior, M. 166
Menéndez, A. J. 89–90
Merton, R. 25
methodological appendix 215–25; operationalization used 215–21; truth tables 221–4, 222*t*, 223*t*, 224*t*, 225*t*
midnight appointments 52
Mitterrand, F. 130
modified structural realism 11
moments, as rejection on formal grounds 107

'National Courts Mandate in the European Union' (Claes) 54–5
national higher courts (NHCs) 20; *see also* constitutional review of EU treaties; coordination problem between 29–30, 30*f*; cross-fertilization processes and 175–6, 179; EU treaty rulings, approaches to *Kompetenz-Kompetenz* in 70–7, 71*t*; findings of research 206–8; future challenges of 211–13; *Kompetenz-Kompetenz* doctrine and 67–8; new decisions of 210–11; with powers of constitutional review 7; research on, in process

of European integration 205–6; statements of *Kompetenz-Kompetenz* 22, 71*t*; treaty ratification intervention by 8*t*
national higher courts (NHCs), ratification and 1–14; decisions on the merits and 5–6; introduction to 1–2; judicial behaviour in processes of 2–6; *Kompetenz-Kompetenz* decisions and 4–5; methodology in analysis of 12–14
national parliaments 101
neoconstitutionalism model 50–1; features of 51
neoinstitutionalism 11, 30, 159
Neuman, G. 132
Niedobitek, M. 103
non-transferable identity of Constitution 147
Nourse, V. 98

open texture of law 25

path dependency 32, 167
Plötner, J. 76
Polish Constitutional Court: Accession Treaty decision 74; decisions on the merits by 61*f*; European clause and 113; holding a referendum and 114; institutional design and degree of independence 161*t*; *Kompetenz-Kompetenz* and 75–6, 84; Lisbon Treaty ruling 56, 178; statements of *Kompetenz-Kompetenz* 71*t*
political-contextual field of study 10–11, 21
political involvement, declarations of constitutionality and 101–2
powers of review 31–2
presumption of unconstitutionality 105
primacy in European clauses 28; EU laws and 118–20
principle of interpretation 171
Putnam, R.D. 5

qualitative comparative analysis (QCA) 6, 13–14, 20, 163, 187–202; declaration of constitutionality and 198–201; defined 187; introduction to 187–8; *Kompetenz-Kompetenz* statements and 188–94, 190*t*, 193*t*; unconstitutionality of EU treaties, national courts and 194–9, 199*t*

Ramsauer, P. 134
Randazzo, K.A. 31, 35
Rasmussen, H. 174
ratification, European clauses and 113–16; legislative chambers and 113–14; referendum holding and 114–15; transfer of powers to EU and 115–16
ratification of EU treaties: constitutional review and 53–6; European clauses and 113–16; *Kompetenz-Kompetenz* decisions and 4–5; by national higher courts 1–14, 8*t*
reassurance strategy 170
referendums 102; holding, European clauses and 114–15; as rejection on formal grounds 108
Regime Politics Approach 36, 42
rejections on formal grounds 107–8
rule of recognition 188–9
rulings on EU treaties, political dimension of 126–52; claimant and judicializing process 127–34; consequences of judicial decisions 134–51; introduction to 126–7

Sadurski, W. 170
Safjan, M. 162
same court/same treaty decisions 167–70
Schäuble, W. 151
Schmitt, C. 25, 50, 146
Schnapper, D. 134, 165
Schönberger, C. 209
Shaffer, R. 98
Shapiro, M. 25, 27
Siems, M. 29, 177, 191
Single European Act (SEA) 1, 9, 59, 100; petitions filed by citizens 128, 129*t*
Slaughter, A.-M. 11, 20, 135
Slovak Constitutional Court 9; Constitutional Treaty decision 57, 100; decisions on the merits by 61*f*; European clause and 112; institutional design and degree of independence 161*t*; *Kompetenz-Kompetenz* doctrine and, absence of 77; powers of EU and 117; primacy of EU law and 120; statements of *Kompetenz-Kompetenz* 71*t*; transfer of powers to EU and 115

Solange decision 30, 68, 70, 74, 90, 102, 172, 176; European clause and 111; powers of EU and 116–17, 118
sovereignty 83–5
Sozialdemokratische Partei Deutschlands (SPD) 60
Spanish Constitutional Court: concrete contradiction and 105; decisions on the merits by 61*f*; Declaración' on the Constitutional Treaty 57, 71, 100; declarations of unconstitutionality 104; European clause and 113–14; institutional design and degree of independence 160*t*; *Kompetenz-Kompetenz* declaration of 71*t*, 73, 79; Maastricht declaration 58, 71*t*
Special Laws 143, 144
specific regulation control 164
stability of political framework 23–4
Stone Sweet, A. 2, 3, 20, 24, 51, 132, 173–4
structural modified realism 3
substantive principles, in European clauses 28
sui generis institutions 7, 10, 40, 158

Tamanaha, B. 21
theories of path dependency 32, 167
Treaty of Nice 9, 59
Tribunal Constitucional 73
Troper, M. 83
two-level game theory 5

ultra-vires 70, 72, 75, 172
unanimity, requirement of 134
unconstitutionality, declarations of 104–7; consequences following 136–47, 137–8*t*; constitutional amendment scenario 139–40*t*, 139–41; eternity clause of Germany and 145–7; as harmless decisions 147–51, 149*t*; new elections and 142–5; referendums as result of 141–2, 142*t*

Van Gend and Loos case 174
Van Rompuy, H. 144
Verhofstadt, G. 144
Voßkuhle, A. 91

Weiler, J.H.H. 11, 20, 85, 174, 175
Wendel, M. 86
Whittington, K. 27
Wieland, J. 70, 85

Zurn, C. 50

FSC
www.fsc.org
MIX
Papier | Fördert
gute Waldnutzung
FSC® C083411

Kolibri 360 GmbH
Ferdinand-Jühlke-Straße 7
99095 Erfurt, Deutschland
produktsicherheit@kolibri360.de